William Torrens

Twenty years in Parliament

William Torrens

Twenty years in Parliament

ISBN/EAN: 9783337153274

Printed in Europe, USA, Canada, Australia, Japan

Cover: Foto ©Suzi / pixelio.de

More available books at **www.hansebooks.com**

TWENTY YEARS IN PARLIAMENT

TO THE

RT. HON. CHARLES PELHAM VILLIERS, M.P.,

THESE PAGES ARE INSCRIBED

BY HIS FAITHFUL FRIEND AND COMRADE

IN MANY LEGISLATIVE STRUGGLES.

January, 1863.

IN

PARLIAMENT

BY

W. McCULLAGH TORRENS

LONDON
RICHARD BENTLEY AND SON
Publishers in Ordinary to Her Majesty the Queen
1893

TWENTY YEARS IN PARLIAMENT

THE PARLIAMENT OF 1865

TWENTY YEARS IN PARLIAMENT

THE PARLIAMENT OF 1865.

Contested Elections—A Majority of One—Admiral Napier—Candidate for Finsbury—Canvassing Difficulties—Tom Duncombe—Recollections of Palmerston—Richard Cobden—Committee on Salaries—John Stuart Mill—Reform—Change of Ministry—Protest of the Tea-room—Lodger Franchise—Monckton Milnes—Disraeli—Artisans' Dwellings Act—Letter of Lord Shaftesbury—Sick Relief and Boarding Out.

Of seven contested elections for Parliament, I was fortunate enough to lose but one. The first was for a seaport town in Ireland, having a constituency of but 250, who were so equally divided that my opponent claimed a preponderance of three only at the poll. On petition, I challenged his eligibility on the ground that he had been born and bred in Maryland, and had not obtained letters of naturalization. His counsel, however, successfully pleaded that, his grandfather having been a British subject before the War of Independence, his posterity in the second generation still owed allegiance to the Crown, and for three days the Committee were occupied with a discussion of the principles of feudal law, whereby they felt bound to decide that Mr. McTavish was, to all intents and purposes then pending, a 'natural-born citizen of the realm.' Thereupon my advisers submitted that, under a statute (since repealed), notice had been served requiring my antagonist within fourteen days to register on oath his property qualification; and that, having neglected to do so, he had incurred as a penalty the loss of the seat.

The Chairman, Lord Harry Vane, impatient at what seemed a contention never heard of before, asked if it was seriously meant to rely on such a point. General Peel, who sat next him, was heard to whisper the Chairman: 'Don't rush your fences'; and after further parley it was found, to the no small surprise of the Committee, that the decision must be in our favour. Four votes were then disallowed as invalid, which left me in a majority of one; and, my opponent having no longer any direct interest in the issue, the Speaker was informed that I had been duly elected.

At the next dissolution, I was invited to stand with the late Sir Charles Napier for Great Yarmouth. The Admiral was a popular hero, full of personal energy and political ambition, and supposed to be just the candidate certain to win the suffrages of the ancient town where Nelson's name was still a household word. In his first address to an expectant crowd, he went incisively through the profession of faith in which he had always been consistent as an advanced Liberal, and he was cheered enthusiastically; only one dissentient fellow-countryman in the throng, after a cautious welcome, warned Sir Charles that, though a brave and noble fellow, he didn't go far enough for *him*. By nature and habit, Sir Charles was, above all things, aggressive, resentful of rivalry, and from the lips outward scornful of opinion. He firmly believed in his genius for command on shore as well as afloat, and cut short cavil, when anyone ventured to hint a doubt, by recalling his naval victory of Terceira, and his memorable storming of Acre by means of Turkish troops, who had so little stomach for the enterprise that he had to lick the malingerers up to the breach with his riding-whip.

An ungrateful Government, however, instead of naming him next as Port-Admiral, thought he might be content with a decoration and being laid up as a spent fire-ship. Charley—as his comrades called him—was slow to believe in such a destiny, and took to sheep-farming and platform politics, in which his first article of faith was to go farther than anybody else. In reply, therefore, to his heckler, he angrily exclaimed: 'What more could I promise, short of undertaking to repeal the Ten Commandments?' Some wealthy Wesleyans present were shocked, but the multitude laughed, and vowed that he was the man for them.

For me there seemed nothing left but the peaceful and practical. I had had some experience in municipal and official work; and learning that the town was seething with sedition against the Sanitary Board for trying to enforce a supply of drinking-water from the distant Broads, in order to abolish unhealthy leakage into domestic springs through the sandy soil, I sought to ingratiate myself by asserting vigorously the right of each locality to decide for itself in such matters.

The Mayor of the town, who had been a middy at Trafalgar, and in civilian old age was the universal favourite with his neighbours, when asked by a pedantic commissioner recently sent down to inquire and report to his dogmatic superiors at Whitehall, attested roundly the longevity of the inhabitants, which could never have taken any harm from the imputed subterranean poison, and being bluntly asked if he drank much water himself, repelled the imputation by exclaiming: 'To the best of my recollection, I never tasted that liquid.' There were other local topics which I endeavoured to use, and in the assurance that I would prove a safe foil for his belligerent eloquence, my veteran colleague, for the first week of our canvass, was in excellent humour. But by degrees the popular disposition threatened to change; and, as there was less variety in abuse of the Admiralty and the Horse Guards than, perhaps, had been expected, the speeches of Sir Charles failed to evoke enthusiastic response, and came by degrees to be pronounced 'all the same over again.' It took but little tact on my part to avoid a similar fault, and at length he declared he would stand it no longer, for on every occasion when he had spoken first and warmed up the meeting he found that I came in for all the applause. 'By all means, then,' I said, 'let us change places.' But this served the purpose no better, and he passionately muttered: 'I see it's no damned use, but I'll never stand with a lawyer again.'

Next night, before he rose, he said to me: 'What are them things you eat before you speak?' 'Only lozenges,' I said; 'have some?' Upon which he put three fingers into the box, and filled his mouth with unsuspected cayenne. The effect may be imagined. He thought I had poisoned him, and henceforth our difficulties rather multiplied.

At the end of one long day of joint canvass we returned to dinner hot and tired, and, having a public meeting to address at night, I resorted to the luxury of changing my dress. On coming down to dinner I saw the Admiral eyeing me with a sinister expression, and then, leaving the room, he reappeared in a few minutes in the full splendour of uniform, and the red ribbon of the Bath across his breast. It was a critical moment, and I felt that any sacrifice to political friendship would be worth making to avert an explosion of temper that would be fatal to our common aims; and, instead of quizzing, I complimented him on never having looked so well before. 'Well,' he said, 'never mind; I have a green Portuguese Order upstairs, and I'll lend it to you for to-night, if you wish;' which, of course, I humbly declined. At the end of six weeks it grew clear that the banking and brewing interests of the borough were not to be beaten in a constituency of some 1,200, and though at the poll I ran one of my opponents hard, the Admiral was left nowhere.

On a subsequent occasion my supporters placed me in a still more advantageous position, but the return being referred to a committee, four of whose members were of the opposite party, and but one of that to which I belonged, my majority of 150 was said to be nullified by certain acts of local partisans, for which, probably, no other tribunal would have found me responsible. I had had enough of the uncertainties and vexations of small boroughs, and resolved to be thenceforth content with the pursuit of literature, unless some constituency independent and numerous enough should fancy that I might serve them usefully in legislation.

In 1864 a deputation from Finsbury asked me to stand at the next General Election, and although one of the sitting members, it was known, would stand again, and two or three City candidates were in the field, they undertook to make me the representative of one of the largest divisions of the Metropolis. I asked Cobden's advice what I should say, and he said, 'Don't touch it; they'll work you to death, and it will be your ruin.' I spoke to Bright, and he asked, 'Who are the other fellows standing?' and on being told, declared they would be no use in debate, or in practical questions about India or Ireland. He offered me a letter of credence to influential members of the Society of Friends; and not without many misgivings I accepted the invitation.

The area to be traversed, the number and diversity of the inhabitants—then counted at a quarter of a million—the sectarian repugnances to be appeased, and the rank and wealth of some of my competitors, rendered a prolonged canvass toilsome, and often disheartening. But ere summer closed Lord E. Seymour, whom Government backed, withdrew, and I began to feel more confidence in being able to cut out for myself practical claims to preference.

Lincoln's Inn, although the oldest and most eminent society within the ambit of the borough, had never been able to assert its claim to name its representative in Parliament, and though but a member of the outer Bar, I had found opportunities already to take such a part in legislative business as rendered me acceptable to many of my own profession. It is difficult to imagine, however, anything more dissimilar than the electoral climate of Old Square and Clerkenwell, except, perhaps, that of Bloomsbury and Stoke Newington. Yet it became part of what I learned to call my pleasing duty to adapt my accents of suasion within the space of a few hours to the bustle of St. Giles's and the quiet of Highbury.

It was slow and laborious work, few of my would-be masters being at home till after sunset, and next-door neighbours, when I was lucky enough to find them, being sure to differ in their politics and creed. To make personal acquaintance with one in ten was impossible, and what assurance that tithe of heterogeneous opinions and interests was likely to afford became daily more a cause for doubt and misgiving among my friends in committee. I persevered, however, and by degrees learned how much more progress in such a case is to be made by a sympathetic listener to the wants and grievances of others, than by the wariest and wisest talk of one's own.

Tom Duncombe had been for years the popular idol, yet he had literally done nothing for his constituents, and it was something new amongst them to be told that one had an ambition to bring the mechanism of law-making and administration into touch with the neglects and deficiencies that rendered life needlessly hard, and fostered the growth and spread of disease. Instead of party rhetoric and rancour, I applied myself mainly to the need, becoming every year greater, of working-men's dwellings fit for habitation; to the want of more numerous schools; to a kindlier system for the relief of the sick in their own dwellings; to a better and more abundant water supply for household purposes; and other questions of an unpolitical but practical nature, which had seldom, if ever, been made the theme of promise or appeal on the hustings.

Few people now recollect the condition of things that then existed in the overcrowded region between Blackfriars and Pentonville, which formed originally the Metropolitan Borough of Finsbury. The wide thoroughfares that now exist between Holborn and Islington had hardly been thought of, and the great viaduct from St. Sepulchre's to St. Andrew's Church as yet was not. No ordinary words can describe the darkness and squalor in which multitudes dwelt, who earned their bread during the daytime in the City or the West-End, and at night thronged the alleys, lanes, and passages that formed a network of inhuman habitation, through which a stranger could hardly make his way.

In company with the medical inspector of the district, or one of the guardians, I made many a pilgrimage through this dismal territory, becoming daily more and more impressed with the need and duty of rescuing the people from a plight whereby, unconsciously, they formed a perennial source of danger to the neighbourhoods all round from the chronic prevalence of disease. I could not be persuaded easily that the region, including several parishes rated at many thousands yearly, and containing an industrious population greater than many independent princely states, was one vast den of fever, small-pox, filth, and involuntary shame.

I remember being taken by one of my committee to visit a court which bore the infernally appropriate name of Frying-pan Alley. It consisted of some dozen houses, none of them having any rear, or thorough draught, every room of which sheltered two or more families, and the approach between the rows was so narrow that I measured it with my walking-cane. Cleanliness in such a place was palpably impossible; but I own that what made the deepest impression upon me, and afforded the most terrible proof that the inhabitants had grown inured to what seemed their inevitable lot, was the fact that not a word of complaint escaped a single lip, or that the notion seemed to prevail that more civilized or Christian dwellings could be provided for the busy crowd.

Henceforth I made it a point at every public meeting to try and obtain authority from the dwellers in healthier districts to plead in Parliament on public and national grounds against allowing the evil any longer to exist, whose details and consequences outweighed socially and morally all others in my mind. By degrees the question, How far a remedy was possible, came to be discussed in the press, and I had often to be content with the chilling compliment that the vague vision of domicile reform was very commendable in a candidate seeking popular confidence, though few practical men would pledge themselves to its realization; and I was warned by a worthy friend in my committee not to rely too much on a topic which he feared the well-to-do majority were not easily moved seriously to consider.

Other difficulties of a different kind beset canvassing in a borough where the registered electors numbered above 23,000. The distribution of representative privilege at the Reform Bill had given the Metropolis two-and-twenty seats, which for a time was considered reasonable; but as the suburbs grew wide and the central districts dense in working population, the political map had rapidly become obsolete; and the suburban hamlets, with their green-lane thoroughfares and modest shrubberies, dotted with brickfields and market-gardens, over which Tom Duncombe, on a high-stepping hack, cantered half a dozen times before an election, and Coroner Wakley visited at the Nag's Head and the Cock at Highbury, was gradually becoming metamorphosed into closely-built rows of streets filled to crowding with retired traders, clerks in City houses, artisans, and workmen of all degrees of thrift and skill, whose names it baffled committee-men and agents to identify on the register.

The eight mammoth constituencies every year required more and more division and redivision; but although Parliamentary reform was talked about and wrangled over, for party purposes, the readjustment of Metropolitan representation concerned nobody in particular, and successive schemes offered no remedy for what was becoming an evil and a scandal. Redress for an injustice so obvious was, indeed, a safe bidding by candidates; but, inasmuch as it provoked no cavil or opposition, my astute friends who wished me well assured me that promises to have the blunders of time amended was only waste of words. Tell a good story if you have one, and make fun of a rival if you can; pelt the existing Ministry for their shortcomings, and give no cause to be suspected of under-working with the Opposition; but don't waste breath on the incontrovertible or obviously useful. My own experience led me to a wider—and I found it a wiser—practical conclusion, and that was: in personal canvassing, as seldom as possible to talk politics.

By way of preface or epilogue at a local meeting, it was expedient to say something definite about one's past votes and future principles; but votes reaped in sheaves in such a community were not to be easily had, and in a canvass extending over eight or nine months were liable to unforeseen and unsuspected mildew. I convinced myself that it was better worth my while, even in a selfish point of view, to listen rather than to talk to the father of five children with a shrewd, anxious wife.

For relief in case of sickness, which practically worsens the conditions of the labourer's family in a degree and to an extent far deeper than the accidental loss of employment or the lessening of wage-earnings, but little provision comparatively had been made by law. The great hospitals provided for accidents and acute disease, but the distress incidental to the many ailments humanity is subject to was mainly without aid or mitigation; and the condition of the sick-wards of the parochial workhouses had become a byword.

The accumulation of orphan children under the same roof, without adequate means of instruction, exercise, or any sort of technical preparation for earning their bread at maturity, filled the humane with pity, but left them in despair. Other evils, like those of intermittent water supply, were felt, even by the better-to-do portions of the community, and in the overcrowded districts added daily to the wretchedness of the household and the increase of the rate of mortality.

These seemed to me infinitely more appropriate subjects of legislative effort on the part of a Metropolitan member than any which could be named within the sphere of party politics; and as I had made up my mind from the first to keep absolutely clear of sectarian disputes and discussions, it became all the easier to enlist sympathy and hope of amendments on the part of the pastors of various denominations. Of course, there were some who objected to this way of looking at public matters as utilitarianism or socialism, and here and there I encountered suspicion, if not antagonism, from fanatical teachers of exclusive theology, who, if they could not convert the suffering multitude to their narrow way of observance and dogma, felt themselves dispensed from the duty of saving their bodies from want and disease.

Two-thirds of the population were habitually absent from home during daylight hours, and did not easily forgive intrusion after dark. General organization, with which we are now familiar, was unknown, and there was nothing for it but to deal with local interests and separate trades.

One instance of the pitfalls of prejudice with which one was unconsciously beset gave me a lesson I did not soon forget. A tradesman who had become the adviser and guide of a great number of his fellows was, I was informed, especially worth conciliating, and I made him a visit accordingly, explained my political views, and of course paid him the compliment of saying I attached no little importance to his support. But either he was out of humour, or supposed he asserted his independence as a Liberal leader by suddenly refusing to give me any definite answer. It was useless, and I was about to leave, when a random thought occurred to me that I might ask if he meant to vote for one of my rivals who, I supposed, had special influence in the locality. 'What do you take me for?' he said, in a sudden rage. 'Don't you know that that fellow was born in this very street?' I begged his pardon, and retreated rapidly.

At an electors' meeting where one was asked to promise all manner of possible and impossible improvements in employment, rating, education, vehicular traffic, etc., we were asked to encourage workmen's clubs, then in their comparative infancy. A competitor who was present offered to answer the question first, and did so somewhat philosophically. The lawyers, he said, had their clubs, and military officers their clubs, and university men; 'and, indeed, the institution is one of great antiquity, for I think I have read that Hercules had a club.' Amid the laughter this excited, it was not difficult to frame an assurance that, though personally disinterested, I might be relied on to do what I could to strengthen the system of mutual self-reliance, inasmuch as I had been for some time an attending and attentive member of the Manchester Unity and the Finsbury Building Society.

But I expressed an earnest hope that they would not expect me, as member for Finsbury, to seek Government aid for spontaneous institutions, one of whose greatest merits consisted in their management and direction by the members themselves. Of course, benevolent but mistaken zeal took exception to the principle thus recommended, and I believe I lost some votes by being outbidden in the opposite direction. But I rejoice to say that in this, as in many other cases, I found no difficulty in securing the cordial support of the great bulk of the constituency in resisting plausible projects of industrial centralization.

The protracted canvass extended over a full twelvemonth, and though ballot was then unknown, and innumerable meetings had been invited to express their feelings preferentially, a general doubt prevailed as to what would be the issue. It came at last in the shape of a declaration of the poll which awarded me 8,640 votes—

a greater number than were given on that occasion for any other borough member.

The new House of Commons was first called together in 1865 to attend the obsequies of Lord Palmerston, and the office of First Lord of the Treasury was occupied for the second time by Earl Russell. And thus, with the exception of Mr. Gladstone, who thenceforth led the Commons, and Lord Hartington, who entered the Cabinet as Secretary for War, the heads of all the great spending departments were in the Peers. The Duke of Somerset, though the greatest aristocrat amongst them, felt the impolicy, if not injustice, of attempting to govern in this old fashion, and frankly offered to retire. But though individually unpopular, he had made himself known in the most discretional of offices, not only for unsleeping energy, but as a man in whom there was no guile. The navy felt safe in his hands, and the new Premier assured him that he could not be spared.

Palmerston, who understood him well, used to tell how he once sent Hayter to the Admiralty to request that the brother of a great supporter might have a ship. 'Can't be; he is growing old, and was never good for anything'; so there was nothing for it but to mollify his disappointed relative, and ask him next week to dinner. Three months later the message was repeated, somewhat more pressingly, but with like result;

and after Christmas the Whip came again with very deferential expressions of regret from Cambridge House that the desired promotion, though it might not be the best, could not be helped. 'Very well,' said his Grace quietly, 'I will give the order to-night, and you will lay my resignation to-morrow before the Minister.' No more, of course, was heard of the matter.

An interesting anecdote was told me by Richard Sheridan regarding his brother-in-law, while he was still Lord Seymour: 'Just after he had made in opposition a caustic and original criticism on the Navy Estimates, I had occasion to cross the floor to ask for some information on another subject from the Treasury Bench. Disraeli seemed to listen without interest to what I had to say, and after I had done rejoined abstractedly, "He's a wonderfully clever fellow; you may well be proud of him." I was delighted with his praise, lost my head, and, like a blockhead, stammered out, "Yes, and I'll tell you what's more, he's a very honest fellow." "Pooh! damn his honesty; that's not the part of him that men value here."'

On another occasion, when a considerable job was said to have been smothered at the Admiralty, then presided over by a peer of high degree, when no one was found ready openly to state the charge and ask for a Committee of Inquiry, Lord Seymour undertook the task with a shrug, saying, 'I believe before I come to the title I shall not be on speaking terms with any of my own order.'

For the rest, four-fifths of the new Cabinet were peers, or their immediate relatives, and the only man of the middle class admitted within the charmed circle was Mr. Goschen. Lord John owned that he had wished to put Cobden in his first Cabinet after the repeal of the Corn Laws but that he had suffered himself to be dissuaded. He then proposed that Charles Villiers, who for years had been the leader in Parliament of the Free Trade Party, should be Vice-President of the Board of Trade, Cardwell being chief of the department, which was naturally declined.

Adverting in conversation somewhat later to the exclusiveness of the Whigs, Bright said: 'Yes, you would have had the man whose policy Peel confessed he had followed play deputy to the man that merely followed Peel.' But times were changing, and the social prejudices which had prevented Lord Russell from conceding the rank of Privy Councillor to William Brown, the influential M.P. for South Lancashire, and to David Hume, the popular champion of retrenchment, had been jauntily swept away when Palmerston kept a seat in his Cabinet open for Cobden in 1859, and wrote a note to Bright asking him to call on him, which accident only prevented him receiving in time for personal acknowledgment.

When Cobden returned from America a few

weeks later, he called at Cambridge House, and was pressed in the most friendly terms to let past differences be forgotten, and to become President of the Board of Trade. But with equal good humour he explained why he thought his position would be a just subject of ridicule if, after all he had for years been saying against what was called a spirited foreign policy, he should publicly join in its administration. Bright told me himself that he possessed a letter from Lord Russell to the effect that, after Cobden's refusal, he wished a similar offer to be made to him, but that Palmerston objected on the specific ground of the violent things he had said in public against the House of Lords.

Cobden's dislike of Palmerston's policy, and his habitual misgiving of his tranquillizing assurances when supplemental estimates were said to be necessary, were inappeasable. A votary of peace at *almost* any price, he enjoyed in an especial degree the confidence of the Society of Friends, and was looked upon by them as a champion of their political tenets not less reliable than Bright himself.

When threats of invasion alarmed quiet people, and the Minister was denounced for provoking despatches, and allowing his organs in the press to impute dark designs on the part of our neighbours, Palmerston was fond of resorting to grave irony or good-humoured banter rather than to serious argument or the calculation of rival force. On one occasion, being sharply taxed with countenancing public alarm, for which the Quakers averred there was no cause, he read, with all the airs and emphasis of serious comedy, what he termed the latest enunciation of their principles from a pamphlet he held in his hand, wherein it was proposed that, should a foreign army reach our shores, Government should at once appoint a Commission to inquire, under a flag of truce, what they wanted; and, failing to obtain a satisfactory reply, that the Treasury should offer reasonable compensation to induce them to return by the way that they came. When the House had done laughing, Cobden, looking pale and angry, muttered audibly: 'That old rogue has got some blockhead to write this stuff, in order that he might use it.'

Charles Gilpin, who professed ardent devotion to the tenets of George Fox, exclaimed: 'I am so sorry to hear our friend talk in this way. I know the writer of the pamphlet, and he is one of the most intelligent and independent men of my acquaintance.'

Milner Gibson, who was intimate with all, but contrived to avoid being entangled in their peculiar tenets, and never quarrelled with anybody, was raised to the Cabinet as an offering to peace, if not a peace-offering; and when the Liberals returned to power in 1869, both Palmerston and

Cobden being dead, he and Bright were included in the Ministry.

I own that I was struck, on re-entering the House after an interval of some years, with its altered tone. There was more tendency to the consideration of social questions, and less of disposition to waive them off with gay indifference by those in power. Palmerston owed much of his influence to his buoyant humour, which, if it never crystallized into wit like Canning's, seldom failed at an awkward turn to jerk him over a dangerous rut in the road, not always without splash, but generally without harm. Baffled opponents muttered that there never was such audacity, but anxious supporters knew that, once beguiled into loud laughter, or even tentative 'hear, hears,' there was no frowning back the majority into the duty of being angry.

In the crisis of his Ministerial life, when a rare combination of domestic and foreign influences threatened to drive him from Downing Street, and the attack was led in the Upper House with characteristic energy and eloquence by Lord Derby, the odds to the last looked overwhelming against him. Sir Robert Peel, not forgetful of the days when they had been colleagues, was generous enough to atone for the gravity of his censure in the Pacifico affair by the confession that, after all, they were all proud of him. Graham and Gladstone, Disraeli and Thesiger, exhausted the resources of their varied skill in provoking the condemnation of the Commons; but, to the surprise and admiration of his frightened friends, on the third night of the debate he defended himself and his policy, as was truly said, from the dusk of one day to the dawn of another, with such temper, dexterity, and force of appeal to the national sense of honour, that he was acquitted of all blame by a majority of four-score.

Next day, in passing through the narrow corridor that then led from the temporary chamber to the Upper House, one swing-door opened to his hand, and at the same moment the other to that of Lord Derby. The manliness of both laughed in the other's face, and Palmerston exclaimed: 'I was just thinking what a clever fellow he was that so nearly had put me in a hole.' 'Ah, but nothing to the cleverness of the fellow that got you out of it!' In fact, they never quarrelled; and I remember once, when the conversation turned on some rumours prevalent of a possible coalition, Palmerston, who had a lurking love for that form of rule, said to me: 'You know, Derby is very Liberal.'

In hours of overwork or diplomatic thwarting, his elastic temperament betrayed depression in other ways than the brusquerie of phrase. Lord Holland once apologized to Talleyrand for going in before him to the Foreign Secretary's room, and returning later in the afternoon he was shocked to find the veteran Ambassador lounging on the same settee. To his inquiry the Prince only articulated, '*J'attend.*' Persons of less importance were unable to rebuke slight with such well-bred disdain. A very loyal colleague used to say that when they met in Cabinet they could generally tell the impending weather abroad from the noble Viscount's whiskers, which, if not in toilette curl, gave warning of European complications.

Graham, though heavy-laden with statistics and quotations as he usually was, often tried to test the skirmishing force of anecdote, and did not disdain, when hard pressed, to affect elaborate fun; and even Lord John, chill and unsympathetic in his ordinary manner, would now and then indulge in an excellent joke or sarcasm worth remembering. I recollect one night, when unexpectedly beaten in division on an Amendment in Committee of no great moment, he seemed less moved than some of his supporters, who had forsaken pleasant tables in Mayfair only to be made, as they thought, ridiculous in division. FitzStephen French audibly denounced the want of proper 'whipping,' and vowed he would not be at the trouble of coming again at short notice. He was not appeased on being informed that the accident was owing to Henry Tuffnell having married a third wife, and being absent for his honeymoon. 'He had no business to be! exclaimed the indignant grumbler. 'He ought to have been in his place.' 'No, no,' said Lord John; 'no man is bound to kiss and tell.

Palmerston's evidence before the Select Committee on official salaries was highly characteristic of the unfailing zest for sarcasm and banter traceable in his most elaborate and business-like statements. While nothing was clearer or more logical in sequence than his narrative of facts in speech or in despatch, he seldom denied himself the bit of fun afforded by a slight pinch of the ear, or by a hinted joke at the expense of a foreign or home critic. Sometimes it was not meant for print, or, if too literally reported, was readily made away with in laughing apology.

I was not of the Committee of 1850, but, like others, was attracted by the eminence of those who had consented to be witnesses to attend its proceedings. Sir Robert Peel and Lord John Russell gave, without reserve, the result of their long experience in administration, and concurred in deprecating as the most anti-popular abuse of public parsimony the lowering of Ministerial or diplomatic salaries. 'I never should have been able to attain the envied position I enjoyed as head of the Government if my father had not left me a more than ordinary estate without encumbrance,' said Peel; and when cross-examined as to whether a Prime Minister's expenditure was not somewhat compensated by the frequency of his dining out, Lord John scornfully replied: 'It never occurred to me to balance the contingencies, but I only know that I was never in debt until I was Prime Minister of England.'

Palmerston came next, and his reputation for liberal allowances and lavish outlay on extras set all who were present more than ever on the *qui vive*. Having answered at great length the Chairman's questions regarding diplomatic service, he was interrogated by Cobden on several apparent anomalies, which he accounted for as the growth of changing times, or as being more apparent than real. Pressed to explain why an Ambassador to Vienna should have three times as much as an Envoy to Washington, he thought it was enough to say that the Minister from Austria here had equal or greater emoluments, and for sake of our dignity we could hardly do less.

'But suppose,' said Mr. Bright, 'the two diplomatists came to the Foreign Office on the same day, and on similar affairs, would more regard be shown to the German than to the American?' The champion of high salaries replied: 'I hope I may say for myself, and I am sure I may for Lord Aberdeen, that the greatest consideration is always shown to the Envoy of the United States whenever he appears at Downing Street.' 'Then,' added his questioner, who fancied he had caught him in a dilemma, 'how is the Government of Austria benefited by this large expenditure?'

How they calculated such things in the Aulic Council his lordship did not remember having ever heard, but he was sure that the Austrian Ambassador thought it a great advantage to have the £12,000 a year. When the ill-suppressed laugh subsided, the advocate of retrenchment asked why diplomatic life at Vienna should cost more than at Washington. Still preserving his air of inflexible irony, Palmerston specified the important discrepancies of equipage and hospitality in the two missions. (Turning to the reporter, he said: 'Don't put this down.')

'Henry Bulwer told me that at a dinner at the White House someone sitting next to him pointed across the table to an occasional waiter, saying: "You see that jane jacket he wears; it was one I gave him." In the capital of the empire all is traditional state and ceremonial; nothing can be more unlike than the social and political ways of the two countries; and the Atlantic Ocean rolls between.' 'Stay,' exclaimed the member for Manchester eagerly; 'what difference does the Atlantic Ocean make?' 'Well,' rejoined the imperturbable Viscount, 'perhaps none'—'The reason,' muttered Henry Drummond, 'why he mentioned it, that, after the manner of Sterne, the world might comprehend what it did *not* arise from.'

Hundreds of questions, the most diverse in

their scope and tenor, were addressed to the head of the Foreign Department, the replies to which, often piquant and sardonic, were modified in the authorized version.

During the period of transition after the destructive fire in October, 1834, when Parliament was obliged to put up with a wooden shanty for its abode, the accommodation was so scanty that men of high and low political degree were often forced into juxtaposition that in the days of the old oak-panelled Chapel of St. Stephen, then reduced to ashes, would not have been possible. When post hour approached, committee-rooms where members could indite epistles to friends afar off were inconveniently full, and even Ministers of State had to put up with the first places they could find at overcrowded writing-tables. Palmerston found himself thus beside a well-known man of business, not remarkable for diffidence in addressing those he wished to be thought to know; and before the Viscount had finished his 'private and confidential' to Panshanger, he was asked by his wealthy neighbour, 'Are there two *h*ens in 'Oniton?' 'No,' said Palmerston at once, 'only one; that's why *h*eggs are so scarce there.'

Many of the familiar faces had disappeared, and many of the best-known voices were to be heard no more in the House; but certain notable additions had been made to the Parliamentary muster-roll, and no little curiosity was excited as each of the new recipients of the popular mandate asked leave to speak.

Westminster had returned John Stuart Mill, from whom much was expected, not only on account of his varied and elaborate speculative writings, but because he was known to have taken an active and influential part for many years in the home administration of the East India Company. His appearance and bearing tended rather to chill such anticipations. His finely-chiselled features and expansive brow seemed ill-supported by his feeble frame, and his gait, abstracted look, and somewhat feminine voice suggested involuntarily the impression of premature old age. Still, when he rose for the first time to address the House, there was intense anxiety to catch every word; and, irrespective of party distinctions, the demonstration of personal respect was manifest.

The subject he had chosen for his notable speech was retrenchment, coupled with the policy and duty of paying off the National Debt while prosperity lasted, lest the time should come when the cost of existence would render it practically impossible. The source of danger on which he chiefly dwelt was that of the approaching exhaustion of the coal supply, which, according to Professor Jevons, was already within measurable distance; and upon the statistics collected by him, the great logician had built up an argument he declared to be irrefutable, and which the most incredulous and reluctant of his hearers felt himself unable offhand to refute.

Before passing to other topics Mr. Mill paused, as though he had forgotten what was to come next. The House cheered as it always does to help a stranger over his embarrassment; but it would not do, and the painful pause continued for some minutes. He appeared to have notes of some sort in his hand, but he did not refer to them; and at length a fickle memory resumed her office, and jilted him no more. It is impossible to describe the contending impressions of the hour.

Roebuck and Cornewall Lewis had been class-fellows with him in Bentham's school, but Lewis was there no more to hear his first essay. Roebuck awaited with interest an appearance in Parliamentary life so long deferred, and characteristically said afterwards, 'I always said he would never do here.' But the lecture—for it was more of a lecture than a speech—produced an effect nobody dreamed of.

Mr. Gladstone, in the course of a highly complimentary speech, welcomed his accession to the intellectual and political strength of the Legislature, and seemed to be so sympathetically impressed with the impending possibilities of fuel-dearth that many were led to apprehend some modification might be attempted of financial policy. Men like Thomas Baring and Edward

Bouverie amused themselves and their friends with the grounds of their scepticism; and misgivings spread lest what soon came to be caricatured as the Jevons crotchet might mislead worthier if not wiser men than the member for Westminster.

The Cabinet decided to grant a Royal Commission to inquire into the national resources underground, who after two years' elaborate research and computation pronounced Mr. Mill's dream to be no better than a nightmare, and we heard of the matter no more.

Although the demand for further electoral reform was neither loud nor general, Lord Russell, on resuming the office of Prime Minister, proposed to lower the franchise from £10 to £7 value, without any redistribution of seats, regarding which the Cabinet were not agreed. The scheme was manifestly incomplete, and would ere long be followed by steps more important in what Mr. Disraeli called the degradation of the franchise.

Several distinguished Whigs, who resented their omission from office, refused their support, and formed the nucleus of a third party, which Mr. Bright stigmatized as another Cave of Adullam, whereunto every man was invited who was discontented or in debt. Their total number did not exceed twenty-four; but, in combination with the Conservative Party, they threatened to obstruct the further progress of the Bill, substituting £5 rating for £7 rent.

Lord Grosvenor led the combined Opposition against the Bill, and was defeated by a majority of five.

Kinglake, one of the most popular and accomplished friends of Government, who felt the hopelessness of their carrying extension of suffrage without redistribution, offered to throw a bridge over the chasm by which they might escape betimes from defeat; and, adopting his resolution that a revised map should accompany any new edition of the register, a further proposal was laid on the table by Mr. Gladstone to reduce the number of close boroughs, and to transfer their representatives to half a dozen counties and towns.

This, like every concession ascribed to lobby misgivings, not Cabinet foresight, only inspired the seceders with further hopes of breaking down the tottering scheme. They were ill agreed regarding the issue to be joined. Was the suggested change wanton, and therefore wrong? or was it too small a patch on the old garment, whereby the popular rent would soon be made worse?

Horsman, who had formerly played the part of superior Radical, had been given by Palmerston the Secretaryship of Ireland, but by neglect of his office, in which he could find nothing to do, he said, worth doing, had slipped the next round of the ladder, and was now only vexed at being out, and resolved to be captious until he could get in again.

He was all for leaving everyone who helped to smash the Bill free to go further or not in reform so far as might suit him hereafter; while Lowe declaimed against yielding to the beginnings of evil, heated up torrents of lava from Burke's 'French Revolution,' and asked, if they wanted examples of all that was violent, venal, and vile in elections, would they not widely extend the franchise?

Whereupon Bright quizzed the malcontent section as resembling a pampered poodle, of which he could not always make out which was the head and which the tail, and the meaning of whose incoherent sniffs and snarls was only intelligible to the owner.

The difference in some places would not have been very considerable, but in several towns of importance, where the standard of rating was high, and in the Metropolis, where rates were to a vast extent paid by the landlord, compounded for in rent, the change would have been little more than nominal.

Mr. Horsman, Mr. Lowe, and Lord Elcho led the attack, and were resisted in debate by Mr. Gladstone, Mr. Bright, and Mr. Cardwell.

The discussion was long and memorable. Mr.

Gladstone's reply to Lord R. Montagu's expression that the working classes, if armed with the franchise, would be 'an invading and destroying army,' evoked a ringing cheer when, in a climax of enthusiasm, he asked, 'Are they not our own flesh and blood?'

Sir Lytton Bulwer next day undertook to answer him, and his mien and tone will hardly be forgotten by any who had the opportunity to observe them.

Formerly conspicuous in advocacy of advanced Whiggery, and something more, he had become a convert to Protection, and repented him of his literary errors in eulogy of Pericles and Aspasia. But he was Pelham still, and on all great occasions relied for effect not less upon cosmetic and attire than upon apt quotation and brilliant antithesis. In the heat and crush of an encounter wherein everybody else discarded the idea of sitting for his picture or dressing for the stage, he could not resist the temptation to indulge in the adornments that had made him in the Park the envy of the dandies, or of what he deemed dramatic articulation that was too fine by half.

Having a night to think it over, he delighted his supporters by challenging the philosophy of the Ministerial leader, which he pronounced perilous in its inevitable consequences. What would he have to say hereafter to the millions who would ask him one day, 'Are we an invading army, or fellow-Christians, or your own flesh and blood?' Would he say, 'For my own part, in my individual capacity, I cannot see that there is any danger in admitting you; but still, you know, it is wise to proceed gradually. A £7 voter is real flesh and blood. But you are only gradual flesh and blood. Read Darwin on the origin of species, and learn that you are Christians in an imperfect state of development'?

The speech was partly given from memory and partly from copious pages in round-hand spread before him on the table, and when it was over he sank back into the arms of his friends, as if in a state of exhaustion.

Coming out of the House, I met Sir George Grey, who was in all things the most inexorable critic of whatever savoured of foppery, and I asked him what he thought of the speech. 'Well, he came down upon us in his war-paint,' was the Puritanic Secretary's reply.

After many debates the final issue was taken on June 19 on the question of rating, on an amendment moved by Lord Dunkellin, one of the most popular of the secessionists, grandson of George Canning, and heir of the noble Marquis who had been Postmaster-General and Privy Seal under Palmerston, but who was now left out. The Government being defeated by eleven in a full House, the Cabinet met, and at once resolved to resign, believing, as was generally supposed, that the Tories, being still a minority, would not venture to take office, and that open coalition with the disaffected Whigs who had helped them would hardly stand the test of a General Election.

Lord Derby would willingly have run that risk for the sake of obtaining such colleagues as Lords Grosvenor and Lansdowne,* Mr. Horsman and Mr. Lowe; but on their declining office he became Premier for the third time, reminding his friends that 'they must prepare to kill their game with their own dogs.'

The failure of the £7 Franchise Bill stirred the slumbering desire for reform, and multitudinous assemblages in the autumn convinced Disraeli, if not all his colleagues, that they must outbid their rivals in the concession of a wider suffrage. The House had no sooner met than he laid on the table a string of resolutions embodying what came to be called the 'fancy franchises.' They would have conferred upon men of various professions and degrees of learning the privilege of voting wherever they resided, in right of their educated intelligence, instead of an accidental possession of house or land, and in an elaborate speech expounding his alternative theory of representation, to use his own phrase in private, 'he tried it on.'

* Fourth inheritor of the title, who had sat nine years for Calne.

But it would not do. In the lobby and the press men of a literary turn called it philosophical: unyielding Whigs called it fantastic: and top-boot Tories said it was humbug.

Slowly and sadly he laid it down, and reported to the Cabinet that they must go much farther or go out. If they could be sure that Opposition would *agmine facto* vote for a £6 suffrage in towns, they might overtrump it with £5: but rumour was rife that a numerous section were pledged to household suffrage, and there was a whisper prevalent that Lord Russell would not disapprove of that course. What was to be done? A meeting of his supporters was called by Mr. Gladstone at Carlton House Terrace, where members overflowed the reception-rooms, and the leader delivered his advice from half-way down the staircase. They must, he said, if they would prevail in the pending struggle, wait for the next bidding of their rivals, and leave the form and time of their own proceeding to their leader to determine as circumstances might require. All who had been in office, or wished to be, applauded the demand of confidence as obvious wisdom; but throughout the hall there were not a few looks of disappointment and suppressed murmurs of regret.

Next day 48 representatives of populous towns and counties assembled in the Tea-Room at Westminster, prepared to warn their eminent leader that the time for half-measures was gone by. A resolution was without dissent agreed to pledging those present to refuse any hard-and-fast line of occupation value if a wider franchise were proposed, and a deputation was instructed to lay the same before Mr. Gladstone.

The deputation included James Clay, Henry Fawcett, and John Locke, and reported a discouraging result of their interview. The former had been for years an intimate and travelling companion of Disraeli; the latter was a trusted representative of City and Borough advanced Liberalism. For some time discordant views were warmly debated at the clubs and in the smoking-room of the House, and in Colonel Gossett's *peculiar*, to which men of all shades of opinion who had brains, and none who were mere babblers, had the *entrée*.

It became known by the end of February that a majority of the Cabinet had made up their minds, as Lord Derby expressed it subsequently, to 'dish the Whigs' by proposing rated household suffrage in boroughs, and that Lords Carnarvon and Cranborne, with General Peel, had in consequence resigned.* No division took place on the second reading or on going into Committee. But on the occupation franchise clause Mr. Gladstone's amendment, enfranchising the occupier, whether rated personally or through his landlord, was overborne by 310 to 289. Lord

* Statement by Mr. Disraeli, March 4, 1867. *Hansard.*

Grosvenor's attempt to limit the rateable value to £5 and an occupying term of two years was negatived.

The Tea-Room section voted on Mr. Gladstone's amendment in the minority, while the Adullamites went the other way. Eventually the anomaly, which appeared greatest in the Metropolis, of householders whose rates were paid in compound by the landlord being, on a legal technicality, disqualified, was swept away by a Bill introduced by Mr. Goschen.

In Committee, J. S. Mill moved the extension of the new franchise to women, but found no more than seventy-three supporters.

Meanwhile there remained unenfranchised a great number of occupiers belonging to the professional classes or possessed of independent incomes, especially in London, who permanently dwelt in parts of houses, and often in the best parts of them. Not being separately rated, their names never came before the registering tribunals, and yet they were confessedly as well qualified to exercise the right of suffrage, if not better than the majority on whom it had been recently conferred.

Nobody disputed a claim which had not been collectively urged before the revising barristers, and I had reason to believe that there was no invincible obstacle in the way of their recognition as fellow-citizens on either side of the House.

But nothing is harder to enforce sometimes than the obvious. Mr. Roebuck and others had given notice of general resolutions on the subject which it seemed to me might have left matters practically where they were, and I therefore, towards the close of the Committee, proposed to add a clause to the Bill enabling every lodger in boroughs to be placed on the list of electors who could show that he had lived in apartments rented at £10 or upwards for the space of a year. In the Metropolis 2,500,000 people dwelt in 300,000 houses, and on an average each house might be said to be occupied by two families. Of these it would probably be less than the truth to say that above 100,000 heads of families would still be excluded, from no presumable unfitness or want of sympathy with the interests of their neighbours. Difficulties in applying a more just and generous rule there might be; but everything really worth doing in comprehensive legislation was difficult in old and varied communities.

After some general discussion, the Chancellor of the Exchequer owned that he saw no objection in principle to my proposition, and offered, if I abstained from pressing for an immediate decision, to authorize the Attorney-General, on behalf of the Government, to confer with me as to the best form of words that would ensure the enjoyment to all persons coming within the £10 definition of permanent lodgers in unfurnished apartments, and that if the Cabinet approved he would himself move the addition. A few days after, Sir John Rolt, one of the best-informed and most agreeable of the members of his profession, intimated his readiness to enter on the task assigned him. He began by saying frankly: 'You know I am individually averse from all the changes we are making; but, being determined on, my duty is to carry them into effect, leaving as little room for harm or abuse as may be; and you may without reserve tell me your case.' There were some possible anomalies to be considered. But after two or three hours' careful review of what had from time to time been the language adopted in other measures of concession, the terms of an inclusive clause seemed free from cavil; and, to my no small gratification, I heard it duly moved from the Treasury Bench, put from the Chair, and carried without a division.

It was said frequently at the time, by some, that lodgers would not take the trouble to register; by others that it was opening the flood-gates through which the representation of property would be ultimately swamped. The experience of a quarter of a century has dispelled both anticipations. At the next election for Finsbury, between 500 and 600 additional voters came to the poll; example gradually told, and year by year, in other great towns as well as in London, the privilege became one of ordinary use, and in 1885 the number of lodgers registered in cities and boroughs in England and Wales was 57,684.

Monckton Milnes, whose boast it was that he was never shy in putting embarrassing questions, told me that when the world was still agape at the Tory Bill granting household and lodger suffrage, he asked Disraeli how he could have brought himself to such a *bouleversement* of all he had been educating the Tories into thinking he thought, and that his answer was: 'It may look awkward, but it was necessary.' We talked on, and I owned my belief that he had done more than anybody to accomplish the emancipation of his race by keeping Lyndhurst up to it. 'But what else,' I said, 'has he done to prove his being a man of political genius?' 'Why,' responded Milnes, 'he did what no other man would have thought of attempting—he invented George Bentinck.' And how wittily true this was will be recollected by those who call to mind how seldom and to what little purpose the noble idler had tried to speak in the House before 1846, and how suddenly he gave up the hunting and racing pursuits of his life, and put himself in training to run against Peel for the leadership of the Country Party.

During the winter Lord Derby was known to have been entirely prostrated by continual attacks of gout, and Parliament, when it met in February,

1868, was informed that he had resigned, and that by his advice Mr. Disraeli had been named his successor. His first act as Premier was a brief intimation to Lord Chelmsford that the Queen had no longer any occasion for his services; his next, to offer the Great Seal to Lord Cairns, thus, as was said by one who knew them both, replacing wit by wisdom. Most of the other members of the Cabinet retained their places.

Mr. Gladstone brought in a Bill abolishing compulsory payment of Church rates, which was feebly resisted and speedily carried; while in the course of a debate on the state of Ireland he announced his conviction that the disestablishment of the Anglican Church in that country was part of the heavy debt of justice long due by Great Britain.

On March 30 he embodied this opinion in a resolution which declared 'that in the opinion of the House it was necessary that the Established Church of Ireland should cease to exist as an establishment, due regard being had to all personal interests, and to all individual rights of property.' This resolution was carried by a majority of sixty-five against the Government.

A dissolution being already impending to enable the expanded constituencies to take their part in the choice of representatives, nobody thought of its being anticipated; and the offer of Ministers to comply with the constitutional rule of vacating their places on the rejection of their policy by the House of Commons was understood to be formal. Disraeli's account of his audience with her Majesty, and of his ready compliance with the request that he and his colleagues would hold on until the decision of the larger electorate should be known, evoked some ironical and some faltering cheers. The remainder of the Session was thereby left free for uncontentious business, and, for one, I gladly availed myself of the improved opportunity for carrying to completion a work which had already occupied three years.

In the Session of 1868 I had the satisfaction of carrying the first Act for the Improvement of Artisans and Labourers' Dwellings, which has since borne my name. Soon after Parliament met, in 1866, Mr. Arthur Kinnaird and Mr. Locke had consented to share with me the responsibility of urging the Legislature to interpose, as it had never done before, for the eradication from our great towns of the dens of disease and degradation in which it was but too notorious that great numbers of the working classes were doomed to wear out life. Lord Shaftesbury had some years before obtained an Act enabling the medical officer of health in any district to report such places as unfit for human habitation, and to authorize municipal authorities to take gradual steps for their structural or other modification. But little or nothing in the way of remedial change was effected in consequence. The Secretary to the Treasury, Mr. Childers, had brought in a Bill enabling his department to lend money at four per cent. to corporations, vestries, or joint stock companies for the purpose of providing better homes for those who lived by daily labour; but it did not appear to any of us who had studied closely the needs and exigencies of the case that palliatives of this kind would ever overtake them, or naturally check their palpable growth, arising from the steady influx of population from the agricultural districts—''Twas but spermaceti for an inward bruise.'

On February 20, 1866, I obtained leave to bring in a Bill to provide in great towns better dwellings for artisans and labourers. There was a hardly suppressed shudder in certain portions of the House at the levity, as it was deemed, with which Parliament was thus invited to deviate from its manifest duty of securing what Carlyle loved to call 'Strength for the strong, want for the weak, and devil take the hindmost.'

Edmund Potter, an able, and in his way an amiable, man, who took care of his numerous employés in evil as well as good times, but who was, before all things, an inflexible utilitarian, reproached me bitterly with lending myself to what he characterized as the obvious beginnings of Socialism. I only replied that there was nothing in human fate which had not two sides the intrinsically good and the convertibly bad. If capitalists were all like him, there would be no need and no excuse for intervention: but with the shameful ripening unto rottenness of the effects of long neglect and permission of rent usury, he ought not to cavil at an attempt to make local authorities stand between the dead and the living, that the plague of labour might be stayed.

Government would only allow our measure a second reading on condition that it should be referred to a Select Committee, which was in due time appointed, containing one Cabinet Minister and two subordinate officials. I tried hard to induce the Home Secretary, Mr. Bruce, to be named, but, being on two important Committees, he excused himself from want of time, though he said he 'would have liked nothing better than to have served. He was sorry that Mr. Childers had conveyed to me the impression that he was hostile to the principle of the Bill. He might have exaggerated objections, but he was entirely with us on its main principles, and, in fact, felt fewer qualms at this onslaught on the rights of property than he himself did.'*

From Lord Shaftesbury we had even more considerate recognition and encouragement. Far

* March 13, 1866, MS. from H. A. Bruce to W. M. T.

from evincing any jealousy that the handle of the plough he had earlier endeavoured to drive through the stiff clay of prejudice should be taken by another, he wrote: 'I have urged Henley to sit on the Dwellings Committee. Mr. Torrens had better speak to him himself.'*

No suggestion could have been more timely. Mr. Henley had sat many years in Parliament, and though a firm, and sometimes sharp, defender of the rights and privileges of the landed proprietary, was recognised amongst us as a man amply gifted with the sense of equity and humanity, irrespective of calling and class. He was easily entreated to lend us the benefit of his shrewd and practical help in dealing with legal difficulties, and I gratefully recall the memory of his essential aid on more than one occasion.

The more sanguine of us were, I own, but feeling our way, and in the Committee we had to encounter from the outset the disheartening agnosticism of the economists *par excellence*, who never tired of reiterating their great non-suit point: 'What, after all, do you mean by a house unfit for habitation?' Long and wearisome discussions arose as to the number of cubic feet that sufficed for the room wherein by night and day a workman, his wife and six children might be left without pity or interference. In vain we pro-

* Lord Shaftesbury to Hon. A. Kinnaird, March 13, 1866.—*MS.*

tested against the futility of measuring legislative duty or justice by the arithmetical test of definition. What was the density of exhalation from cesspool or sewer which constituted an indictable nuisance? Or what was the contiguity to dung-heap or knacker's yard that in a Christian State should be left as good enough for dwelling to unnumbered dependents upon daily labour?

We pleaded earnestly that local authorities should be charged by law with the constructive responsibility of allowing the cumulation of such mischiefs without corrective interposition, and that owners of property in cities and towns, whose rentals were swelled by the deadly competition for shelter near places of work, should be held bound to overhaul and repair the buildings out of which their luxury was fed.

But such questions were novel and distasteful, and after several contentions in argument, and deliberation on amendments—some to do less, some to do more, and some to do nothing at all—we found our first project of remedial legislation so tattered and torn that it became a serious question whether it were not better to let the Committee report directly against the Bill. This, however, upon reflection, our critics did not think desirable, and the Government draughtsman was instructed to put together instead a permissive scheme upon the basis of letting the dead bury their dead as heretofore, generally speaking, but permitting philanthropic vestries and corporations to submit to the Lords of the Treasury, in certain cases, proposals for gradual amelioration.

Mr. (now Lord) Thring favoured me in the course of a few days with the result, which he was good enough to say should not be circulated among the members of the Committee until it had received my signature of assent. With the approval of my colleagues, I answered that as, either in substance or in form, no part of our proposal was retained in that which he was directed to offer, I could not presume that the intention could be regarded as identical; and that, as I failed to see how the object contemplated by the House in its reference was likely to be attained, I must decline altogether adopting the substitute proposed.

When we were next summoned to meet, nothing was said on the subject; but, with the assistance of Mr. Henley and others, we gradually rebuilt most of the outworks that had been broken down, and when submitted to Lord Shaftesbury for his consideration he wrote: 'The Bill will do fairly enough if got into operation, though the delays are many. But I fear that it will seldom be put in motion. The substitution in Clause 5 of an officer of health appointed by the *local* authority, and not by any independent power, instead of the Clause 5 in your own Bill, will seriously restrain the operations you desire. All the clauses following are injuriously affected by the new Clause 5.'*

Mr. William Chambers, then Provost of Edinburgh, hailed with infinite satisfaction the reform we had in hand, and wrote to Mr. Maclaren, who sat for the Scottish capital, begging that the Bill might be extended to towns north of the Tweed: 'The grand difficulty we have to contend against is the rapacity of a pack of proprietors who pick up old buildings for a few pounds, let them at monstrous rents to poor wretches, and insist on getting enormous sums for these edifices when any sort of improvement is projected. Parliament has never properly dealt with this evil. What we want is a power to peremptorily shut up old, half-ruinous buildings, by which means we could easily buy them for improvements at their proper value. If I had now this power in Edinburgh, I could half renovate the old town, and build hundreds of houses of a good kind for artisans. Should the Bill, improved so far, be extended to Scotland, I will gladly give it my support.'†

The change of Administration led to the postponement to another Session of nearly all opposed Bills; but in 1867 we had little difficulty in carrying a carefully revised and expanded edition of the measure, which, in compliance with suggestions from various quarters that fuller statistical infor-

* To W. M. T., June 13, 1866.—*MS.*

† Edinburgh, February 23, 1866.—*MS.*

mation should be had before it was passed, lay over until the following year. We were then more fortunate, and when taken up to the House of Lords we were gratified by the intimation that Government would take charge of the Bill in Committee.

Pressed at the last moment by some proprietors of importance, the Duke of Richmond consulted me at the bar, where I anxiously watched its progress, whether we would not be content to allow the compulsory clause for demolition to be modified so far as to be rendered permissive. I told him that the alteration would not only quench the growing belief in effectual legislation, but would probably drive many now likely to be satisfied to more debatable demands. Individually, his Grace concurred with the new Premier in preferring what the Commons had agreed to, and no further idea was suggested of limiting the scope of the enactment.

When it had obtained the Queen's assent, Disraeli asked me to call on him at Downing Street, and after some characteristic expressions of gratulation, inquired what advances we expected the Treasury might be asked to make in the course of the next year or two. My sanguine anticipations did not put too high the figure that local bodies would at first require, and I named £100,000, on which he said: 'You shall have double that if you want it.' It was some time, however, before London vestries availed themselves of the promised aid.

Great distress, intensified by sickness, had prevailed throughout two-thirds of the Metropolis during the winter and the ensuing spring. Parochial workhouses had fallen into bad repute for humanity and guardianship of the public health, and in 1867 an Act was passed intended to establish dispensaries for the sick, distinct from the ordinary refuges for the infirm and infant poor.

In many instances, the measure proved to be insufficient, and Government, with much applause in the press, announced their intention to build and equip, out of an additional rate which industry just then was ill able to bear, a number of vast edifices for different classes of disease, under the direction of what came to be called the Metropolitan Asylums Board.

In common with the most thoughtful and enlightened medical practitioners, many of us deprecated this course of proceeding as entailing needless burthens on the ratepayers, ill calculated to afford the best means of mitigating the miseries of humble life, and as being wholly at variance with the cheaper and better system that, after the famine in Ireland, had been found to work admirably there by means of well-appointed dispensaries, while throughout Scotland and England each locality had, time out of mind, remained charged with the care and cure of its own sick.

Mr. (afterwards Sir John) Lambert had specially been sent to Ireland in 1867 by Mr. Hardy, then at the head of the Poor Law Department, to inquire into the subject, and he reported that nothing could be better adapted for the purpose of giving timely aid to the fluctuating numbers of the population who intermittently fell under the calamity of fever or other epidemic, that the mortality was comparatively small, and the cost specifically low, three-quarters of a million having been relieved in the year out of a population of six millions, at a total expense of £118,000; while numbers of orphan or destitute children, instead of being cast into the workhouses to grow up unfit for self-reliant labour, were boarded out, and thereby better fitted to bear their part in peasant or artisan life.

I had myself been gradually impressed for some time with the growing evils of aggregation in medical relief, and had spared no pains to obtain from military as well as civil authorities, abroad and at home, testimony as to the comparative worth of severing or huddling together the wounded and the stricken.

Dr. Sutherland, of the War Office, assured me that, with the exception of special cases, the percentage of recoveries where the sick were subdivided among separate dwellings was greater in all cases than when they were removed to a distant hospital, even though the surroundings were far superior to those of their own homes.

Numerous friends who had served in the Crimea testified to the same effect, and I had the satisfaction of quoting in debate the touching words of the first and best of witnesses—Florence Nightingale: 'I have come to believe that the hospital system is an intermediary stage of civilization. At the end of a life spent in hospital work, to this conclusion I have always come—that the poor are always better relieved at their own homes.'

Nor were witnesses wanting in the daily experience of manufacturing and mining existence. Sir James Simpson told me that from minute inquiries he had instituted in the border counties he was enabled to state that, of 2,098 cases of amputations of limbs of persons treated in their own homes, only one in nine died, while of 4,937 treated in great hospitals in England, Scotland, and the North, one in three ended fatally.

I visited personally, with the assistance in each case of the principal officer in charge, the chief hospitals of the Metropolis, and learned that, while the wards at Guy's, Bartholomew's, and Charing Cross were crowded with sufferers from accidents, internal maladies, phthisis, and fever of every description, other great institutions were obliged to leave their spacious wards empty, some from want of funds, and others, as at King's College, where they had been, in despair, obliged to refuse admission to obstetric cases, from the fatal experience of contagion.

The Ministerial Bill, however, being pressed, I moved as an amendment that, before voting the expenditure of great sums on building estimates, and committing Parliament to establishing a fresh staff of permanent officials, a competent Commission should be issued to investigate the whole subject, and to ascertain how far further medical and surgical relief might be best administered without breaking up the people's homes or branding them with pauperism.

But I pleaded in vain. Coming out after the division, Mr. Bright said to me, in a low tone, 'There was no answer to the case you made.' I could not help rejoining: 'Then, in mercy's name, why did you not vote with me?' He muttered something I could not hear, and went away. I thought of Shiel's words on a former occasion, when I had provoked the ill-humour of Government by saying in the House something that might be distasteful, but was only true: 'That's what renders critics on one's own side formidable; but, remember, those that make themselves formidable must prepare for a long fast.'

Abuses of the indoor system of relief in the Metropolis, grimly exposed and caricatured by Dickens, remained still uneradicated until Mr.

Gathorne Hardy introduced his Bill for the amendment of the Poor Law by the general concentration of inspection and control in the governing department, and the erection of district infirmaries for the various classes of disease not provided for in the great hospitals. Vast establishments were at the same time created in the suburbs, to which children were to be transferred from time to time from the parochial poor-houses, partly on the plea of securing better health, and partly on that of severance from the demoralizing influence of destitute and dissolute parents.

Without impugning the aim of these costly changes, or encouraging a niggard cry certain to arise against their burthensome character, not a few of us, who had become acquainted with the actual working of local distress, challenged on wider, and we thought better, grounds the strides thus indicated in the system of centralization. For one, I could not defend the laxity and heartlessness too often shown by Boards of Guardians, and I resisted every suggestion, frequently urged, that, because poverty could never be expected to cease out of the land, it were better to leave things alone.

I had no objection to the rebuilding of workhouses, expensive though they might be, or the institution of separate wards for the shelter and care of the decrepit through age, or the helpless through overwork or accident. But I deprecated earnestly the resort, advocated by the department, to vast aggregations of misery, even under honest and experienced medical direction, as tending to maim, if not destroy, the ties of local sympathy and family obligation.

The same objections seemed to apply to the accumulation of multitudes of poor little creatures within the prison walls—for such they necessarily must be—of district schools, where the children could by no possibility learn anything to fit them for ordinary ways of life, and be brought up in the graduated experience of give and take, without which they could only be flung out into the world to lie and cheat and steal for their bread as occasion offered. It was said, on the other hand, by the doctrinaires, that everything was to be gained by the exclusion from the eyes of the young of the temptations and indulgences of ill-regulated mature pauper life, and by the magical advantages of absolute uniformity in the processes of elementary education.

With several of my worthy colleagues in the representation, I strove to resist this tendency to artificialism, and I am bound to say that at every local meeting, where the impending changes were discussed, I found a ready and cordial response to the counter-policy we advocated. It was, of course, comparatively easy to denounce the inevitable jobbery of contracts and subordinate patronage we feared; but it never was equally clear to me that busy, tired, and unreflecting constituents, whether working men or traders, entered fully into the moral and social aspects of the case as we endeavoured to explain them.

What we said in favour of local and household relief was all very well; but perhaps it was not a bad thing to have the crippled old grandmother placed comfortably for the rest of her days, though her people couldn't see her more than once in a way; or to have a clean, lightsome, healthy school-home provided, not only for destitute *Jinx's babies*, but for the ever-accruing crowd of orphans and foundlings. It grew clear to me that unless we could suggest practical antidotes for the specious remedies propounded from Whitehall, our struggle in the press and in Parliament must end ere long in the usual—*probitas laudatur et alget.*

Mr. Goschen, who succeeded to the Chairmanship of the Local Government Board, was impressed with the belief that, had great central schools and asylums been built ten years earlier, they would have tended materially to keep down the increase of pauperism, which had begun to assume threatening dimensions. The wisest and best of my friends in Finsbury assured me that this idea was fallacious, and that the truest, as well as the most Christian, security of the hard-driven poor against sinking into the depravity of despair was the cherishing and strengthening, by every means, of the family tie. Instead of cut-stone places of imprisonment for the sick and decrepit, I said I would spend any amount of grants or rates that might be necessary on human aid and human skill. Believing, as I did profoundly, that the chances of recovery from ordinary illness or hurt lay quite as much in the humble consolations of affection and tenderness as in the drugs or cataplasms of the physician, I would have the same system of out-door sick-relief applied in England which we had tried with such eminent success in Ireland after the famine.

Under the dispensary system, myriads of sufferers had been, at comparatively little expense, rescued from death or the contraction of chronic infirmity, who would probably have risked their lives sooner than go into distant workhouses; and as for gigantic asylums or monster schools, they were happily unknown. But as an alternative and an antidote I proposed a systematic plan for the boarding-out of poor children in suitable places, where they might, especially if orphans, be domiciled and taught useful employment as part of the family. Of course, I was told that such a scheme was chimerical and impracticable. I replied that if it were only impossible, I hoped it would be acted on—experimentally, at all events—as I never knew anything that was worth doing that was not at first pronounced impossible; and though I met with every species of discouragement from official quarters, I had the satisfaction in due time of finding the suggestion nip the shell, and after a time shown to be able to take wing in a very expanded sphere.

The boarding-out system has not only spread throughout every portion of the realm,* but has been, by adaptation and the surpassing self-devotion of benevolence, like that of Miss Rye and the Rev. Styleman Herring, rendered an auxiliary instrument of annual emigration to Canada and the Far West. Like every other human invention, it is liable now and then to break down in isolated cases, because cruelty and covetousness lurk in the dark places of the earth, and cannot be always even detected for denunciation. But in the main this way of escape for desolate and deserted childhood is no longer impeached by either doctrinaires or dialecticians.

The General Election of 1868 dispelled the dream of the Conservatives that their gift of household suffrage would be requited by a renewed lease of power: a majority of more than one hundred recalled the Liberals to office. In Finsbury the seat of my colleague was ineffectually challenged by an eminent Queen's Counsel, who disclaimed opposing me, and I was returned once more at the head of the poll.

* See the admirable report of Miss Mason, the inspector for the department, 1890-91.

At a public dinner soon afterwards given to my worthy colleague, Sir Andrew Lusk, and myself, I thanked my new supporters without distinction, creed, or party, asking no question of individual motives for conscience' sake. I knew that Conservative Lincoln's Inn and Bloomsbury had contributed freely to the result, and I own that I was glad that, as at Dundalk and Yarmouth, I had been able, without any compromise of principle or furtive pledge, to obtain the suffrages of the out-numbered minority who had seldom, if ever, voted before.

On one curious incident ot the struggle I forbore to dwell. At mid-day during the contest, when passing the warehouse of a well-known firm in the iron trade, I stopped to ask for a small account which I remembered was due to them. When handing me the receipt, the foreman said: 'Everybody here, sir, voted for you before nine o'clock this morning, except our Mr. Charles, who is not very well, and has not been in town as usual; but,' he added consolingly, 'if he don't turn up by three o'clock, I'll take care and record his vote for him.'

In vain I deprecated the proffered aid, assuring him that the franchise could not legally be exercised by deputy, and that the act, though well meant, might help to set aside the election. I shall never forget his sceptic look as he rejoined: 'Oh no! you won't do me, sir, for the vote's as good as any in London.' And I was absolutely unable to convince him of his error.

Before I had recovered my electoral equanimity, I was told by an officious friend that in another district the poll, by some sleepy mistake, had not been formally opened till three or four minutes after the appointed time; but as nobody had objected, many hundred worthy citizens — not having the terms of the statute in that behalf before their eyes—had actually registered their votes, and gone away rejoicing. A score of years have come and gone since then, and I fear we are not yet done with the pedantries of electoral enactments.

THE PARLIAMENT OF 1869.

The Irish Church—Abuse of Patronage—Henry Bulwer—Lowe's Budget—Spurgeon's Lecture at Islington—State Aid to Emigration—Irish Land Act—London School Board—Debate on Income Tax—Bernal Osborne—Immature Recruits—Witnesses at the Commons' Bar—Friendly Societies—Empress Eugénie—Charity Commissionership—Dismissal of Officers—Case of Pyne—Irish University Bill.

At the meeting of the new Parliament all party thoughts were felt to be subordinate and almost irrelevant to the coming redemption of Mr. Gladstone's pledge to deal finally with the Anglican Church in Ireland. Disestablishment was regarded as a question which had been settled by a decisive majority at the late election; but regarding disendowment there was a great variety of opinions. The staunchest Whigs in and out of office had always been for levelling up, as it was called. Lord Russell had propounded his plan for triple redistribution, and Lord Grey advocated the purchase of glebes and manses for the Catholic clergy and Presbyterian ministers out of the surplus revenues about to be sequestered. Whately and Arnold were dead, but their counsel, fearlessly avowed in their writings, led the political convictions of Broad Churchmen everywhere, and a remarkable sermon by Dean Stanley in favour of Christian comprehension breathed new hopes of compromise on the paramount question of the day.

The chief peers and commoners having estates in Ireland were known to favour some such mode of reappropriation, and the silent acquiescence of the tenantry, both in the North and the South, was illustrated by one of Mr. Trench's sinister tales of agrarianism, in which he represented a conclave of Ribbonmen as coming to the conclusion that—'Maybe, if we had once a hold of the Church lands, the landlords' lands would be 'asier come at after.'

It was currently believed that the Vatican would greatly prefer a parting of the old ecclesiastical raiment that had once belonged exclusively to the Catholic Church; whether with or without a *paulopost* future step in the progress of restitution, controversialists in England could not make up their minds. Thus confluent if not collateral streams, having their sources wide and deep, were flowing with apparently increased depth and breadth towards compromise.

At length the memorable day arrived, and in a speech of marvellous ability the Premier announced that the Protestant establishment founded by Elizabeth should cease to exist: that, under certain conditions, its dignitaries and ministers should be entitled to preservation of their life interests, and that the surplus accruing from episcopal, capitular, and parochial endowments should be devoted to charities not already provided for by the Poor Law, such as asylums for the care of the imbecile and insane. His tone was throughout moderate, and almost regretful. The financial details were more complicated than those of any of his most celebrated Budgets; but their ingenuity and clearness, if they did not really make them intelligible to half of the audience who crowded every corner of the Senate House from floor to roof, were wholly free from the distracting or perplexing irritants of party rhetoric. Opposition listened throughout with bated breath and forlorn hope that acquiescence was not yet inevitable, but when Disraeli, in a few despondent words, assented to the first reading without debate, and agreed that an early day should be fixed for the second or decisive stage, the feverish assembly broke up rapidly; and, with a sense that the fight of centuries was drawing near its close, every man betook himself to his own home.

I happened to pass near the Conservative leader in the cloisters, as he muffled to resist the outer air, and could not help asking him what he thought of the speech. 'Oh,' he said, 'perfectly wonderful! Nobody but himself could have gone through such a maze of history, statistics, and computations.' And then, after a pause: 'And so characteristic in the finish to throw away the surplus on the other idiots.'

It is but fair, however, to record how ready upon critical occasions he was to acknowledge the marvellous versatility of his great rival. I do not remember to have ever heard him countenance the fault-finding disposition of others, whom party or personal prejudice impelled to disparage Mr. Gladstone; and I have more than once heard him pay unqualified tribute to his limitless resource of argument and of language. But he laughed all the same at the restless activity in business, with which he could not sympathize.

In a division some years after on a foolish question, which found no other supporters than Mr. Wharton and Major O'Gorman, I found myself in line with Disraeli; and as we slowly paced along he was asking me some commonplace question, when I was inadvertently jostled against him by one who hurried to be early past the tellers' bar. To account for my seeming inadvertence, I pointed to its Right Honourable cause, on which Disraeli only said, 'What an ardent creature!'

Gladstone's eventual reply in debate may have been intended to allay ill-disguised feelings of discontent on the part of those who, for forty years, had implicitly followed the guidance of Lord Derby on the Irish Church Question, and their apprehensions that they were about to be a second time let down as they had been on household suffrage by their less orthodox chief.

But after a few days the ripples on the surface of the stream disappeared, and a stranger visiting the Park or dining out would hardly have perceived that what had always been deprecated as a revolution was about to be enacted in Committee of the Lower House without anyone pretending to foresee what the course of events might be in the Upper.

On questioning a noble friend of mine somewhat abruptly as to what the Lords would do with the Bill, he languidly replied, 'What Bill?' and when I named it, he said, 'Some will stay away, I suppose, and the rest will let it go through.'

The details are matters of history; but I cannot help noting a practical suggestion submitted in writing to the First Minister, and which, after so many years, I own I still regret found no favour in his eyes. I proposed that the surplus, if it could not be used for a triple endowment, should be permanently made the capital of a trust fund, to be employed in the creation by letting or sale on easy terms of farms at long leases under the Crown on fee simple at a quit rent, with a view to the creation of the agricultural middle-class, the want of which in two-thirds of Ireland was the social and political want of wants—greater in evil than any other.

Mr. Gladstone did not dispute the existence of the want or the facility which the occasion afforded for meeting it peaceably and safely. But he said in conversation that he thought it was better to deal with one great change at a time. I could not forbear reminding him that that was not Bacon's opinion, who, acting upon the opposite maxim when in power, had advised that in Ulster, as elsewhere, it was often better to change several great things than one.

My reasons for voting in support of the measure were, in the main, historical, and I endeavoured to give authentic illustrations of the lamentable results of expropriating the whole of the ecclesiastical property of the island to the clergy of one-tenth of the population.

The earliest and best memories of my life were interwoven with feelings of respect for the teaching of the Anglican Church in Ireland, and regard for its devoted ministers, several of whom were of my own family. Education served to strengthen attachment, and the knowledge acquired in after-life deepened the conviction of the purity and worth of those engaged in its parochial ministrations, when and wherever congregations were allotted to their care.

It was not their fault if, in more than half the

country, the community adhered to the faith of Rome, and that even in Ulster the numerous descendants of Scottish settlers remained Presbyterian. Penal laws had not converted the former, and the lure of rich endowments had not won over the latter. But neither persecution by statute nor invidious preference in the appropriation of property originally given for the use of an undivided community could reconcile the great majority to such a state of things.

It was not pretended by Government that the Establishment was a missionary Church, nor was it expected that its rites and functions would have become co-ordinate with the religious wants of the nation.

During the whole of the last century, and by every Administration, it was used systematically and shamelessly as a supplemental means of patronage, its dignities and revenues being without scruple conferred upon relatives, dependents, or creatures of English Ministers.

It would be wearisome to trace throughout the details of episcopal jobbery practised without scruple, or even the shabby semblance of reciprocity, but a summary of the abuse of official power in a single diocese must suffice.

If anywhere consideration might have been shown for devoted loyalty at the Revolution, and unswerving fidelity to its principles in Church and State, one might have supposed that it would have been manifested in the choice from among the clergy of Derry of deserving men to preside over them. But the see being one of the richest in Ireland, it was offered in 1717 to Nicholson, whose political services were deemed insufficiently requited by the poorer See of Carlisle. What he understood by the proposal is disclosed in a letter to Archbishop Wake that has been preserved for our learning.

He had for some time been Clerk of the Closet, and on taking leave of his Majesty was much surprised by the command to take up his residence henceforth in his new diocese. 'I was stunned at this, but professed that, as I had hitherto, I would personally attend the duties of my charge. Had I known a fortieth part of what I have since heard and seen, I would not have gone into that kingdom for the Primacy. *Sed jacta est alea*: go I must; God's will and the King's be done in righteousness.' Further dismayed by what he heard on his way of the disordered state of things, he asked to be furnished with an escort of dragoons; for 'the worst of his condition was that when come to the place where he hoped for rest, he found himself in an enemy's country.'

The every-day aspect of life in Ireland at this time, scarred by sectarian wounds, and haggard with the too palpable signs of the lack of reproductive vigour and of social health, is vividly depicted in his private correspondence with Archbishop Wake, to whose influence he owed his honours of lucrative martyrdom. The Establishment as a parochial institution was almost everywhere in ruins. Churches were dilapidated, glebes let out to farm, incumbents holding four and five benefices to eke out the means of living, and ill-paid curates obliged to ride half a dozen miles to perform their various duties at irregular intervals.

The squalor of the peasantry and the evidences of general neglect were all along his route too observable by Nicholson. He had 'never seen in Picardy, Westphalia, or the Highlands, such dismal marks of hunger and want of employment. The poor creatures dwelt in reeking hovels, and had generally no more than a rag of coarse blanket to cover them. These miserable serfs tilled the ground to the very top of the hills, in the service of their lords, who spent their rack-rents in London or Paris, leaving them but a ridge or two of potatoes for the support of themselves and their children. They might be seen trudging to some out-of-the-way chapel to Mass, or to a funeral or a wedding, with a priest in the same habit as themselves.'

The Leinster clergy usually lived in Dublin, leaving their parishioners to the priests of the old persuasion. Three or four were lately seized on landing from abroad; but the magistrates admitted them to bail, being more lenient to the

Secular clergy as natives than to the Regulars sent intermittently from France and Spain.

For ten years his immigrant lordship dwelt in summer on the banks of the Foyle, where he tried with little success to enlist the Presbyterians against the impoverished but outnumbering Papists, and in winter, like most of his episcopal brethren, living in the capital, to attend the House of Lords and the levées at the Castle. He was succeeded by his friend Dr. Henry Downes, who from a vicarage in Northamptonshire had been made an Irish prelate, and who seems to have been an amiable but colourless man, of whom no good or ill has been recorded.

Not so obscure in the annals of unsanctified jobbery was the case of the next occupant of the see. Thomas Rundle, a fellow-student at Oxford of a brother of Lord Chancellor Talbot, had become known as a disciple of Whiston, whose unbelief in Mosaic inspiration he was wont to illustrate by the jest that, had he come by at Mount Horeb before the ram was caught in the thicket, he would have laid Father Abraham by the heels. Finding his heterodoxy was not the best way to advancement, he grew more reserved, took orders, crept into favour at Bishop Auckland, and besides other preferments obtained a prebendal stall of Durham.

In 1733 Lord Chancellor Talbot nominated him to the See of Gloucester, but such an outcry was raised by Mr. Venn and other devout Churchmen that Sir Robert Walpole, who never before had been suspected of ecclesiastical qualms, thought it needful to interpose; and after much discussion it was agreed as a compromise that Dr. Benson should have Gloucester, and that Rundle should have Derry. 'What do you say,' asked Pulteney, when writing to Swift, 'to the bustle made here to prevent the man from being an English Bishop, and allowing him to be good Christian enough for an Irish one? Surely the opposition or the acquiescence must have been most abominably scandalous.'

Even Primate Boulter, the most Ministerial of all Ministerialists, could not refrain from telling the Viceroy 'how sorry he was that the public service had made it necessary to give the Bishopric of Derry to Dr. Rundle, because your Grace cannot but be sensible it will give a handle to clamour here.'*

Then followed in episcopal order Reynell, Chancellor of Bristol; Stone, brother of the Duke of Newcastle's secretary; and Barnard, Dean of Rochester. The succession of the unfittest of imported prelates culminated in 1768, when to the honourable and *ir*-reverent Frederick Harvey was confided the spiritual care of the Established Church in Derry.

For five-and-thirty years this matchless proof

* To the Duke of Dorset, February 20, 1735.—*MS.*

of what an Established Church can be brought to by the abuse of political patronage amused and amazed not only the inhabitants of Ulster, but of Ireland generally, by the vagaries of his career.

By the death of his elder brother he became a temporal as well as a spiritual peer; and though seldom attending in his place as a legislator, he was fired with the crazy ambition of being the head of an armed revolution.

Fond of show and lavish in expenditure, there was no caprice of luxury or hospitality in which he did not indulge, and no whim of demeanour or license in talk which he seemed to think unbecoming. If Nature had not given him the capacity of a statesman, she furnished him at least with all the histrionic talents of an actor, and he would alternately play the part of high priest in his cathedral, and cynical champion of Voltairian opinions at the head of his own table; courteous and generous as Ordinary at the visitation of his clergy, or arrayed in purple, he would perform the chief part in procession surrounded by volunteer cavalry to overhaul Parliament and the executive authorities.

Tradition has not yet forgotten all the illustrations that once were rife of his versatile and voluptuous criticisms on sculpture and paintings, and monuments still remain of his ambitious taste in architecture. His eccentricities of action and language were equally lawless, and I remember hearing from a friend far advanced in life, who in his youth knew Lord Bristol well, that in the excitement of convivial discussion he did not shrink from declaring his doubts whether the Author of our religion was not an impostor. A venerable clergyman who was present exclaimed that if that were so, his lordship had better resign the See of Derry. 'I should to-morrow,' was his reply, 'if I could find a better one.' Failing to win or keep the favour of the multitude, he betook himself in later years to foreign travel, and resided for a long time in Italy, where at length he died.

Such were the eight wise men of the East who were sent during the last century to maintain the cause of Establishment in Ireland.

Judgment was at length pronounced by the Commons by a majority of upwards of five score.

What would become of the Bill in the Upper House? Its absolute rejection by whatever numbers was felt to be impossible; but might not changes be made that would reconcile Conservatives and Liberals who agreed in regarding the day of sectarian ascendancy in Ireland as past, and who wished to see concurrent endowment established in its stead? All who held this view, like Pitt and Grenville, Burke and Grattan, either voted for the second reading or stayed away.

No debate in our time drew forth so great a diversity of genuine eloquence, or from first to last commanded an audience so capable of appreciating its claims to remembrance. Every seat and every inch of standing-room in the narrow galleries set apart for the members of the Lower House was occupied from the beginning to the end, as was the space ordinarily filled below the bar; while on the steps of the throne were crowded Privy Councillors, Ministers, and sons of peers; and the diplomatic seats were shared by the most distinguished leaders of rank and fashion.

The loftiness of the building, and the historical recollections haunting the great issue challenged, lent histrionic impressiveness to the scene; and, worthy of the occasion, the chief actors, lay and episcopal, performed their respective parts. Prelates menaced with the extinction of their sees, and prelates not unnaturally fearing in the *paulo-post* future for the stability of their own, deprecated vehemently, but without arrogant bitterness, the recent plebiscite of the electors and the vote of the Commons; but seven only ventured to speak of compromise in any form of the anomaly it was proposed to remove.

Tait, recently elevated to Lambeth, Ellicott of Gloucester, and Selwyn of Lichfield, were, it was well known, willing to sustain Lords Russell, Grey, Salisbury, and Stanhope in restoring, after the long night of deprivation, a moderate portion of the ecclesiastical property theretofore enjoyed exclusively by the clergy of one-tenth of its traditional owners; and attempts were made in various forms during the progress of the measure to modify in this sense the inevitable change.

Earl Grey would have postponed the preamble, which asserted the theory of demolition by levelling downwards, and gave utterance to the sentiments of Whigs and Peelites generally in favour of the national endowment of religion without regard to sectarian or social distinctions; but Government deprecated discussion on such a point until a later stage. The most memorable speech on the second reading was that of the Bishop of Peterborough.

Excepting Wilberforce, he had no rival among the spiritual peers. I never can forget the hush of curiosity that greeted him when he rose, or the sense of admiration wherewith his hearers followed him throughout his superb though unavailing protest against the legislative abolition of the hierarchy of which his grandsire had been a conspicuous chief, and under whose rule his own youth and prime had ministerially been passed. I have heard that his fellow-countrymen, Lord Cairns and Lord Salisbury, concurred in the opinion that the speech was unsurpassed by any that either of them had ever heard. Yet such is the unaccountability of human judgment under the unconscious sway of opposite prepossessions, that not long after, when I asked Mr. Gladstone at a reception at the Foreign Office what he thought of the discussion, and especially of *the* speech, he replied, with emphasis: 'I think it the worst in matter and in manner I ever heard.'

Two veteran combatants reiterated after forty years their opposing confessions of faith upon the question. Lord Derby from the cross benches, where scarce intermittent pain seldom allowed him to appear, repudiated with the intensity of his early days his conviction on imperial grounds of the value of what he did everything but call the Garrison Church.

The old Rupert zeal for Protestant ascendancy and royal authority rang in every note of that silver-trumpet voice. In youth, like the daring Greek, he had laid himself down athwart the highway of change, and risked the life of his ambition on being able to arrest the impending course of things;* and more than any other influence his determination had kept back the change.

While he was a possible Premier, no one ventured in direct terms to propose it; and now that he had renounced by reason of physical suffering all share of responsibility in Government, he would not abate one jot or tittle of the

* See his speech for the maintenance of the Irish Church in 1826.

shibboleth of his youth. Equally unbending on the contrary, though bent even lower by infirmity and age, Lord Russell hailed with satisfaction this long-postponed realization of his early desire, though he threw all the weight of his authority into the scale still supposed to be trembling as to which way sectarian levelling in Ireland should be brought about.

No criticism, spiritual or temporal, of the measure approached in bitterness that of Lord Westbury, who not long before had been forced to relinquish the Great Seal by a Cabinet of which most of the existing Ministers were members. The keenness and quaintness of his wit, and his consummate affectation of concern for the interest of religion, amazed and amused an audience till then pervaded by a genuine desire to reason with candour and discuss with gravity the painful and trying subject. But as if to dispel any lingering belief of nobler or better aims than those of high comedy, the ex-Chancellor ended his singular harangue with the finical utterance: 'My lords, I feel that it is all in vain, for I am like John the Baptist preaching in the wilderness.'

Lord Cairns, now Leader of the Tory Party, was generally believed to agree with Disraeli in desiring that the Church Bill should pass, in spite of their protestations. He had actually paid a visit to Dublin not long before, in the hope of persuading the Irish Chancellor Napier and the

Archbishop of Dublin to agree to amended terms of compensation in Committee, which, if rejected by the Commons, would justify the throwing out of the Bill by the Lords.

But it required all his forensic subtlety to deal with the matter in this elastic fashion, and his elaborate address, at the end of the fourth night, nominally against the second reading, but really suggestive of the compromise he had offered to make with Lord Granville as to details, was listened to in silence by the Opposition, who feared that, as in 1829 and 1846, they were again about to be let down.

They had been so long accustomed to the Cavalier style of Lord Derby, that they did not understand the Calvinistic gravity and enigmatic special pleading of the ex-Chancellor. There was not a gleam of humour about him, and, what was worse, no social sympathy or political force.

Lyndhurst was a wholly different man. He was essentially an idler and a gossip, was up in every bit of scandal of the town, and knew well the state of the odds. He was afraid of neither the Court, the pulpit, nor the mob; and, what was more, he was not to be cowed or turned by the murmurs of his own party, when, as happened in the case of the Corn Law and the Jew Bill, he had made up his mind to go against their prejudices.

Lord Cairns created the impression that he was always speaking from a brief, and that he was ready, if his instructions were changed, to crumple up any number of his platitudes and put them in his bag.

When at length the division was called, we who were permitted to retain our places in the stinted nooks set apart for us of the Commons beheld the two Archbishops take their stand in front of the throne to signify their resolve to vote neither for nor against the second reading; and we watched the minority troop to the left of the bar, while the outnumbering majority filed to the right of the throne, one of the latter only —the Bishop of St. David's—wearing lawn sleeves.

Among the non-contents the eye looked in vain for the episcopal tribune who had been the loudest in the ringlead of resistance, but who now had seen reason to mutely slip out of the fray.

At Christmas he had tried to draw Archbishop Trench and the Irish Episcopate into a hollow way of compromise between retrenchment of dignities and emoluments, and unavailing resistance to national repudiation, and on their refusal he hoped to vindicate his claim to Apostolic intrepidity by denouncing the sequestration of the revenues conferred by Elizabeth on the Anglican hierarchy in Ireland as savouring of sacrilege and sin; but at midsummer his devious course changed once again.

In the prolonged struggle, who could tell whether the shrouds of the English Establishment might not be caught by the flaming spars of the doomed squadron? or, if there was risk of such a contingency, was it not rather the part of the Right Rev. Lord of Oxford, likely to become a Most Rev. Lord of Winchester, to let one fire-ship drift harmlessly out to sea?

The majority of thirty-five for the second reading was made up chiefly of Whigs like Russell, Cleveland, and Grey, who had always been opposed to an exclusive endowment as to a sectarian ascendancy in Ireland, and who frankly owned that they wished the opportunity to be used for the purpose of what was called levelling upwards.

Archbishop Tait and Bishop Ellicott warmly supported in Committee the adoption of this policy, and seven of their brethren voted for various amendments to create glebes and manses for the Catholic priesthood and the Presbyterian ministry.

At length a clause of this nature, supported by Lords Salisbury, Abercorn, Carnarvon, and others, was carried by five, and the Bill was sent down to the Commons with this and other changes of minor importance, to be rejected peremptorily at the bidding of the Prime Minister.

While the rank and file of the Radical contingent was changed by the levy *en masse* of household suffrage, some non-commissioned officers, and a good many of brevet rank on the Whig staff, reappeared in the new Parliament. I found myself sitting beside one of the latter, Sir Henry Lytton Bulwer, who had in the course of forty years filled a curiously varied succession of diplomatic posts, from time to time reappearing at St. Stephen's, but seldom, if ever, tarrying there long enough to inscribe his name on popular memory as a legislator. Like his more distinguished brother, he had early aspired to literary fame, and in 1825 had given to the world a volume of personal notes and comments on the memorable life-and-death wrestle in the Morea, which fixed the attention of all the Cabinets in Europe, under the dilettante title of 'An Autumn in Greece.'

With no other flag he sallied forth from Knebworth to contest Hertford, but was quizzed and bantered out of the field by Thomas Duncombe, who bade his followers ask why they should be called on to become 'the publishers of a nerveless duodecimo, which in London would not sell, because there was nothing in it to buy.'

Obtaining, however, a seat for Wilton, and voting throughout for the Reform Bill, he was employed by Lord Palmerston on more than one special service abroad, and he acquitted himself with such colourless zeal as to be thought worthy of adoption as a permanent confidant of the department. As Secretary of Legation at Brussels and afterwards at Paris, his sagacity and aptitude ripened under favourable auspices into what was called, by no unfriendly critic, a very fair genius for intrigue; and his 'France, Social and Literary,' followed by his 'Monarchy of the Middle Classes,' gave him an exceptional character for industry and information above more pretentious claimants to diplomatic preferment.

In the critical juncture of 1840, when a heedless expression might have brought on war, he happened to be Chargé d'Affaires at Paris, and he acquitted himself so much to the satisfaction ot his superiors that he was soon after appointed to Madrid.

I hardly at first recognised him from his delicate and depressed look, greatly altered since we had met last in a distant and different scene. As Minister to Spain, Sir Henry had accompanied the Court of Queen Christina to Barcelona, and at his table I was a guest with MM. Mon, Pidal, and other members of the Government who had paved the way for that of Narvaez.

In a dilapidated palace overlooking the bay, his Excellency had given us a dinner curiously characteristic of his ambition to rival his more celebrated brother for originality and finesse in affairs of the cuisine. I remember asking one of the richly-decorated courtiers near me if he knew accurately the *component delicacies* of each fairy dish of which we partook, and this Hidalgic dignitary replied that he had only been able to make out the ingredients of one of them; but he supposed they were imported from afar, and their flavour and odour were divine.

His Excellency was equally fantastic in his wines, and it took so long to appreciate discriminatively the specimens of diplomatic caprice that I found myself after dark in danger of being left ashore for lack of a waking boatman to pull me off to the vessel in which I had come. Though always a valetudinarian, it was his rule to affect gaiety in costume and conversation; few people could be pleasanter when he chose, even among men: and women were wont to pronounce him delightful for nearly a fortnight, after which he relapsed into his inveterate habit of pathetic self-contemplation. Whether he really believed that invalid airs, equivocal elixirs, and stimulating pilules kept awake political or feminine sympathy, I know not; but the presence of a variety of medical confections in the ledge of the seat before us gave signs of preparations for taking part in debate.

Expelled from Madrid in 1848 for reading the Spanish Ministry a course of lectures by Palmerston on their sins and shortcomings, he had been sent on a more important embassage to

Washington, with instructions to negotiate with Secretary Clayton the Boundary Treaty, which bears jointly their names; and subsequently he was chosen by his confiding friend, the head of Foreign Affairs, to succeed Lord Stratford de Redcliffe at Constantinople. His repute for discretion was hardly maintained in that difficult post, and he was tempted to use its prestige to speculate in certain profitable investments on the shores and in the islets of the Dardanelles, that provoked severe comment at home.

But he enjoyed his embassy beyond description, perhaps more thoroughly and intensely than any of his predecessors had done. Lord Ponsonby had lived there the life of a sybarite, but he had never done otherwise anywhere else. Meantime, indulgence had not, therefore, for him equal charms of novelty; and, ambition being burned out within him, he let affairs take their course without being at the trouble, like his successor, Sir Stratford Canning, of trying to direct them, or reaping the pleasure that overreaching rivals and colleagues affords. Like them, he swam in his gilt caique and fared sumptuously every day. But he was too *blasé* to have any real gratification in the round of dreamy enjoyments, or to be amused by the glitter of costly shows and toys. He had spent his patrimony, had grown old, outlived his faith in Charles Fox, and come to look upon the Egyptian question as a bore.

The great Elchie, who preceded and followed him, was a man of another nature. He had spent the best part of his life in half-suppressed enthusiasm for the Moslem cause. As an outwork against Russian aggression, Palmerston felt and thought with him, and chose Henry Bulwer for a reliable instrument to speed the execution of the reforms sanguinely stipulated for in the Black Sea Treaty.

But Bulwer cared in reality for none of these things. He had gone to Stamboul to enjoy the distinction and luxury of an envied post, and, as ill-natured critics whispered, to repair his fortune; and he would not abridge the term of his opportunity if he knew it by a single day. Why should he scheme or plot to circumvent his Muscovite rival at the Porte about trivial or equivocal matters that, from embers fanned into sparks, might kindle Europe into flame, and for his pains put him out of favour with some future Secretary of State? The welfare of Greece might in the second aorist of diplomacy be affected perhaps slightly, perhaps not at all, by his non-interference at Yildiz Kiosk; and some writer in the *Débats* or *Allgemeine Zeitung* might aver that, but for his indifference, the Meridites would not have ventured to rebel. But what thanks would he get in Downing Street, or what credit at St. Stephen's, for fishing in shallow waters?

Fastidious in his tastes and his pleasures, he

was afflicted with few scruples in private finance or expenditure; and, surrounded as he was continually by adventurers of all kinds, with flattery on their lips, and plausible projects of improvement and development in their hands to which Pashas, and Effendis, and Western bankers lent their names, he was gradually induced to lend his likewise, and not unfrequently, it was said, to profit by the fluctuations of the money market. One transaction in particular became the subject of severe comment in England. He had bought an islet in the Sea of Marmora for £4,000, on which he had built a villa, surrounding it with gardens such as the luxurious in that climate love. Its intrinsic worth might be disputed, but the public only knew that when tired of his bagatelle it was purchased by the Khedive of Egypt for four times its cost. Cossack and Gallic sense of propriety was shocked at such want of dignity and reserve on the part of the British Envoy.

Palmerston, however, was not to be twitted by party criticism into giving him up; and on his return to England, after his five years' embassy, he received many proofs of confidence and promises of future employment elsewhere. 'Only,' said his noble friend, 'don't buy any more islands.'

After the Viscount's death his Excellency, who had been, and hoped to be again, an Ambassador

Extraordinary, thought himself neglected; and, that his pretensions and services should not be forgotten, he contrived to get himself returned for the borough of Tamworth by household suffrage.

When reminded of our former meetings, he relaxed easily into quiet chat about change of scene and climate, and 'Edward's transfer to another sphere,' and the marvellous development of 'Vivian Grey,' as he had once been known among the dandies, into a leader in legislation. Though never intimate with him, I gladly availed myself of his disposition to be friendly, and there was something so idiosyncratic in his whole performance in public and private, that I own I took more than usual interest in observing him.

Attention was naturally given by the new House to whatever fell from so old a Parliamentary hand, but it was hardly rewarded for its pains. Without the physical power that sometimes lends music and meaning to common-place, and without a touch of his brother's fluency or fancy, his discourse seldom rose above the level of a cautious despatch in a half-developed crisis, the pros and cons of alternative courses being marshalled in a chill, pedantic style. He did not pretend to be the mouthpiece of even a section, or to be prepared to give more than a preliminary opinion on any of the contingencies that might arise. The one idea evidently uppermost throughout was that of an unexplained mode of dealing with some pending affair, whereby its author felt certain it might be made to redound to the interest and honour of England. While keeping up the forms of party attachment, what he called his sense of public duty, he was constantly devising embarrassing questions, grounded on correspondence within his previous knowledge, but of which he was too wise to give anything more than a suggestive and tantalizing glimpse.

Meanwhile, he was chiefly occupied in carefully elaborating the materials placed in his hands by Lady Palmerston for the historical memoirs of the late Prime Minister. From nearly his own entrance into public life, forty years gone by, few had had more constant opportunities of hearing, if he did not always heed, the current talk of English foreign affairs; and during the greater portion of the period he had been one of the trustiest and supplest in working out the venturous, but on the whole successful, policy of his director-general. There was hardly room for misgiving as to his intense desire, to call it by no higher name, that the work should tend to strengthen the general conviction that Palmerston had carried the assertion of British power and pre-eminence throughout the world further than it had ever been carried before; and it was not in human nature that one whose subordinate career had been closely interwoven with the many vicissitudes of such fortune should fail to do his best in its illustration.

He had given notice of a motion for the production of papers, which Lord Clarendon had told him it would be imprudent, if not mischievous, to lay on the table. In the desire to dissuade him, the Under-Secretary was instructed to call on him and hint some additional reasons why he should refrain.

Sir A. Otway found him in bed in one of his most languid and desponding moods, weary of the ingratitude of public life, and too ill to talk about papers. My hon. and gallant friend did not think it necessary to press the object of his visit, and he reported at Downing Street that the motion might for the present be considered at an end.

His chief, who knew his man better, said quietly: 'He'll be there,' and accordingly, at a quarter to six, when idle questions were running off the reel, the glass door opened, and the Right Hon. Member for Tamworth sauntered in, carelessly attired to hypochrondriacal perfection, trailing a warm overcoat over one arm, and with the other embracing a bundle of confidential documents. It all came to nothing apparently; but before many months reasons were discovered for making up her Majesty's mind to the grace and expediency of summoning Sir Henry to the House of Peers.

Surprise was not concealed among the Whigs at the nomination of Mr. Lowe as Chancellor of the Exchequer, Lord Russell being especially outspoken on the subject; and sceptic curiosity waited to see how, with his signal defects of vision, he would be able to deal with the distracting details of exposition should he venture on excursive variety in his Budget.

It was said, indeed, that he had disclaimed any pretension to originality, and when it disclosed unexpectedly no little diversity of fiscal resource, there were not wanting critics who insinuated that its best points had been thrown him by the great master of financial magic at the head of the Treasury.

With the rank and file of his party, his candid impatience of what he deemed their political ineptitude had rendered him personally unpopular, and his recent exploits in the field of electoral reform had shaken whatever degree of confidence in his judgment had previously existed among thoughtful politicians.

The odds were, therefore, heavily against him when he rose to make his statement of the national liabilities and revenues for the year, and his numberless mistakes of figures as he tried with high magnifiers to read his elaborate notes filled the reporters during the first half hour almost with despair, and his few official friends with something like dismay.

Yet I own my sympathy thawed unbidden, as I followed him in the performance of his task, and beguiled me, before he was done, into a feeling of respect for the self-reliant courage and intellectual elasticity of the man that could bear him without wincing or faltering through such a sea of difficulties.

His speech in the hearing could be compared to nothing but an exceedingly bad proof of a recondite author, who, one was sure, knew what he meant to say; and in the reading next day in the *Times*, with all the literal errors left out, it was logical, lucid, and very much to the purpose.

Why he should have been offered the second place in the Board of Treasury, and why he should have accepted it rather than some other Cabinet office, in which his normal infirmity would not have been brought so painfully into view, I never understood at the time or since; but I must avow my dissent from Lord Russell's opinion that Cardwell would have been the better man.

Few men in my recollection seem to have been more overrated. In precision impeccable, and in formality first-rate, his leading aim consisted apparently in saying Amen to Sir Robert Peel as long as he lived, and then to Mr. Gladstone. What was said by Charles II. of a much greater man might always be said of him—that he was never in the way, and never out of the way.

Lord Chelmsford, asked for his definition, replied: 'Macaulay was said by Sydney Smith to be a book in breeches; had he lived long enough, he would have called the Member for Oxford a pamphlet in pantaloons.'

But he had an inexhaustible knack of evasion when questioned regarding awkward particulars. After a remarkable instance of this sort of demi-official ambidexterity, his colleague, who knew him *intus et in cute*, but who strove to keep up the amenities expedient between Parliamentary yoke-fellows, was bullied by a baffled questioner to say whether Cardwell's solemn answers were not often contrary to fact. 'No,' said Neate, tugging slowly at his huge cigar; 'I think you are wrong. Cardwell always speaks the truth, but never too much of it.'

When, after being left out for a time by his Peelite patrons, the late Mr. Gurdon Rebow was told by the Whip that Cardwell was to be Secretary for Ireland, he exclaimed: 'Oh, really; we all thought he was dead!'

Irish humour, which seldom misses its mark, recognised his effeminate character by dubbing him on public occasions as the Right Hon. Miss Cardwell; and when, in evil hour for the content of the Service, he was made Secretary for War, and his term of office was signalized by the passing of the Abolition of Purchase, he was only regarded as the administrative telephone of Mr. Gladstone's views.

The ways of the clubs towards political men are inscrutable, and their idiosyncratic rules vary widely. After the break up of the Tory Party in 1846, the friends of Sir Robert Peel remained in the Carlton, a majority of its members treating them as adversaries in Parliament, but in private as old friends.

As the breach widened during Lord Aberdeen's Ministry, an attempt was made by Lord Ranelagh and a few vehement partisans to compel the most distinguished of the Peelites to withdraw; but upon examination it was found that no authority existed to warrant the expulsion of a member on the mere ground of opinion legitimately expressed. Much indignation, however, was excited by the abortive attempt; and some of his colleagues in the coalition proposed at Brooks's that Gladstone should be invited to join without ballot. This, however, could not be done without unanimity, and several of the old Whigs refused to concur in waiving the prescriptive rule.

If Pitt, Granville, Fox, and Grey, Melbourne, Russell, and Palmerston, were content to abide the anonymous test, why should not their successor? The proposal of his name was, however, relinquished. The Reform Club, less exacting, voted in highly complimentary terms his and Lord Granville's admission as honorary members.

Beside the occasional delivery during the recess of lectures on popular but unpolitical topics for the benefit of local institutions in the borough, I was sometimes asked to preside when an unfamiliar speaker of reputation lent his aid. The deacons of Arundel Square Chapel induced Mr. Spurgeon to give them an evening on any topic he might name, their senior member taking the chair; and I was somewhat perplexed by the announcement in print that the subject chosen was of all others the inflammatory one of 'Candles.' I felt bound to ask our friend if his purpose was controversial, and received a frank assurance that it was nothing of the kind. I was therefore ready to welcome him on the appointed evening, and on inquiring what time his address was likely to take, was met with the significant reply: 'Haven't a notion—just as the maggot bites.' I own my confidence, however, in polemical peace somewhat shaken when, on assuming the chair, I saw arranged before the lecturer a curious variety of candelabra, candlesticks, and taper-holders, with their appropriate lading of wax all trimmed and ready to blaze. My fears, however, were dispelled by the opening words of the speaker, who took for granted that his audience contained good-humoured people of all denominations, ready to smile, though not perhaps to laugh, at a frank and friendly discrimination of their several characteristics. 'Here, for example, is the unmistakable scarlet of Rome, predominant in size and height above all its episcopal rivals, and set, as you see, on a highly artistic and gorgeous support. It is not my business here to kindle contentious flame, but, after all, we must own that if lighted up it would, as some might desire it would, give a blaze proportionate to its rare dimensions.

'Next in size and significance comes the cathedral purple of Canterbury; and then the yellow and frugal symbol of Presbyterianism.' Caustic, but never cynical, observations followed on the differing colour and capacity of each well-known sect; and, last of all, the smallest and most exclusive—the Plymouth Brethren—typified by a minimum taper in a little writing-table candlestick. 'Well,' said Mr. Spurgeon, 'most of you know my opinions, and that I am not in the habit of mincing them; but I try to remember, and I would have you try to think, that all who profess and call themselves Christians can do good in their way; and in this wicked world there is more to be done than all of us put together can do.'

Colonial interests found during the Session of 1870 several able and energetic representatives in Parliament. New Zealand, by the lips of its envoys, pleaded earnestly for financial aid in the shape of advances to complete the railways and other public works indispensable for the development of its rising industry. The Treasury was, however, deaf to importunity, and Lord Granville, as Colonial Secretary, though bland and sympathetic in tone, as was his habitual wont, on all occasions endeavoured to dissuade deputations who waited on him from urging the matter in the Commons as one of Imperial concern. The newspapers were content for the most part to report that the gentlemen forming the deputation thanked his lordship for his obliging consideration to their statements and withdrew.

But we were not disposed to abandon the cause we deemed alike one of policy and justice. In most of the great towns there had been during the winter and spring an increasing superfluity of able-bodied labour, arising partly from temporary depression in trade, but in great part also from the crowding into the centres of industry of spare hands from the agricultural districts, stimulated silently but steadily by the changes lately made in the parochial law of settlement, which filled young people of both sexes with the new hope in life, that if they could earn anyhow but a few months' wages, and were then compelled to seek public shelter and relief, they would no longer be liable to be remitted back to their place of birth, where not a chance of employment any longer awaited them.

In concert with several correspondents in

Birmingham, Liverpool, Manchester, as well as London, I sought to cumulate and classify facts descriptive of the prevailing lack of independent means of subsistence by a large portion of the working population; and in conference with Sir George Grey, who had been Governor of the Cape as well as New Zealand, and Sir Dillon Bell, the Agent-General for the latter, I undertook to bring before the House certain proposals for aid to emigration, which we sincerely believed would naught impoverish the old country, but make new colonies rich indeed. Numerous public meetings discussed the various forms of the proposal, and petitioned for its adoption in some form, but month by month rolled by without our making apparently much impression on the mind of rule.

I remember Lord Granville telling me in private, with a gentle suavity all his own, that he had consulted Mr. Goschen, then head of the Poor Law Department, and others of his Cabinet colleagues, and that on principle they were all opposed to lending pecuniary aid to emigration. There was nothing for it, therefore, but to leave our people to their fate, or to try what impression could be made on Parliament.

In an attentive but thin House I did my best, by the space of forty minutes or more, to show that there was urgent need of greater facilities being not only afforded, but contributively created, between the central and the outlying portions of the realm. It was no answer to say that imports and exports were increasing, joint-stock banks multiplying, splendid residences rising both in country and town, and the general fact becoming yearly more palpable that England never was so full of realized capital before. The history of civilization in every age and clime proved that, with great opulence great poverty, and with great luxury great misery, was constantly apt to grow, and if we were justly proud of the triumphant results of limitless invention, boundless enterprise, and fearless freedom of competition, it was our duty to make to ourselves friends of the mammon of commerce by providing out of our abundance for the honest poor that cried. An Act had been passed during the Session securing the means of living to Irish tenants, a million of money being devoted to this purpose. Was it unreasonable to ask what could be done, though not in the way of agrarian grants, to improve the condition of classes of our countrymen who were as little importunate? Above a million of money was voted annually, nominally, for the postal service, but practically for the provision of floating hotels for the great comfort and expedition of first and second class travellers. Those subsidies were professedly granted for postal reasons, but they had the inevitable effect of combining great luxury with great speed for those persons who were able to travel at high pressure and great expense. Why, then, should not the working classes have their fair share of the advantages of improved transit? In every railway Bill a provision was inserted that there should be third-class carriages, and why should we not have, in like manner, third-class ships? It would be possible, without any appreciable increase of national burdens, to enable many thousand families to emigrate, who were now unable to do so. If each adult paid £3, and each child over twelve 30s., the difference might be made up by one-third from the Exchequer and one-third from the colony, whose local authorities should from time to time decide what additional hands they required. The present Government had decided upon concentrating our troops at home, but surely if we withdrew force we ought to plant affection.

The motion was seconded by Lord G. Hamilton, and the debate adjourned at the instance of Mr. W. H. Smith. Government refused to give any direct aid to emigration, but eventually yielded the advance by loan to New Zealand for public purposes.

Gradually, however, competition has brought down the charge for steerage passengers to a third of what then was usual; and beside liberal inducement in the shape of land at nominal rents, Canada has done a great deal to develop the primeval forest, and to fill with merchandise the vacant haven.

In memorable language Mr. Gladstone, when unseated for Oxford University, told the electors of Lancashire that thenceforth he was unmuzzled, and that his legislative mission would be to cut down the upas-tree of misrule in Ireland, the topmost branch of which was the Established Church. The next branch destined to legislative lopping was, he said, the power of the landed proprietary to exact exorbitant rent, and to evict the tillers of the soil for non-payment.

The grievance, embittered as it was by absenteeism, had been reported on five-and-thirty years before by the Commission to Inquire into the Condition of the Poor in Ireland, of which Archbishop Whately was chairman and Sir G. C. Lewis and I were assistant commissioners. The abject plight of the peasantry in the southern and western counties, and the prevalence of pauperism consequent on the want of employment, were reaffirmed by a subsequent commission in 1843, presided over by Lord Devon; but no change had been effected in the deplorable state of things except by the ruthless hand of Famine, and the subsequent exodus of many hundred thousands beyond sea.

An Act from whose remedial efficacy great benefits were promised was passed in 1849, for the sale of encumbered estates by peremptory process, in the expectation that at the abated price English capitalists would largely become the purchasers, and would introduce better systems of culture in husbandry. Sitting for an Irish constituency, I ventured to propose, as a supplementary measure, that on all such estates, pending the compulsory transfer, substantial tenants not in arrear should be entitled to claim renewed leases for thirty-one years from the Court, at a rent not exceeding the Government valuation, and the best men acquainted with the circumstances of the country warmly approved the proposal.

But, as it did not wear the official stamp, it was of course rejected; and thousands of occupiers, whose homes would have been made safe, and whose interests in the preservation of law and order would have been ensured, were driven into exile, or into improvident contracts for their holdings without leasehold permanency. How often have I subsequently heard bitter exclamations of regret that this special but moderate concession was not made in time!

In 1870 Mr. Gladstone undertook to go a great deal further, and the Land Act, which after no little contention he succeeded in passing, legalized all over Ireland the tenant right of Ulster, gave compensation for unexhausted improvements, and secured the tenant compensation for eviction, if not provoked by non-payment of rent. To a certain extent these provisions proved remedial, and checked for a time the tendency to agrarian violence and crime; but ere long the old evils of over-population and want of remunerative employment overpassed the slow growth of agricultural improvement. Tithe had ceased to be a cause of quarrel between classes and creeds, and rack-rents, with their inevitable appendage of evictions, became the wider and deeper subject of contention. The gilding of the first Land Act thus soon became dim, and it was not until after several painful years of suffering and violence that a second and more sweeping measure was proposed.

Responding to the prevalent demand from all parts of the kingdom, Ministers resolved on proposing a comprehensive scheme of elementary education, and on Mr. W. E. Forster, as Vice-President of the Council, the onerous duty devolved of maturing its provisions and furnishing the detailed information that might enable Parliament to see its way in fulfilment of the popular hope.

Aid was already contributed by Government to the voluntary schools of various denominations, and thus a million and a half of children received primary instruction. As many more grew up in ignorance, and it was for this shameful remnant that Parliament was asked for the first time to provide. In every parish, or union of parishes, the ratepayers, it was proposed, should triennially elect a Board having the power to impose a rate to the amount of threepence in the pound, to erect suitable buildings, and to appoint competent teachers.

Government declared their object to be to 'take care not to destroy in building up, not to pull down the existing system in introducing a new one; to complete the present voluntary system; to fill up gaps, sparing the public money where it could be done without, and welcoming as much as they could the co-operation of those benevolent men who desired to assist their neighbours.'*

The Treasury inspection and veto throughout being retained by the Committee of Privy Council, each Board would be enabled to obtain loans from the Treasury, repayable in thirty years, and attendance at the Board or at some voluntary school between the ages of five and fourteen was made compulsory.

The difficulties of applying the scheme in the Metropolis seemed almost insurmountable, but on this Ministers were desirous of having the advice of those who represented its wants and capabilities in Parliament. The discussion of the varied and complex subjects raised occupied the greater part of the Session.

In London a great fear fell upon all who wished well to the advancement of popular education, lest the inequality of the new burthen of rates between

* W. E. Forster, in introducing the Bill, February, 1870.

districts obviously so unequally fitted to bear them should beget hostility to any and every system waterlogged by such injustice. St. George's, Hanover Square, was yearly multiplying palaces, and comparatively few children of humble parents would need the smallest possible rate in aid of its richly-endowed voluntary schools; while the struggling industry of Bethnal Green and Shadwell would be speedily crushed with the weight of the new taxation if Board Schools were to be maintained out of strictly parochial resources.

Finsbury was one of the districts that could not be classed with either extreme of realized wealth or fluctuating wages, and the self-denying and indefatigable men of various creeds who there, as elsewhere, had long sustained popular schools out of the margin of their limited, and sometimes narrow, incomes, expressed their strong desire that some better method of dealing with London as a whole should be substituted for Mr. Forster's plan.

When the Bill had made good progress in Committee, I called together my colleagues and laid before them suggestions which had been carefully matured for an amendment, dividing the capital into three great circles—one for the south of the Thames, one including the City and the East End, with a view to adjust the diverse capabilities of educational rating, and the remaining third including the vast area from Westminster to Highgate.

We were unanimous in agreeing to the proposed amendment, which, among other advantages, appeared to hold out the promise of administrative competition between the three powerful bodies it was proposed to create. Mr. W. H. Smith and I were appointed to communicate with Government on the subject, and on more than one occasion we had long conferences with the Vice-President of the Council, who gladly gave up the clause for parochial Boards, but whom we could not persuade of the advantages of our triple scheme.

If an amendment were moved to omit the provisions for parochial building and rating, and to constitute a new municipally elected body for the whole Metropolis, to be called the London School Board, Government would agree to support it. As an experiment which might thereafter be modified if necessary, I consequently moved the alteration that had been agreed on, upon the condition that the limit of threepence in the pound, which from the first had been held out as the inducement to the House to take its educational leap in the dark, should be faithfully adhered to. Lord John Manners seconded the motion in terms that carried the sympathy and support of a great majority of his friends, and the comparatively few tares that appeared in the field of discussion were easily bundled out without burning.

When, however, the Bill in its progress through

Committee came to be printed, the limit of rating had disappeared; I gave notice, accordingly, that I should move to insert words rendering the maximum rate for schools threepence in the pound.

Mr. Forster, while profuse in acknowledgment for the change accomplished in the machinery about to be set up in London, deprecated earnestly what he called the unnecessary imposition of a rigid rule. The Metropolitan members, however, whose educational patriotism had begun to feel rather nervous at the opening prospect, loudly indicated their dissent, and the Prime Minister thought it necessary to interpose.

Addressing us in his most beguiling tones, he assured us that our apprehensions of an excessive burthen were altogether groundless. Government had carefully considered the possibilities which the Bill involved, and he could give us the assurance that the rate could never exceed, if it ever reached, threepence in the pound. I do not pretend that we were all convinced, but we thought, perhaps weakly, that such an undertaking, though general in terms and transitory in duration, was some guarantee against the excesses of pedantic caprice or ostentatious prodigalities in architecture.

The House had grown weary; the weather was hot, and an early prorogation was the consuming hope in the breast of the majority. We had little choice left, and after trying to accentuate, and if possible rivet, the expressions of the wily Minister of Education, we were forced to submit to the inevitable. What has happened since, and how painfully our forebodings have been fulfilled, it would be superfluous to say.

By my own constituents and generally throughout London, a feeling was expressed that the chairmanship of the new Board should be conferred on its Parliamentary author. I need hardly say that I should have valued highly the distinction, and that, being responsible to the public opinion of those who were to pay the rates as well as to the administrative approval of those who were to impose them, I was likely to strive consistently for the fulfilment of the guarantee of Mr. Gladstone that the amount should never exceed threepence in the pound.

But Ministers were bent on setting a coronet upon the head of their new department, and, relying on the love of the municipal middle class for lords, they engaged an ex-Governor-General of India, who had never been in a common school in England since he was a boy, and who knew next to nothing of the texture and fibre of Metropolitan life, to be the first chairman. A relative of Mr. Forster's agreed to propose him, and I regret being unable to forget that more than one distinguished member who had voluntarily offered me his support apologized to me for being unable to keep his word. Lord Lawrence found himself out of his element, and eventually relinquished the post, for which he proved singularly unfit.

General disappointment arose at the Chancellor of the Exchequer's proposal of twopence additional on the income-tax, to meet the deficit on the year, created by the abolition of the shilling duty on corn, which, it was said, nobody felt, and which imperceptibly lowered the current price. Ministers, however, had a majority of eighty-five on going into Committee on the Budget, and the question was raised on an amendment moved by me on the first resolution that the tax should be reduced from sixpence to fivepence in the pound.

The tax on matches had been devised in the hope of saving the middle classes from heavier direct taxation, to which the Chancellor of the Exchequer owned his aversion. The sentiment was creditable to him, and ought to be kept in mind. Public opinion had compelled the withdrawal of the match-tax, and then for a few days an increase of the succession duties was relied on to supply what was wanting.

But this also proved impracticable, and nothing remained, it was said, but a resort to that exaction which Sir Robert Peel had only resorted to as matter of necessity, and had promised to retain only for three years. Yet now, in departure from all financial pledges and traditions, when they had in their hands the actual means in moneys numbered to meet the deficit by suspending the payment of long annuities, Sir Robert Peel's example was cited as authority.

The cases were neither identical nor similar. The only long annuities existing in 1842 were engagements between the Treasury and private persons, a breach in the payment of which would have been a breach of public faith; the long annuities since created were mere entries in public book-keeping by which so much Consols held by the Treasury were converted into long annuities, held by the Treasury also.

Paying off debt as fast as we were was a duty and policy none would dispute; but paying off debt when we happened to be *un*-able was the mere pedantry of financial consistency, for which it was provokingly hard that the public should be compelled to pay.

The guardians of a great and varied community would not, I trusted, deal so inequitably with the great and deserving classes who were already too heavily laden. Why shear only the flock they had already fleeced, and leave the rest of the sheep unshorn?

The wisest statesmen in times past had always carried in their minds the equity between to-day and to-morrow, the capability of the country to bear an extra weight of taxation during a single year to secure a particular object, and the spreading of taxation over all the years that were to be benefited by it. If there was justice to be done between classes, there was justice to be done between years.

The alleged deficit was made up of three items —new primary schools, purchase of army commissions, and new military stores. We did not grudge the large grant this year for education. But what did we get for the money? Every penny of it was outlay for future years. It might ripen five years or ten years hence. But why should not the ripening years help to pay for it?

I did not say, Do not build schools, but, Do not lay the whole of the cost on a single year. A man might want an additional two-pennyworth of cream, but was that a reason for keeping an additional cow?

With reference to the stores, why should the profits and wages of to-day be over-weighted with the whole cost of the £1,600,000 which it was supposed to spend on extra munitions and stores? Were the accumulated cartridges, the surplus powder and ball, the rockets, torpedoes, and shells to be fired away by Christmas, or before the end of the current financial year?

Of all the expedients at the disposal of the Government for raising the money they required, they had selected the one which the Prime Minister himself had condemned in the strongest possible terms, when in Opposition he had said:

'It tends more than any other tax to demoralize and corrupt the people: not from the extent of its levy, nor from the fault of those who levy it, but from the essential nature of the tax itself. It is a source so productive, an engine so convenient, it is so easy to lay on a penny or twopence at a time, that so long as you have the income tax a part of your ordinary revenue, you need not think of effective and extensive economy.'

Here was condemnation broad, sweeping, and plain. We had been used to look to the right hon. gentleman as the great financier of the Liberal Party, and with that article laid down as one of the cardinal items of our creed, we had a right to expect his Government would not be the Government to resort to a tax so condemned by his own lips.

Let them remember what had happened at the close of the Great War. Lord Liverpool's Government refused to pay off troops, and to reduce direct taxation, relying on the majority, theretofore unbroken, to support them. But the House, to their amazement, suddenly slipped out of their hands. Brougham and Whitbread, Romilly and Russell, denounced the keeping up of an income tax to liquidate debt, which they agreed should only be done when there was a clear surplus, and a section of the supporters of Ministers, led by Wilberforce and Baring, broke their ranks, voted with the Opposition, and, by a majority of thirty-nine, scattered the financial scheme of Mr. Vansittart to the winds.

Did the combination of forces that then fraternized deserve the name of an 'illegitimate combination'? Yet that was the phrase now applied to the coincidence of opinion between opposite sides of the House which this unlucky proposal made manifest. But the country thought then and the country thought now—the better, not the worse, of honourable and independent men who differed in their political leanings when they preferred the good they could in common accomplish to a blind subservience to the cause of Party.

The Chancellor of the Exchequer had been somewhat spoiled by the impunity with which he had disregarded public opinion. I owned that in those days of indiarubber principles it was something to find a man possess the hardihood to stick to his opinions when he thought he was right. But what of the man who came forward to defend measures some of which he had admitted to be wrong?

Indifference to the passing breeze of public favour was high merit in a statesman. But when they saw one child after another born only to be deserted, charity compelled them to doubt the paternity of each and all. First they had one with three heads, which the populace declared to be a monster, and which, after three days, was abandoned; then they had one with two heads, and that was likewise forsaken; and now they had one born in convulsions, which had come into the world 'scarce half made up, and that so lamely and unfashionably,' that it seemed extremely doubtful whether it would ever be able to stand.

The Chancellor of the Exchequer did not battle for these children that were called his as he was wont to do for his genuine offspring. If the right hon. gentleman had propounded what he thought right, and adhered to any one of his Budgets, though I might not have been able to support him, he would have had my respect. But these three Budgets could not be all right, and there was not one of them that had not been condemned by public opinion.

Mr. W. Fowler, a staunch Liberal, and regarded as an authority in banking circles, ridiculed Mr. Lowe's assertion that suspending the reduction of the long annuities for a year would be a breach of faith by the Treasury. The former long annuities were contracts to pay private individuals, which if broken would amount to an act of public insolvency: the existing long annuities were simply conversions of Consols made liable for a term to so much higher interest, and were literally bargains made by the nation with itself. Everyone had heard with astonishment the astounding reference made by Mr. Gladstone to

Sir Robert Peel, because in 1842 he did not suspend the annuities he had to deal with, which, in point of fact, he had no power to touch. The sole question was whether suspending the Sinking Fund, or adding so much additional charge to the taxes of the community, was more just.

Mr. Goschen insisted on the duty of rigid adherence to the financial policy in paying off debt. In answer to Mr. Goschen, Mr. Osborne scoffed at compelling members to follow Ministers into the lobby as a profession of confidence and support of a twice-amended Budget of which they disapproved.

When challenged by the Premier to verify his ascription to him of strong condemnation of the course now pursued Mr. Gladstone, asking 'When and where?' sat down, awaiting the proof—instead of rising in his place, his imperturbable critic quietly exclaimed, 'Go on!' and in the general laughter that ensued Mr. Gladstone's argument was resumed.

The Leader of the Opposition concurred in the amendment, and was highly complimentary of the manner in which it had been brought forward. The honourable and learned Member for Finsbury was perfectly justified in his remarks with regard to the long annuities 'in the able and exhaustive speech which was fortunately delivered when the House was full.' It was a complete fallacy to pretend that there was any identity between the long annuities of Sir R. Peel and those that had to be dealt with at that time.

The First Minister, notwithstanding, repeated his contention, and sarcastically twitted me on what he was pleased to call unacquaintance with the subject, having betrayed me into an expression of surprise at the definitions of securities given by him. The question, he insisted, was not who were the holders or the claimants of the long annuities, but of the nature of the claim which the Treasury was bound to meet under the existing system. The Opposition were free to object on public grounds to a mode of finance they disapproved, but he regretted that they should have been led into error by misguided members below the gangway.

The Liberal members thus reproved for their independence numbered 14, and the previous majority for Government of 85 was reduced to 46 in a House of 542. The result called forth numerous gratulations, not only from constituents, but influential persons elsewhere. It was, however, an exercise of independence not to be forgotten.

In the earlier days of the Session of 1871, the temper of Ministers was severely tried by an outburst of bitter but broad humour from various quarters. Conspicuous among their assailants was Bernal Osborne, who, failing to rally to his signal of discontent any section of English or Scotch

Radicals, was driven, as he said, to make friends of electoral unrighteousness at Waterford by posing as one of the excluded Irish Liberal members whom the great Cabinet-maker had treated with disdain. With curious unconsciousness of the ridicule he provoked by assuming the character of a mock Moses, he jokingly recalled his past adventures in search of an easy seat.

For years he had intermittently praised, and every now and then quizzed, Government measures, expecting to be at last found indispensable; but it availed nought. Frown and tremble with emotion though he might at their distress at particular intervals, he never could get up the suspicion of a Whip that he was really alarmed or alarming; and when the fit of *malaise* was over, he could be as friendly and funny as ever from the fourth bench behind Ministers, and sometimes as serviceable too.

When Gladstone, abandoned by Oxford and rejected by Lancashire, was fain to put up with a Metropolitan seat, and a Tory member timidly tried to obstruct an important measure by arguing that the present was not the fit time, Osborne exclaimed, 'Not the right time, sir? We take our time from Greenwich!'

A supercilious Chancellor of the Exchequer neglecting once to satisfy his curiosity as to the component elements of a round sum in the estimates, he repeated the question for the third time with a broad insinuation that there must be something wrong with the money. Piqued at last into answering him, the financier named half a dozen items, and then rashly began a dignified reproof; but thinking better of it before he got very far, he stuck fast at, 'I treat the imputation with——' Osborne interjecting, 'Oh yes, I know—with silent contempt,' amidst laughter at which his opponent was glad to sit down.

Some years after I told the story, without the names, at Horsman's table, where the forgetful wag happened to be, and when the laugh was over, he said, 'That's capital; who said it?' giving me the unlooked-for opportunity of responding, 'Your target was Charles Wood, and thou art the man.'

The Bill to provide exceptional means for baffling and punishing Ribbonism in Westmeath having led to heated debate, Ministers proposed to refer it to a secret Committee, where witnesses might speak without reserve, and even members of the House might be refused the privilege of listening. The only precedents that could be cited were from the evil days of the Regency, and the taunt was reiterated by Opposition that Government did not know what to do or recommend, and wished to throw the responsibility on Parliament.

Osborne seized the occasion to vent his own grievance. Without fear of rebuke or retort, he ascribed their perplexities to the constitution of the Cabinet, which he proceeded to vivisect limb by limb. The whole mischief, he averred, had its origin in the preference of the First Minister for Whig marionettes when forming an Administration which could in no sense be said to represent the sister kingdom. The Cabinet had lately been whitewashed—that is to say, they had been shuffled, only to come back to the old position of 'as you were.' He wanted to know how far they represented the House of Commons, and how far the feelings of the people of Ireland.

There were fifteen gentlemen, but in every turn of the kaleidoscope there reappeared a combination of the old materials. They had got back the old family party, and, true to their traditions, they were, in the words of Sheridan, not content to knock their heads against existing walls, but wantonly built up walls for the purpose. They were all respectable men, more or less gifted; but what specific knowledge had they of Ireland?

He had not a word to say against the noble lord (Hartington) who, he was glad to see, accepted the thankless but responsible office of Chief Secretary. But the only man with any practical knowledge of the difficult and disorganized country was the Member for Louth, who was accordingly removed from the Castle, and sent to the treadmill of the Board of Trade, of which he before knew nothing: and one never looked at the official list without reading over the door, 'No Irish need apply.' The Member for Limerick, who had long been waiting in the ante-room, supposed to possess the confidence of the people and the priests, was of course not considered worthy of confidence, and was sent aside to the dead-letter office.*

We were about to disperse to enjoy at leisure this pasquinade, when a whisper of 'stay' arrested our steps, and the voice and gesture of the Solicitor-General for Ireland seemed to promise that perhaps, after all, the cynic might have met his match.

No dumb guardian of the flock ever watched with angrier eye a skirmishing assailant of the fold than, from beside the Speaker's chair, the rough-and-ready legal sheep-dog 'from D*a*rry, dear,' awaited the master's look to go for him.

Dowse was known to men of all parties as a genial, outspoken, self-made man, brimful of a certain coarse humour, utterly fearless in choice of phrase, and ready on all occasions to give as hard as he got. The Treasury Bench did not contain any respondent more apt in reply, and no one who heard him will ever forget the crackling of his gibes and jeers, or the uproar of mischievous mirth they provoked.

* Mr. Monsell, now Lord Emly, was made Postmaster-General.

It was made a complaint, he said, that the Member for Louth, who knew Ireland well, had been removed from the Castle, and sent to the treadmill of Trade at Whitehall. But would the Member for Waterford object to work that treadmill? If not, within a few months they might depend upon it they would lose in silence and gratitude all the amusement afforded by his patriotic wrath.

He was proud, he said, of being an Irish member, and everyone must be glad that, when he failed to find rest for the sole of his foot at Dover, he fled to Waterford, where refuge was found for the destitute. But he was an Irishman, though not *pro re nata*, and would probably remain so till the next General Election.

Defence or excuse for the system of administrative disfranchisement impugned there was none, but from that day the ruthless but comical Parliamentary pugilist never hinted that he was ready to take off his coat without fixing attention in its most listless mood.

Osborne chafed not a little at finding himself in the plight of the drummer whose lash had been wrenched from his hand, and he could not conceal his vexation. Someone asked Dowse how he looked when pacing the lobby afterwards. 'Oh,' he replied, 'like a man with the toothache in his mind.'

The authorized version of what occurs at St.

Stephen's embalms but little of what helps to make the tedium endurable, and some of the good things I recall with the freshest sense of admiration for their unpremeditated wit are not graven on that vast collection of legislative tombstones kept by Mr. Hansard.

One of these I must note ere parting company with my learned friend. A colleague who sat next to him one evening in a half-empty House was annoyed by the too-audible snoring of a Highland member engaged in cattle-farming, who, after trudging about town in wet weather, and dining heavily, devoted the rest of his day to the performance of public duty, and, settling himself on the fifth bench behind the Government, took his rest undisturbed by debate, but was ready to vote as often as wakened. His attitude was original and unique, and from below the ruddy face could be seen between the soiled feet of the fore-shortened form. 'Do look round at that fellow,' said the disgusted Lord of the Treasury. 'Pooh!' said Dowse: 'it's only another case of the foot and mouth disease.'

Complaints were rife of the way in which recruiting was habitually practised, and of the number of youths of the humbler classes who were beguiled into premature engagement in the service without contributing permanently to its real strength. Medical experience testified how practically unfitted were beardless recruits to endure the wear and tear of laborious discipline; still less to exposure in foreign climates, ere their frames were knit or their bones were grown. The concurrent testimony of physiologists, whose judgment was above suspicion, and of veteran commanders, whose confessions must be taken at a minimum, pointed to the need of some check being peremptorily placed on the reckless and wasteful practice whose evil fruits were gathered at the public expense in the hospitals, crowded from time to time by youthful invalids returned from abroad.

Medical reports had frequently been made from Netley of the deplorable numbers thus sent back, after brief service in the tropics, to be treated for awhile as indoor patients, and then to be remitted to their village homes to linger out a profitless existence, or from incurable disease to die.

In company with a well-known member of the College of Surgeons, Mr. Jabez Hogg, I visited Netley, and no doubt was left in my mind that the case in the departmental blue-books was rather under than over stated.

The late President of the College of Surgeons, Mr. Guthrie, who in early life had had great experience in the Peninsula, and who as a writer was of European fame, felt bound, in season and out of season, to press upon every Minister of War the hideous and hateful evils of premature enrolment for foreign service. Professor Parkes,

Professor of Hygiene at Netley, who had had great experience in camp and hospital in India and the Crimea, in his work on hygiene, spoke of the danger and loss from immature enlistment. The age of eighteen was too low; the youngest recruit should be twenty or twenty-one. The process of ossification had not even begun to be completed at eighteen, especially as regarded the spine and long bones, the epiphyses of which did not unite to the shaft of the bones until a much later period.

Our visit was made to Netley for the purpose of being certain of the injury to the military service by the enlistment into it of growing youths. The age was seen to be too low, as boys under eighteen years of age were every day enlisted for both ordinary service and service in India. The evils resulting therefrom led to Parliamentary action, and at a much later date to Lord Airey's Committee on army reorganization.

Parliament accepted twenty as a safe limit for India; but, as the minimum for recruits remained at eighteen, the regulation soon fell into disuse, or became of little value, since the young fellow on his enlistment fixes his own age, subject only to the further check of the medical officer, who is obliged to determine the question himself by his development or 'physical equivalent' to the age stated.

The sanctity of the oath administered to the

recruit goes for little or nothing, as it is systematically disregarded; and so long as he answers to the regulation of 5 feet 4 inches in height, 33 inches in chest-girth, and 115 pounds in weight, he is, as a rule, accepted for the line, because the medical officer experiences a difficulty in rejecting him.

Professor Sir Thomas Longmore, a surgeon of great experience, said: 'No rule whatever can be laid down for the height of growing lads between seventeen and twenty years of age, because the diversity is so great; and, more unfortunately, the powers entrusted to the recruiting authorities are so largely used in dispensing with the physical qualification that the medical officer finds himself and his advice constantly set aside. So that, in fact, there is still a very excessive waste going on in the army during the early years of the soldier's career, which is in great part due to a want of strictness in the first examination of the recruit.'

We were received at Netley with courteous attention by Sir William Aitken, the Professor of Pathology in the Army School there, the well-known author of a standard work on the growth of the recruit and the young soldier; and from him I gathered many important facts with regard to hospital administration, and the wider and more debatable field of the hygiene of the social organism, more especially in relation to early enlistment as an important factor in the conversion of the raw recruit into the effective soldier. Sir William had frequently insisted on the grave responsibility which attaches to the War Minister in this respect, and his advice, founded on long experience, was ably sustained by that of Sir Thomas Longmore, Professor of Military Surgery, who took us through the pathological collection of the museum, and explained in detail the slowness of the growth in years of adolescence of the long bones, and the tardy perfection of the epiphyses, without which men supposed to have reached their prime are liable to break down on unusual strain.

I had the good fortune to be well acquainted with Sir John Burgoyne in Ireland, and he told me how often he had remonstrated against the system in question, but to no purpose; and that he felt the opportunity now offered for invoking the authority of Parliament was one that ought not to be neglected. If recruits were difficult to be had of the full age of manhood, at least a rule might be enforced that the Queen's shilling should not be offered to boys under eighteen years of age, and forbidding their being sent beyond sea before they were twenty-one.

In concert with the late Colonel Anson, I gave notice of an amendment of the sixth clause which, as it stood, left the notorious abuse uncorrected, and the feeling generally expressed on both sides of the House as well as in the press was so unmistakable that the Secretary of War proposed to withdraw the clause without any renunciation of its purport, to which we strongly objected, not only as an attempt to evade discussion of a subject of acknowledged importance, but as a deviation from the established practice regarding Government Bills in Committee. Lord E. Cecil, Mr. Disraeli, and Lord Elcho supported this view, and the clause was postponed, and we had time to accumulate testimonies to the truth of the pleas of humanity and policy we urged before the question came on for decision.

After three months had been spent in discussing the varied interests of the officers, it could hardly be thought unreasonable that a day should be given for considering those of the rank and file, and I consequently declined to withdraw the notice which stood in my name. At length a day was given for its consideration,* and I appealed to the patience and patriotism of men of all parties to give their verdict according to the evidence I had to lay before them.

The engrossing topic of the day was still the Bill introduced by Secretary Cardwell for the abolition of purchase. Royal Commissions and Select Committees, and numberless political essayists, concurred in advocating the change, which would emancipate the army, it was said, from the aristocratic monopoly which had sub-

* June 19, 1871.

sisted from the time of the Revolution, and hold out to the gallant and meritorious youth of all classes the competitive rewards of military ambition. Over-regulation prices paid by rich subalterns for promotion had become an unendurable scandal, and though innumerable criticisms on every part of the proposal gave rise to animated, and often angry, debate, the great preponderance of opinion in the Lower House was in its favour.

The Army Estimates for the current year exceeded those of the preceding by £2,800,000, and the Government project of military reform was the consideration offered for this large increase of public burthens. Ministers drew upon the confidence of the House, and it had accepted the Bill. Of many points debated concerning purchase, nearly all had been ruled in their favour.

In a speech of considerable length, I pointed out that, while the whole patronage of the army was about to be transferred to them from the neutral trusteeship in a Commander-in-Chief established by Mr. Pitt, and which had lasted for well-nigh eighty years, the property qualification for commissions was to be abolished, and the Government of the day was thenceforth to have the whole power of selection. The embodiment and control of the militia, which had for centuries belonged to local authorities — wisely as Bacon, Pim, Summers, Walpole, Fox, and Russell thought—

was to be concentrated hereafter in the hands of the Administration. The consideration held forth for all this transfer of power and expansion of supplies was the promise that we should have not only a better officered army, but an army so complete and so reliable that all misgiving as to danger from without should at once and for ever be extinguished. The profession of arms was to be encouraged and rewarded in promotion by merit, and the complement of regular troops was to be completed up to a force of 200,000 men. But when we were asked to provide permanently for this great array, we naturally supposed that Ministers spoke of men. The House agreed to the enhanced price, taking for granted that what was purchased would be of standard weight, and the article up to sample—some guarantee for a proper system of enlistment, some warranty that the condition of the recruit in age as well as health should be sound—surely no unfitting stipulation for Parliament to make on behalf of the people.

The question of recruiting, far from being subordinate or incidental, was one that went to the very quick of army reform; and Ministers having withdrawn their only enlistment clause, no other course remained than that which I proposed, of adding a new clause to the Bill before we parted with it in Committee, forbidding the sending in future of immature youths out of their native land. In a letter of the Duke of Wellington in 1811 to Sir H. Torrens, then secretary to the Commander-in-Chief, there were the significant words, 'Government have never taken a comprehensive view of the subject of recruiting;' and he went on to explain how short-sighted the policy had proved of sending him feeble and ineffective rank-and-file instead of reliable reinforcements. Lord Hardinge told the Sebastopol Committee in 1854 why he had been unable to furnish Lord Raglan with the support he required in the Crimea, that 'our peace establishment was so low on the outbreak of war, and that after making the first effort to send out 25,000 men we could do nothing more than send out young recruits, made partly perfect in drill in a couple of months; but instead of bone and muscle they were nothing but gristle. In the face of the winter, it was impossible for them to endure hard work and inclement weather like seasoned men.' And Lord Raglan, when informed that 2,000 more recruits were ready to be despatched from home, wrote that 'the last sent were so young and unformed that they fell victims to disease, and were swept away like flies. He preferred to wait.' Sir de Lacy Evans at the same time wrote that 'the drafts sent to him were quite too young to bear the strain of the winter encampment, and of the work in the trenches.'

Most of the distinguished men who held command in the Crimea had passed away, but one remained whose jealousy for the honour of the country he had served so well, whose sympathy for the troops he had so often led in danger, and whose clear and calm discernment in all that related to military discipline, had not been dimmed by years. Sir John Burgoyne wrote to me saying: 'Your principle of preventing the employment of youths under twenty-one years of age on foreign service is both important and just. Each regiment should always have a battalion at home, in which might be youths in a state of progress with others older in the service. Such battalions would form valuable reserves.' Public opinion would no longer allow the War Department, in the words of General Daubeney, 'to go on year after year shipping multitudes of boys to the tropics, to their inevitable destruction,' for no better reason than that it had long been the practice, and that it would be less trouble to let the practice continue unchanged.

Lord Sandhurst suggested another plan, namely, that youths might be enlisted in militia, which in some respects would be identical with the home battalion, from which the corresponding regiment liable to serve abroad might make up its complement of men above twenty years of age; and after six years with the colours they might return to form part of the reserve. The Secretary for War might perhaps suggest a third alternative, which officially might be deemed still better. Then by all means let them have it. The House would not be nice as to form or nomenclature, so that the country escaped the reproach of the present yearly holocaust. Let not the Minister deceive himself with the notion, however, that the question, once raised, would ever be allowed to sleep again until the people of this country had got security for the total abrogation of this reckless and ruinous malpractice. I would not do him the injustice of alleging that with the power already in his hands he had year after year neglected to use it; for I thoroughly believed that, until Parliament interposed with a high hand, no civilian Secretary of State would ever be able to bring the evil system to an end.

It was like what occurred regarding the abolition of slavery, which most of the old planters declared to be impracticable. Year after year the demand was made, the evil admitted, and vague promises given by Minister after Minister that orders would be issued to lessen the mischief, and gradually to work the cure. But slavery would have gone on until our day if the House of Commons had not insisted that it should be abolished peremptorily and for ever. Setting aside all considerations of humanity and cost, was it conceivable that we should passively rely on imperfect materials for national defence, with no better justification than the huckster plea of cheapness in the labour market?

In conclusion, I moved that a clause should be inserted in the Bill providing that no person hereafter enlisted as a soldier in any regiment of cavalry or infantry of the line should be called upon to serve out of the United Kingdom until he had attained the age of twenty years.

Sir Henry Storks, on behalf of the Government, stated that no opposition would be made to the adoption of the principle contended for, if embodied in an Address to the Crown instead of a clause in a statute; and in conformity with the general feeling of those present I consented to adopt that course.

In due time her Majesty was advised to send a message in reply that orders should be forthwith given to carry into effect the wishes of the House, and I received many congratulations on having at last obtained an assurance that the department would desist from a practice which could no longer be defended.

For a time the public conscience was appeased, and the royal word was ostensibly kept. But the humane intentions of her Majesty have been too frequently neglected, and the Duke of Connaught's evidence before Lord Wantage's Committee of what has since occurred in India under his own observation conclusively proves that nothing less obligatory than the words of an Act of Parliament will suffice to protect undiscerning youths from being drawn into undertakings for which they are physically unfit.

In the Lords the Purchase Bill met with a very different reception. It was denounced in eloquent terms as wantonly democratic in its aim and tendency, and obviously bureaucratic, by the substitution of selection for seniority in every step of advancement. No exertion of personal or family influence could persuade more than half the peers to attend the discussion; but the Duke of Richmond's amendment for indefinite postponement was carried by a majority of two to one. Lord Derby, who objected to the measure, though not to the principle, had incidentally dropped in debate the assertion that the Bill was unnecessary, inasmuch as the Crown might, without violating any statute, put an end to the practice. A noble friend of mine is said to have exclaimed: 'Then we are free to do what we want by the admission of the opposite party.'

The Cabinet met early next day, and resolved that Lord Halifax should convey their unanimous advice to the Queen to adopt the course thus suggested; and, to the infinite surprise of both Houses, they were informed that a royal warrant had been signed declaring purchase of commissions at an end.

The peers were very wroth, and several Whigs of note who had previously supported Government, including Lords Russell and Romilly (then Master of the Rolls), pronounced the act to be an ill-advised resuscitation of prerogative of evil example. Lord Cairns objected strongly to the course adopted as unconstitutional; Lord Westbury refused to defend it, and the Master of the Rolls, though a staunch Whig, said that 'since the Bill of Rights there had been no instance of such an interference by the Crown with the Legislature. The cases cited by the Chancellor were really not precedents at all; and the legality of the warrant being open to question, the opinion of the judges ought to have been previously taken.'

In the Lower House Colonel Barttelot, Mr. G. Gregory, Mr. W. Fowler, and Mr. Fawcett, concurred in objecting; but sooner than risk the total loss of the measure, on whose elaboration Parliament had spent so much time, I proposed an additional standing order declaring 'that, whenever any Bill shall henceforth be returned from the Lords with amendments, the same shall not be taken into consideration if it shall have been brought to the knowledge of the House that, subsequent to the passing of such Bill by the House, any material provision thereof has been withdrawn from the cognizance of Parliament, by any act done, warrant issued, or proclamation made by the authority of the Crown.'

At considerable length I argued the question historically, pleading earnestly against the course being drawn into precedent. But the Attorney-General, Sir R. Collier, Sir William Harcourt, and the Prime Minister, defended the issue of the warrant on the ground that, as the purchase of commissions did not originate under any statute, its inhibition in future did not require one, and my suggestion was overruled.

Although the practice of allowing petitioners of distinction who thought themselves aggrieved to plead for redress at the Bar of the House, and of hearing witnesses in support or confutation of facts of undisputed questions of privilege, had for some time gradually fallen into disuse, the Representative Chamber had never renounced its time-honoured right to sit as a Court of Parliament to pronounce judgment of exoneration on those whose conduct was unjustly impugned, and to condemn and punish offenders with expulsion, fine, and imprisonment. In proportion as the electoral bases widened, and the legislative cares of empire multiplied, instinctive reluctance seems to have arisen to the exercise of judicial functions.

Time was when a President and a Lord President of the Council, or a Keeper of the Great Seal, did not disdain being heard in self-defence by the Commons against political charges, and within the memory of living men the connivance or innocence of a Prince of the Blood in the sale of military commissions by his mistress had occupied the House for many days together, chiefly in the cross-examination by any member who chose to put questions to the conflicting witnesses at the Bar. Later on O'Connell, in his own name and that of his fellow-believers, had been suffered to claim admission to his seat as Member for Clare without being returned a second time under the Act of Emancipation that was already practically agreed to; and some few cases not worth recalling had kept alive the tradition of an inherent power in the People's House to sit betimes as an independent and unappellate Court of Equity.

An incident in Irish agitation in 1869 of little interest or moment had led to the summoning of the Mayor of Cork to answer his alleged presumption in publicly questioning the conduct of Parliament; and had he not prudently exculpated himself by retractation and apology, there was every prospect of valuable time being wasted in the endeavour to make out distinctly what his worship had said and what he had not said from the conflicting testimony of numerous witnesses. When relieved from the apprehension of a profitless proceeding, it occurred to not a few unconnected friends of constitutional usage to inquire what would have been the course of procedure with regard to the taking of evidence. The custom appears to have been to send the witnesses who were required to bear testimony, when called on, to appear at the Bar of the House of Lords, or before a Master of Chancery, to be sworn; but no instance could be cited of the Clerk of the Commons administering the requisite oath to a person in that capacity.

I asked Speaker Denison whether he saw any reason why we should not assume the right in all respects to regulate our own proceedings, and though by temperament he was averse from any change not sanctioned by usage, he confessed that he had often wondered how the anomaly pointed out had so long been permitted to exist without question. With the approval of several men of experience on both sides, I moved for a Select Committee to inquire into the subject, and had the satisfaction of seeing it composed of men well qualified to conduct its proceedings.

As chairman, I had the privilege of receiving the evidence of the Speaker and his distinguished predecessor in the Chair, Lord Eversley, both of whom, as well as Sir Erskine May, expressed the opinion that the alteration suggested ought to be made. No serious difficulty arose, and the report of the Committee was unanimous in its favour. I had reason to believe that neither the Chancellor nor Lord Redesdale, the Chairman of Standing Orders in the Lords, was disposed to object; and in 1871 I had the satisfaction of seeing a Bill founded on the report of my Committee assented to by the Peers.

Within a few days of the prorogation, a Bill was brought down from the Upper House entitled the Friendly Societies Commission Bill, consisting of sixteen clauses, the main object of which was to create a new court, consisting of two commissioners to be appointed by the Treasury, for the hearing of all causes affecting benefit and building societies, with power to summon any person before them as a witness, and to call for the production of books and papers, and clothed with authority to fine and imprison directors and officers who might be deemed culpable through negligence or malfeasance.

One of these commissioners was to be authorized to institute any inquiry into past and present transactions, and to hear and adjudicate, sitting alone upon the issues that seemed to him involved. In short, to do and decree anything heretofore only recognised as legal when decreed or done by one of the Supreme Courts of Law. A certificate of indemnity might be granted by him to any person giving testimony before him, though the same might otherwise legally amount to defamation.

There had been little if any discussion in the Upper House, and there were few left in the Lower to debate the proposal; but looking at the multitudinous interests involved, and the novelty of the jurisdiction it was proposed to set up, I deemed it my duty to remonstrate strongly against its being read a second time, and the Home Secretary agreed that legislation on the subject should stand over till next Session.

When the various societies throughout the country were made acquainted with the provisions in detail, their surprise and irritation were great; but journals that assumed philosophic superiority to popular feeling, and sought to maintain the old ideas that laws for the industrial classes ought to be enacted without consulting them as to how they were likely to work, lamented the opportunity lost of fitting upon them a harness which other orders of society would not endure.

I had during the autumn no little correspondence on the question with the active directors of building and benefit societies both in town and country; and at a public meeting in Holloway, of which I was chairman, I explained fully the reasons why it appeared to me inequitable and unconstitutional that to a new tribunal so inquisitorial and so arbitrary the best portion of the working and humble middle classes should be given over. If Parliament thought that a poor man was wronged, it should appoint a public prosecutor, whose duties should be as in Scotland, Ireland, Belgium, Italy, France, and everywhere excepting among ourselves; but that was only safe where it was made to apply in any case, civil or criminal, which came within the confines of an Act of Parliament.

But the great benefit of these societies lay in their teaching men to combine habits of thrift with habits of discernment—the true means of popular education. I was tired of the incessant talk then in fashion about the greatest amount of book knowledge to be crammed into the heads of all. Having written some books myself, and read a great many, I had come to the conviction that the civilized world was not a mob of fools before the invention of printing, and that, great as its benefits had been, it would never be a substitute for practical education in the varied business of life.

It is needless to say that most of my hearers went with me; petitions poured in from all parts of the kingdom against the creation of a separate jurisdiction. Other measures of a more reasonable kind had their origin in the House of Commons, and drew together men of opposite parties in maturing them, and the obnoxious project was heard of no more.

Having frequently enjoyed the advice and aid of Blanchard Jerrold in matters connected with the organization and extension of benefit societies, in whose development he took an active and enlightened interest, I learned through him that a desire was felt by the Empress Eugénie to be made acquainted with their practical working, and that the principles and practice of the system should be brought to the knowledge of the Prince

Imperial. My name being mentioned as that of one who had given great attention to the subject, I was not surprised at receiving an intimation that a visit at Chislehurst from my friend and me would be very acceptable, with special reference to the subject of inquiry; and as the preparation of materials for the life of the late Emperor was then in progress at Camden Place, the time was easily chosen for an interview.

We were received by her widowed Majesty alone, and without the least shadow of ceremony or reserve. Attired in simple black, and anxious to place her visitors at their ease, she said she would endeavour to understand the details and distinctions of the exemplary mechanism of self-help which she rejoiced to find so much relied upon in England by the working classes, and which hitherto had not made the same way to prevalence in France. The people there were marvellously frugal, and at every age accustomed to self-denial; they were willing enough to combine socially and industrially, and the wide dissemination of the sense of property ought to facilitate greatly local associations to make safe its possession, if the way of management were sufficiently made known.

I endeavoured to explain generally the precise objects to which our institutions were carefully limited; their freedom from political or sectarian exclusiveness, and the efforts which were constantly made in Parliament by men of opposite parties to render their accumulated savings more secure. Provision against sickness, accident, and old age, and the encouragement of voluntary thrift on a moderate scale for the purpose, was the basis of our unpretentious but widespread building societies. We thought it not only useful, but essential, to bring the subscribers to each benefit society together with perfect freedom to discuss from time to time what should be done with their funds, and who should be chosen to take care of them; and in this way we believed that a mutual education of the old and the young was promoted, not according to any rigid method or form, but with a cheerfulness, and often with the unconsciousness, of neighbourly good humour. The connection between all the societies using the same fraternal name—such, for instance, as the Oddfellows, which now contains 695,687 members—was a galvanic battery whereby each contributive portion silently added to the strength and importance of every other, and kept all the stronger for being parts of one great whole. We had never had to regret the perversion of the system to factious or unconfessed objects, sectarian or political, and we were therefore the better able to ask the Legislature for such judicial protection as we required by registration and audit, because we could fearlessly claim to be at once the most soberly democratic and the most selfishly conservative of institutions.

The Empress asked many questions, evincing a keen perception of the practical worth and the difficulties of working societies, and, expressing her gratification at the different light they seemed to cast upon the lot of labour, begged that we would see Prince Louis, and endeavour to enlist his sympathy in the cause we had so much at heart. He had been already prepared to expect a visit, and with affability received us in his study, which was full of engineering plans, books, and drawings. He had just returned from examination at Woolwich. He had studied hard, and looked tired, as it was late in the day; but his manner was eager and winning, and he evidently was resolved to do his best to understand the nature of the explanatory reports we offered when he had more leisure fully to comprehend them.

A few years rolled by, and the hopes of usefulness we had cherished the privilege of being instrumental in stimulating were darkened out in a far-distant grave. I saw the bright, ambitious face of the young Prince no more, or the sympathetic features of her, the remnant of whose chequered life was at the time in question devotedly wrapped up in the dazzling contingencies that in the distance seemed linked with his possible career. Since then men of science and of benevolence in France, as in Germany, have directed more attention to the examples of automatic provision for accident, disease, and age; and the uninterrupted success in England of associations like the Manchester Unity of Oddfellows is now recognised year by year more widely, and applied more generally to secure similar results.

To some who may not be familiar with the mute but eloquent facts of the case, it may be enough to cite the latest authentic testimony on the subject with regard to the investment and outlay of the past year. In the present year the Unity consists of 4,594 lodges. The capital of those that have sent in reports is nearly seven millions sterling. With the addition of the funeral funds, the total capital reaches £10 10s. 1d. a head. Last year £635,535 was paid to members for sick benefits. In the last eighteen years £14,476,152 has been received by the Manchester Unity, and £10,343,173 paid out: and in the same period the capital of the sick and funeral funds has risen from three millions to seven millions.

The just exultation universally felt at these splendid results of self-help naturally inspires distrust of alternatives, however benevolently meant, that—directly or indirectly—would rely on Government contribution or control. Money at Whitehall can always be had cheaper than money withdrawn from the till; and the proposal is, therefore, always plausible that the revenue and the credit of the State may fairly be made contributory to the self-denying thrift of the people. But official intervention necessarily implies official interference, subjection to the ever-encroaching imposition of official power, and step by step to the attenuation and ultimate extinction of self-respect and self-dependence in the best classes of those that live by labour. From provision in an Oddfellows' lodge for accident, sickness, or death, the decline may not be sudden, humiliating, or obvious to relief by State pauperism. But to that the downward change must inevitably come. Not only in the frank and friendly confidence of the lodge where I often spent a pleasant and instructive evening, but in the House of Commons, I always did my best to keep this sentiment in remembrance as vital for the well-being and self-respect of the many; and I had on more than one occasion to resist the supercilious arguments of persons in authority who could not be easily brought to believe that any practical assurance of good was valid without a stamp.

Let me freely own that the same desire to encourage, preserve, and fortify the collective instinct of local and independent self-management inspired me always when dealing, as I had frequently to do, with legislation regarding building societies. An amending Act providing better for registration of societies, for the appointment of trustees, and for the audit of accounts, was carried by me, much to the satisfaction of the numerous associations that bear that name.

With the active co-operation of Sir Stafford Northcote, we did not deceive ourselves with the expectation that risk of loss from want of judgment or want of honesty in special cases was thereby obviated. But we believed, undoubtingly, that the practical education which such societies imparted in the duty of weighing betimes the character and disposition of those with whom the direction of each society's affairs was entrusted was in itself an inestimable good.

We could not help seeing the pain and sorrow which pecuniary failure in any instance must entail, and the damage it must inflict upon the credit of similar associations all round. But we thought that, upon the whole, inoculation with official guarantee would prove worse than the disease. I think so still; but I would not upon that account, if I had a voice in discussions which late unfortunate events seem to foreshadow, reject any reasonable improvement in the system of audit or registration.

Looking disinterestedly, but deliberately, on the future prospects of building societies, I would earnestly advocate the limitation of investments on mortgage or in public companies of the funds paid in by members from time to time; not because such investments made by those that can afford to wait for their realization when wanted are not in a thousand instances safe and wise, but because the form of these particular associations does not admit of their being to an unlimited extent adopted.

Misadventure and mistake there have been, and will again no doubt be, in these as in all other financial undertakings of vast and varied extent; and having regard to what we have recently seen in the highest commercial sphere, as well as the humblest, no true friend of thrift and put-by will reject or discard supplemental provisions that may be suggested by reliable men of experience for better management in future; but I fervently trust that no influence of panic will beget an appeal to Government, because it has always money at command, to take in the institutions and do for them.

We shall have wheat and tares growing together until the harvest of all things, and that is a law of nature which cannot be possibly prevented; but in the main, I believe, no such crop of good was ever reaped in this country as has been by the free action of co-operative bodies like these.

One word more upon a sinister objection often heard in private, which to-morrow may be cynically echoed in public, against building societies—namely, that if a man by their aid finds himself after ten or twenty years his own landlord, his house costs him more than it would have done if he had hired it on lease, or borrowed the money to buy it from a wealthy neighbour. Yes, and the same thing might be said of his buying for his wife a really serviceable gown in preference to one at two-thirds the price at the cheap shop; or to purchasing for himself a coat that will long keep out the wind and rain o' nights in preference to attempting one of shoddy, incapable of resisting the winter's blast.

But, after all, building societies, extensive as they have become, and fruit-bearing morally and socially, form but one division of the advancing host of progress. The Manchester Unity wears the blue ribbon without envy or cavil on the part of its comrades, who wear other facings, and are less heavily equipped for the war against want. Benefit societies, under a variety of names, have during the present century grown to a magnitude that, had it been foretold thirty, twenty, or ten years ago, would have been called fabulous.

Mr. Brabrook's recent evidence before the Labour Commission, as Chief Registrar of Friendly Societies, shows that the invested capital of the various friendly societies in the United Kingdom amounted in 1891 to about two hundred and eighteen millions sterling, of which the building societies account for nearly one-fourth. Every Chancellor of the Exchequer would like to have such resources to play with in Consols for the purpose of paying off debt; but when it is remembered that the automatic working of these remarkable inventions of popular industry is to save from waste the small surplusage of weekly earnings and directly to reinvest them in the trade of the neighbourhood whence they have been gleaned, while to absorb them into the Government purse would be at best to lighten the weight of two and a half per cent. on the national debt, it behoves all who live by labour, and all who patriotically wish to sweeten its breath, firmly to resist the beginnings of such an absorption.

Towards the close of 1872 I had reason to believe that after the division on the income tax, and the ungracious manner in which the chairmanship of the School Board had been disposed of, Mr. Forster, if not others, rather wished for an opportunity to promote me out of Parliament. The occasion seemed to present itself on the retirement of Mr. Erle from the Charity Commission, of which the Vice-President of the Committee of Education was chairman. One day I received very unexpectedly from Lord Granville, as head of the department to which the Commission appertained, a friendly note offering me the vacant appointment, which, he said, had the recommendation of being for life, but implied giving up Parliament. The position was one I had never thought of or desired, and, preferring what my old friend Shiel called 'the fascinating vicissitudes' of life at St. Stephen's to the influence and ease of a quasi-judicial life, I thanked my kind friend, as I had always found him to be, and declined. Still more to my surprise, he wrote next day asking if I cared to have a Red Ribbon of the Bath; but neither did this seem to me a temptation.

Hearing that Disraeli had been detained in town in the autumn of 1872 by the illness of his wife, I called one day to inquire, and found him much depressed and complaining of the loneliness of London in the depth of September. He had hardly seen anyone to speak to for a week. He drove out generally in the afternoon beyond the suburbs, and tried to realize in his own mind the changes wrought by the speculative builders everywhere; but there was no recalling the topography of antediluvian Middlesex (*i.e.*, before the Reform Bill), and as for distinguishing places, terraces and crescents from one another, nobody could do that but a surveyor or a rate-collector. No apathy of the mental faculties could betray him into Pall Mall, and he thought he was sometimes better inhaling what was called the fresh air of Hyde Park through the open windows of his study, two pair up.

The name of his former colleague, Colonel Tomlin, with whom he had sat for Shrewsbury, drew forth a passing protest against men in politics being yoked together in representation. 'At first,' he said, 'we contrived to get on peaceably, and as long as I was nobody we did very well; but when I mounted he conceived the most unreasoning aversion towards me, which I tried to appease, but I soon discovered it was no use. He is the most ill-tempered man I know: governed by jealousy, wholly unaccountable in his political leanings from time to time; but I believe he is coming to the conviction that whatever I advise or say is wrong.' In reply to an expression of a hope that Lady Beaconsfield was gaining strength, he said, 'They tell me she is better, but you know what better is at eighty-three.'

Several cases of hardship had arisen in which officers of acknowledged courage and experience were removed from the army upon the report of courts of inquiry, without the opportunity of offering testimony on oath, or the privilege of appeal to a public military tribunal under the Articles of War. The Duke of Wellington had left on record the characteristic disapproval of the system as a bad substitute for courts-martial according to the Mutiny Act; and other eminent commanders, while maintaining its necessity for the preservation of discipline in the field, concurred in avowing the opinion that it had better be dispensed with in garrison.

I was induced to look carefully into the numerous cases on record by the painful incidents that had arisen out of the removal of Colonel Dawkins, who had served with great distinction in the Crimea, and that of Captain Hawtree, who had risen from the ranks, and in a course of eight-and-twenty years had behaved with exemplary fortitude and loyalty in the estimation of his regimental superiors, and yet was cashiered without even being told the cause.

I appealed to the generosity and justice of the House whether there was a pickpocket collared by the police, or a welsher on the Newmarket course, or a burglar caught in the act with centre-bit and jemmy upon him, who was not certain of more justice than they had given this man. Very recently an officer was accused at head-quarters in India of inebriety. A court of inquiry, after examining many witnesses, all of whom denied the allegation, unanimously reported that no case was made out. Yet within a month he was dismissed without any reason being given.

I cited many instances of former times and of our own, and especially the weighty opinion of Wyndham, than whom no more honoured name was ever associated with the discipline of the army, that the members of a court of inquiry 'were a set of advisers, and not judges, or, if judges, judges who were to judge of nothing but whether the matter ought to be submitted to judgment. But to pervert the tribunal is to produce a strange, anomalous, and inconsistent proceeding—a trial which is no trial; for it can neither condemn so as lawfully to inflict punishment on the guilty, nor lawfully acquit so as to protect the innocent.'

I concluded by moving for an address praying her Majesty to order that no officer should be dismissed the army without the option of trial by court-martial. The Judge-Advocate replied that the practice, though sometimes complained of, often afforded the means of getting rid of a member of the service who would not himself desire to be publicly arraigned, and that consequently the alternative would rarely be availed of. On a division, 50 voted with me, and 110 for maintaining the practice.

Beside their legislative duties, members for populous places have long had demands on their time and attention of a very different kind. They are not unfrequently called on to intercede with the Executive on behalf of persons summarily condemned to fine or imprisonment for some act of violence or breach of public order at variance with the tenor of their previous lives. Criminally charged for the first time, and unable at short notice to bring vindicating proof of provocation, the accused found himself debarred by an effete rule of law from being heard on oath in his own defence. The overweighted magistrate, having before all things to preserve the peace, saw no escape from sentencing an industrious and well-conditioned head of a household to incarceration, or the infliction of a penalty not easily paid unless the one-sided testimony of the police were to be injuriously discredited.

Friends and neighbours appealed to the Home Secretary, and asked their member to support their memorial, alleging facts that might have been considered by a Court of Criminal Appeal, had such a tribunal existed; and the difficulty was obviously great to determine how far this prayer ought to be pressed on the Minister.

Several respectable tradesmen came to me one evening in the Central Hall to represent the hardship done to the son of an old and esteemed neighbour in Pentonville for taking the law into his own hands under intolerable provocation. A young watch-case maker in regular work was walking with his wife through a crowded thoroughfare on a summer's evening, and, stopping at a tobacconist's to replenish his pouch, allowed the expectant mother to walk on. Overtaking her in a few minutes, he found her much distressed by the brutal conduct of a tipsy scoundrel, who still addressed her in shameless epithets, and without parley he felled him with a blow.

The real misdemeanant swore next day informations for an assault, and the bystanders, who cheered the promptitude of his punishment and then passed on, were not present as witnesses in a case they probably thought of no more. To his bewilderment, the accused was not allowed to tell his story, and the lips of his wife were closed by the same rule. She was sent away weeping, and he was committed to Coldbath Fields for three months' hard labour.

Upon inquiry, the incidents of the injustice appeared to be clear, and I asked for a reprieve. Mr. Bruce, always humane and just, hesitated, from the number of applications made to him, between which it was impossible confidently to discriminate; but when I vouched for the facts of provocation, and asked what he would have done himself in like circumstances, he replied frankly, 'Knocked the fellow down.' 'Then,' I exclaimed, 'my man is free'; and after the inevitable formal delay the order came for liberation.

Three weeks had passed, and when turned out of the prison gate he seemed dazed, and could not be persuaded that he might return to his home close by. His mates extolled the Secretary of State, to whom I told them the reprieve was due, but at the next election it took some argument to persuade them that it was their duty not to plump for me.

The Speech from the Throne announced that the long-deferred subject of University education in Ireland was about to be dealt with in a form worthy of legislative regard for 'the advancement of learning' and 'the rights of conscience.' The opposition, though well meant, served from the outset as an alarm-bell. Mr. Disraeli, with all due reverence and respect for both, said he had not found it so easy to reconcile their distinct, though not necessarily incompatible, claims; for 'he had never failed in meeting with warm support when he projected any measures for "the advancement of learning," but there had always been received in a more chilly way any reference to the rights of conscience. He should be greatly mortified if the solution, after all, turned out only to be the sacrifice of a famous and learned University in order to substitute for it the mechanical mediocrity of an Examining Board.'

Mr. Gladstone in one of his most elaborate speeches, introducing the Bill, stated, as the fundamental ground for academic reform, that, from the exclusive character of the endowment and administration of Trinity College, out of 1,179 students in arts, less than 150 were Catholics, a disproportion which he did not shrink from characterizing as miserable and scandalous. Modifications had from time to time been made in the rigour of exclusion that had prevailed from the days of Elizabeth to our own time, and the Queen's Colleges had been instituted by Sir Robert Peel, with an Examining University Board connecting them, which it was hoped, from their neutral character as regards theological teaching, might appease distrust and satisfy the wants of the Catholic community. But the manifest disparity of inducement and encouragement which these institutions afforded, and the objection on religious grounds taken from the first by the Catholic hierarchy to the system of education they afforded, left the inequality and injustice as obvious and as flagrant as before.

The Bill proposed to transfer the government of the existing University from the Provost and senior Fellows, then exclusively of the Anglican communion, to a governing body of whom a large proportion should be from time to time chosen by the various provincial Catholic colleges throughout the kingdom. It proposed to hand over the theological faculty, with its endowments, to the governing body of the disestablished Anglican Church, and thereby to leave the character of the University in future intact from all provocatives of polemical difference or contention, and that £15,000 a year should be set apart out of collegiate funds to provide in future for the Chair of Anglican Divinity. For a preliminary period of ten years the new Senate should consist of persons of various denominations named by Parliament. After that period it should be elected by the colleges, Protestant and Catholic, which were to be placed on an equal footing of academic endowment, the great object of the entire change being that the youth of various Churches should be brought up in the companionship of learning and truth. But for this Ministers thought it indispensable that Chairs of Moral Philosophy and Modern History should be omitted from the curriculum. The laughter with which the announcement was greeted was truly said to sound like the knell of the Bill. But the only protest uttered on the occasion was that of Mr. Mitchell Henry, who, though representing one of the large Catholic constituencies, did not scruple to declare that the measure was one for the destruction of University education and the substitution of another system, the like of which was not to be found in any other portion of the globe.

A fortnight was given for the consideration of the scheme, and it was taken almost for granted that the second reading would be carried by the usual Ministerial majority. But in the interval the Irish Bishops, resenting their not having been consulted on what was offered condescendingly as a boon, resolved to advise their representatives to reject it. Even when this had become known, there were confident predictions that the measure would, as was said, 'pull through.'

After two nights' controversy, the amount of Liberal defection became more obvious. Among the Nonconformists, few, if any, shook their heads when pressed to promise by their Whips; but amongst old Whigs and earnest Churchmen it was palpable that growing dissatisfaction widened. On the third night Secretary Cardwell, dubbed the safest mouthpiece ever leader had, was put up to offer new conditions in the nature of possible safeguards against ultramontanism; but these, though shaped with pedantic ambiguity, when vivisected by unsparing criticism served, as was well said, only to exacerbate Catholic distrust without recalling Whigs or Anglicans to the Ministerial blind-fold.

It was vain to make the House believe that if the Bill survived a second reading it might be transformed to any extent in Committee. The measure was too long expected, and too portentous in aspect when it came, to be transformed in its essential features. It must, said Mr. Dodson, have a new title, a fresh preamble, and another set of clauses; and that was a course without example in the history of legislation.

Whatever doubt existed in the minds of Catholic members as to how they should vote was dispelled by the disingenuous offers made by Cardwell, that, if the Bill were allowed to go into Committee, its authors were ready to effect a change of front. One of the most independent and enlightened dissentients told me that, personally, he thought the best solution would have been a fully endowed college on all fours with Trinity, both being within the sphere of Dublin University, as Christ Church and Oriel are at Oxford. This, he confessed, might involve trouble and friction at first as regarded the governing body: but in time it would come right. College life would be denominational, and University degrees have a uniform Christian stamp. But after Mr. Cardwell's speech he felt that he could not support the measure. That speech gave up everything that made the proposal valuable.

Mr. Gladstone felt it necessary first to attenuate, and then to repudiate, the suicidal concessions of his lieutenant; but it would not do. Forty-five of his usual supporters, of whom ten were English or Scotch* members, swelled the majority of 287 against 284 that threw out the Bill.

Some days elapsed before the consequence of the event was definitely made known. Mr. Gladstone's resignation being tendered, Mr. Disraeli was called on by the Queen to say whether he would undertake to form a Government; and this, after some deliberation, he stated in writing he was not prepared to do before a General Election, there being a majority in the existing House of Commons of more than eighty on the general character of public policy. The Adminis-

* They were Henry Fawcett, Edward Bouverie, W. H. Foster, Edward Horsman, Sir R. Peel, R. Aytoun, E. Akroyd, A. Herbert, G. Whalley, and W. M. Torrens, while Sir J. Trelawny, Lord E. Fitzmaurice, Colonel Anson, Peter Taylor, Sir T. Lloyd, Montagu Chambers, and E. H. Burke were absent without pairing.

tration therefore resumed office, though not without foreboding on the part of its chief that the omens of success upon resumption were not encouraging. It became subsequently known--unauthentically, but I believed at the time, and have not since learned any reason to doubt—that Mr. Gladstone ascribed his loss of power some months later to his failure to carry the Irish University Bill.

A great change had come over the spirit of Conservative dreams of rule, and though many honest and earnest members of the party made no secret of voting against the Irish University Bill because it manifestly aimed at raising the standard of priestly instruction in literature, science, and art, there were also many who sincerely opposed it in the belief, as they said, that 'it would have put out the eyes of Protestant education.'

There were passages in the 'Memoir of Lord George Bentinck' that had taken away the breath of pious and patriotic country gentlemen, who were not altogether restored to confidence by the speech on the second reading of him who they feared would one day mislead them into the wilderness of Pantheism; and their misgivings were not laid to sleep by casual cynicisms on his part at the expense of what they termed wanton dropping of decorous reserve.

Monckton Milnes, who in social life floated impartially between sects and parties, and who delighted in nothing so much as indelicate candour on religious subjects, loved to tell how he had once enjoyed the opportunity of tormenting Sir Robert Inglis, whose bigotry, he said, was the best bred and best tempered in the world, by asking him gravely, after a hopeless discomfiture on the subject of Maynooth, whether it never occurred to him to reflect upon the significant fact or, indeed, concatenation of facts that during his Parliamentary life he had always been defeated on the topics he deemed of most importance: and how with imperturbable kindliness and grace, sanctified by an exquisite tinge of reverence, the venerable baronet replied, 'Yes, I thank Heaven that it has been my lot to hang heavy on the wings of Time.' The irrepressible Member for Pomfret only laughed, as, indeed, he was ready to do on all manner of occasions.

Monckton Milnes was wont to tell how, when they were intimate, Dizzie would often say, 'Whatever you may hear of me, remember I am always two things—a Radical and a Jew.' Nor was this mere idle paradox. He had hardly won this envied pre-eminence of recognised adviser of the Protectionist Party in the Commons, when on the motion of Lord Blandford nearly the whole of them signified their intention of voting against the second reading of the Jew Bill. Sooner than succumb to the humiliation of staying away or speaking against his recorded opinions, he left his seat on the front Opposition bench, inducing Lord George Bentinck to do the same, and both took their places on the second bench during the debate, and waited until they were recalled by their friends to their posts of indispensable leadership when the discussion was over.

One who had rare opportunities of observing and appreciating the outflow of his feelings in private life, averred that he never ceased to speak with deference and attachment of Judaism, and with a sort of mystic homage to the part it had played in the history of the world; while he never disparaged the destiny of Islam as a great reconstructive force, or betrayed the slightest disposition to undervalue the moral and social worth of Christianity as a ruling faith. Religious exclusion and disability on any pretence and in any disguise he looked upon as foolish and wrong.

I never shall forget his satisfaction when, in conversation, I cited the words of an almost forgotten follower of Canning, Mr. North, who, when asked on an Irish hustings would he go the whole way of toleration towards the Catholics, exclaimed: 'I cannot bring myself to use deliberately that presumptuous word toleration; it is nothing but the old intolerance with a padlock on its lips.' The day of legislation, however, in this spirit had not come, and the friends of sectarian equity in the privileges, dignities, and rewards of University education regarded the foundering of the project of 1873 as but too likely to preclude for another decade or two a settlement of the question.

At the close of the Session Mr. Lowe quitted the Commons for the Upper House, where, contrary to expectation, he failed to make any impression in debate, and was soon forgotten as a contentious politician, Mr. Gladstone taking upon himself the duties of second place at the Treasury in addition to those of First Lord.

Though Ministerial pluralism had since the fall of Peel gone out of fashion, there were precedents for it not a few in former times. Arrogant Sunderland, when Lord-Lieutenant of Ireland, insisted upon having the Privy Seal; and Walpole would not undertake to rescue public credit from the disaster wrought by the South Sea scheme unless he were conceded both first and second place at the Treasury.

His pupil and successor, Pelham, held both offices, as did Lord North, the younger Pitt, Addington, Perceval, and Canning. As peers, Liverpool, Grey, Melbourne, and Derby were ineligible for the post of Chancellor of the Exchequer, and they did not seek further responsibility by taking additional office. But the Duke of Wellington on becoming Premier thought he might retain the command of the army, and he was only dissuaded from the attempt by the remonstrance of Lord Lyndhurst, who had the courage and discretion to tell his chief in Cabinet that the union of civil and military primacy in the same hand would be looked upon as unconstitutional.

Historically, the difference of practice, acquiesced in without serious or notable objection in days gone by, may be interpreted by the future annalist of matters of fact as indicating that when the head of the Administration happened to be a peer he forbore to take secondary executive office, and that when a commoner was Prime Minister it was thought not unreasonable that his authority should be reinforced by a twofold mark of distinction.

There were, of course, party cavillings when the Member for Greenwich was gazetted, in August, 1873, as Chancellor of the Exchequer without vacating his seat for the Metropolitan borough; but the polemic in the press upon the subject gradually ceased without apparently contributing materially to weaken his influence with his pledged supporters, and the public at large hardly found leisure to listen to the controversy. Trade was good, and remunerative enterprise continued by leaps and bounds to gladden the heart of speculation, and to fill to overflowing beyond precedent the coffers of the State.

Ere Christmas it was certain that a considerable surplus of revenue would enable Government further to hasten the liquidation of debt, or to lighten the burthen of taxation. What could Government desire more?

In answer to the question casually addressed to an able and experienced observer of events, whether such unexampled prosperity might not tempt the Minister to anticipate the period of dissolution, he said: 'I don't profess to understand the mystery of temptation, but I am sure that a man who with fifty majority and many millions of a surplus dissolved Parliament would not long remain Minister.'

George Glyn was still the Premier's chief adviser. As Whip he had borne the brunt of many a hard struggle with indomitable energy, and with a gaiety of temper to which his worthier successor, Mr. W. P. Adam, was a stranger. But after the defeat of his sanguine calculations on the University Bill, he began to share the misgivings of his chief, that the tide of fortune was on the ebb. Soon after Parliament was up, the death of his father called him to the Peers, and, inheriting a large fortune, he was content to take the all but sinecure office of Paymaster-General without salary rather than cease to have a consultative voice in affairs.

In most respects a greater contrast there could hardly be than that presented by the new Secretary of the Treasury, whose personal and political character was summed up in the expression that 'there was no humbug about him.' He was not suspected by anyone of being hitherto in the secrets of Government; and the nominal disposal of patronage transferred to his hands from a predecessor who seemed to delight in playing with it as with the odds, or each fresh deal of cards, was to the unselfish and sincere Member for Clackmannan a source only of anxiety and concern; for he knew that from the one who was preferred gratitude was not to be hoped, while from the ten who were disappointed on each occasion, ill-will, if not spite, might be reckoned on.

George Glyn cared for none of these things. He had quitted Lombard Street for Whitehall to aid in piling up balances of another kind, and as long as he was able to discount political scruples for this firm in which he was a junior partner, he was willing to forego much of a life of pleasure. At the Pay Office he would still be at hand; and, with the accurate measure of every politician in his head, he might be consulted on all occasions confidentially: or, freer now to hear what the world was thinking or saying than he had been of recent years, who could tell but he might find veins of influence theretofore unworked, which his trained astuteness might show the way to develop without troublesome and tiresome discussions in Cabinet?

Unluckily the Prime Minister listened to Lord Wolverton once too often—to the undoubting assurance of his priviest of Privy Councillors, that he might still by a bold stroke of financial policy retrieve his decline in popular favour, and stifle the vexatious question about re-election for Greenwich in consequence of his becoming Chancellor of the Exchequer. The apathy of the country was not to be trusted. It must be startled into consciousness by a *coup de main*, and Adam might be allowed to post some more of his gentle suasions to friends at a distance that they would make it a point to be in town betimes; while captious colleagues in Cabinet had better not be consulted unnecessarily, but allowed to doze at their country seats or to linger a little longer abroad until recalled by the stunning news of a dissolution.

THE PARLIAMENT OF 1874.

Government Nominee beaten—Nawab of Bengal—Hartington and the Leadership—Russian Invasion of Turkey—Indian Troops summoned to Malta—Life of Melbourne—Extradition of Foreigners—Isaac Butt—Parnell—Bright.

THE bye-elections in the recess, though not numerous, rather attenuated the Ministerial muster-roll, and the Leader of Opposition summed up what he termed the signs of the national desire for a change of policy in letters to various independent members of the Conservative organization. But Parliament stood prorogued till February 5, and no one of cool judgment on either side doubted that it would be suffered to outlast its sixth Session. On January 24 I was amused at breakfast by a paragraph read aloud by one of my family, which in the profundity of legislative wisdom I treated as an editorial jest, announcing an imminent dissolution. When convinced at last, by reference to an address to Greenwich, that the decree had really gone forth, my breath was again taken away by learning that the immediate cause was the authoritative confession that the Cabinet had lost its necessary influence in directing public opinion, and that the new departure requisite for its recovery consisted in the offer to abolish the income tax, and the creation of a number of peasant boroughs instead of those which might be spared, as still belonging to the upper classes.

I called together my leading friends in Finsbury, and invited their judgment on the occasion. With a single exception they called on me to stand again, but advised me to refuse in their name any response to the financial project until we knew what new taxes were to be imposed in lieu of the six millions that were to be given up.

Meetings were hastily called in various districts, and the situation sententiously discussed by the comparative few who attended them. The constituency had grown rapidly of late years, and the discord of sections and factions had become so sharp that I was not surprised at mutterings of opposition; but in a few days these took definite form, when a respectable artisan, long known as holding extreme opinions, announced his candidature with the significant preface that he had not half a crown of his own to meet the expenses of a contest, but that he had reason to know they would be forthcoming.

We soon became aware how this riddle was to

be read, and before the contest was over the pay-master-general of elections was so confident that his golden seed would fructify that he told the late Mr. H. W. Wills at the Reform Club that, whatever else might happen, they were certain to get rid of me. The contumacy of a share in the Tea-room mutiny might have been forgiven, and the sin of helping to abolish flogging in the army; but that an LL.B. of Dublin University should refuse to aid in putting out the eyes of Protestant education in Ireland was sedition deserving political extinction. I was adjured by more than one anxious friend to give some penitential pledge of party loyalty in future, and warned that, there being no time for anything like deliberate discussion, or even exceptional canvassing, the best committee would be unable to ascertain how the odds lay in the ballot, now for the first time put to the test.

I had worked too hard and, as they owned, too successfully on unrequited but independent lines for ten years to think it worth while putting on second-hand livery. The historical labours I had laid aside to become a representative of their vast borough often beckoned me back to retirement, and, if it must be so, they would hear no word of complaint from me in having to fall back on *Torrens Vedras*.

If the constituency preferred a sutler of the Treasury to an independent fellow-citizen from

Lincoln's Inn, be it so. But I would neither be bullied nor jostled off. They went away misgiving, and when they were gone I had an impatient summons from Clerkenwell, where a numerous body of watch-case-makers had met to consider what they should do, and had come to the conclusion that not only they should vote for me, but for nobody else, in the quadrangular contest impending. Their governing impulse had nothing to do with politics, but the diversion was refreshing.

The day of polling came, and the result proved more satisfactory than my good friends had hoped. Ten thousand and ninety-nine votes placed me at the head of the poll, and the Treasury nominee was left nowhere. The balance of parties was overthrown, and a majority of fifty summoned the Conservatives to power.

In the evening of the day of declaration there was a meeting at Exeter Hall which I had almost forgotten having promised to attend, and being cheered on appearing upon the platform with a call to speak. I thought it sufficient in few words to say that I took it as a welcome for being one of the first survivors of the wreck, and if I were asked what I most attributed my good-fortune to, I would simply say, 'Ten years' adherence to two simple rules of political arithmetic—asking for nothing for myself, and trying to be useful to every class that deemed my aid serviceable.'

Bernal Osborne, having lost Nottingham, had,

to the surprise of not a few, been returned for Waterford. As a happy illustration of the need for representative revision, he gave a retrospective account of his own Parliamentary experiences, beginning with Wycombe, where Disraeli had been signally rejected, to Middlesex, which he was unable to hold after he took office under Lord Aberdeen. Then his cares as a shepherd of the Nottingham lambs, who showed little gratitude for the tenderness with which he carried the weaker ones in his bosom. 'But,' he added, after a dramatic pause, 'I went further, and I fared worse.'

Though he had voted for years unflinchingly for every useful—and, in a lower tone of ineffable significance, every useless—demand of Celtic democracy, he was hunted, he said, within an inch of his life because he would not pretend to be a Repealer. Well known in the neighbourhood, however, and a favourite with all who loved hilarity, he contrived to win the seat, whereupon the disappointed multitude were suddenly seized with the notion that they might cancel the election by extinguishing their Saxon conqueror.

His committee, he said, thought matters looked so grave that they insisted on his making his escape over the roofs of some adjoining houses—'Evasit erupit,' as the poet says. The timely expedient of flight succeeded; but, unluckily, after wandering over tiles and gutters for some distance, he was tempted by an open dormer window to descend from aery height, and, mistaking the position of the household cistern, unintentionally plunged into the middle of it. The crowd, balked of their prey, broke forth into derogatory songs and shoutings, and next day enjoyed the circulation of a handbill which declared that ever since the member had been in the water there had been no need in the house to boil a kettle for tea.

In the previous Session Mr. Haviland Burke had brought to the notice of the House the unjustifiable course pursued by the Government of India towards the native Prince of Bengal, whose hereditary rank and guaranteed income had been ominously threatened, with the cognizance, if not the sanction, of the department at home. I had voted for the inquiry asked for, and heard with amazement the Under-Secretary state, without repudiation by his superiors in office, that the existing Nawab Nazim had no pretension to be regarded as a native Prince, with whose ancestors the East India Company had made treaties of territory and finance, and that the latest of such alleged conventions, if it ever existed, did not deserve the name of a treaty at all.

The policy of annexation recklessly carried into effect by Lord Dalhousie, though subsequently renounced by Lord Canning while its sanguinary fruits in the Sepoy Mutiny still strewed the ground, and absolutely repudiated by the advice of Lord Derby in the memorable proclamation of the Queen, that she would regard her Asiatic subjects as entitled to the same care and consideration as those of English birth, still haunted the minds of all those who, in the words of Bright, felt it a duty to see justice done to India.

For some time Syud Ali had resided in England, whither he had come to make his appeal for protection and security against the encroachments and exactions of the Executive at Calcutta; but he had been unhappy in the choice of his advisers and agents, who were treated with disdain at the India Office, and were wholly unable to obtain for him the payment of heavy arrears long due, or any assurance that his current revenue would be made good.

The late Major Evans Bell, who had, by dint of courageous importunity, wrung from the department satisfaction of somewhat similar demands for the Rajah of Sattara and other victims of proconsular pressure, earnestly besought me to bring the case forward in Parliament, and promised his assistance if I would undertake to publish in a popular form a summary of our acquisitions in Southern Asia, and of the obligations we had nationally incurred by taking over those of the East India Company.

During the recess I wrote and published a volume entitled 'Empire in Asia: How we came by it. A Book of Confessions,' which unavoidably affronted the vanity of red-tape and provoked the lisping censure of Quietism of every well-bred degree, but which startled into earnest sympathy men like Bishop Fraser, who felt that we owed a great debt of reparation, and Henry Fawcett, and drew from the wary Leader of Opposition the condensed criticism, 'You have struck a true note.'* When put fully in possession of the correspondence and of the documents that constituted the Nawab's title-deeds, I resolved to try what could be done towards rescuing him and his family from impoverishment and humiliation, and after several unavoidable postponements, I moved on June 26 for a Select Committee to inquire into the circumstances of the case which I had to lay before the House.

More than a century had elapsed since the great joint stock company whose assets and liabilities we had taken over accepted fiefs and became taxgatherers under the Princes of Bengal, the progenitors and predecessors in the male line direct of the petitioner at the Bar, all of whom had undeviatingly remained true to British interests, and never in any turn of fate or conquest swerved from the friendship pledged in the most specific and even solemn terms.

Before 1770 five of these memorable conventions had been interchanged. Moorshedabad

* Letter from Mr. Disraeli.

remained the capital of the decadent but still dignified Power, and while under Hastings and Wellesley conquest spread its sway all round, and unavailing resistance disappeared, no change took place in the original relations between the European Power becoming paramount, and the descendants of a long line of Moslem Viceroys who never seemed to have harboured a doubt that they and their progenitors had been dealing with a noble and truthful Christian State.

The Company preferred the way of diplomatic acquisition. They trafficked with successive Nawabs, and step by step won peaceably their way, never firing a shot in anger, but bargaining for each jaghire and pergunnah, each privilege and function; and it would be ineffably base, contemptible, and infatuated to higgle or to huckster about the price which they agreed to pay. By the latest of these treaties the contents of all that had gone before were ratified, and the yearly sum to be paid was fixed at sixteen lacs of rupees. Yet we were, by some strange hallucination, led officially to disbelieve in the existence of the instrument itself, and for the marvellous reason that there was no Prince with whom it could have been made.

To the seeming amazement of the Under-Secretary, and amid bitter cheers of reproach, I produced the treaty, with its twofold signatures and seals, which I invited anyone who might be curious to read, mark, and inwardly digest for himself. Could it be said that though the instrument were genuine we were not bound to a descendant of the party with whom it was made? What would become of half the subsisting engagements we had with foreign Powers if such a doctrine of evasion were avowed? And was it to be pretended that we might take advantage of our own strength in cases where the disparity was great, not daring to whisper a menace of a similar kind where we shrank from provoking a quarrel?

Appended to the treaty were the words: 'This agreement, by the blessing of God, shall be inviolably observed for ever.' Would anyone have the face to aver that this grave engagement by a Christian Power was but profane levity, or that, either in badinage or blasphemy, the Company consecrated what they deemed a good bargain worth keeping for a hundred years, while the Government of her Majesty, her royal pledge as a Sovereign *non obstante*, were free to cast it to the winds?

One of the best and worthiest men who ever sat in Parliament, Lord William Bentinck, when Governor-General, refused to allow civil suits to be brought against the Nazim, because 'his Highness had been recognised by the British Government as an independent Prince, and the national faith was pledged for nothing being carried into execution derogating from his honour.'

Did the Nawab doubt that faith would be kept with him when Lord Canning wrote to him that he might rely that the 'just regard to the honours and dignities due to his hereditary rank, guaranteed by the stipulation of existing treaties and long-established relations observed by former Governors-General, would on his part be fervently fostered and punctually fulfilled'?

The Under-Secretary deprecated the reference to a Committee, and, as representing the department, denied the binding obligations of the treaties. He was answered by Mr. Serjeant Sherlock ably and conclusively, and feebly supported in the theory of repudiation by Mr. Beckett Denison, the departmental theory being denounced as untenable from every point of view by Sir John Grey.

The debate was adjourned, and before it could be resumed, there were symptoms of a change of policy on the part of Government, who were no longer unwilling to entertain definite propositions for a settlement of Syud Ali's claims.

A long conference ensued, and it was finally settled that the arrears should be liquidated, and provision made for the various members of the family, it being stipulated that at the next accession to the dignity the title should be changed from that of Nawab of Bengal to that of Moorshedabad.

Mr. Gladstone's desire to be relieved from the

responsibilities of Leadership being again made known in a letter to Lord Granville, the Liberal Party had to consider whom they would choose as his successor. The claims of Mr. Forster were urged by not a few men of judgment and experience, on the ground of his assiduous devotion to public business, and his recent success in carrying the Elementary Schools Act to completion.

But many of us, for reasons unnecessary to state, preferred being led by one in whom we could all equally confide, with his characteristic way of saying neither more nor less than he really meant, and abiding by his word. Doubts were cast upon his consenting to undertake the arduous duties of the position, while injudicious flatterers of the Member for Bradford would have it believed that his own pretensions were insidiously depreciated to secure the nomination of another.

In accordance with the wish of several independent members, I wrote * offering our support, and asking Lord Hartington if he would undertake to act if chosen. He replied, with thanks, that he had personally no desire for the position, expressing his regret at the difficulties in the way of Forster's nomination, and his readiness to remove one of them by refusing to be named when the party met, if that would ensure general

* January 21, 1875.

contentment.* It ended as we had hoped; no division of opinion was publicly made known, and Lord Hartington became our leader.

Mr. Gladstone seldom appeared at Westminster during the Session. Happening to meet the Premier one morning sauntering leisurely on the Park side of Piccadilly, he entered freely into the few salient topics of the day, and in answer to my question whether he thought his great rival had finally bid us farewell at St. Stephen's, he said quietly, 'There will be a return from Elba.'

He took my arm, and we walked on for some time. At the corner of St. James's Street, a right rev. prelate, in passing, took off his hat and bowed very low. Disraeli looked hard at me, as if curious to know what I thought of the egregious obeisance, and then said: 'I made him a bishop, but I forget his name.'

What those who hated Disraeli never tired of calling his inveterate cynicism, and what his admirers used to cite as his mere love of sarcastic fun, cost probably not a few adherents. But its indulgence was uncontrollable, and when an avowed adversary did not furnish cause, one of his own rank and file occasionally became the unconscious object. I say the unconscious, for it is simply incredible that in wantonness one so meditative and even calculating of influences con-

* January 24, 1875.

tributory to the maintenance of his own, would have cracked a joke over the head of an unoffending henchman.

One instance may suffice to explain what I mean. There voted steadily in the party, without faltering or flaw in debate, a worthy fellow, whose peculiarity of look and gesture would have made him easily caricatured, though I do not remember his having ever been so. A question being asked which no one else could be trusted to answer offhand, Disraeli, putting up his eyeglass, looked along the bench, and whispered to the colleague next him, 'Where is our hippopotamus?'

Notwithstanding his desire to increase the number of his supporters, he would sometimes risk the enrolment of a recruit for sake of an epithet or an epigram. Among waverers between opposite parties, there was a young man of family well connected with both, who was rather possessed with an idea of his own personal attractions, more readily acknowledged at Almack's or at Ascot than in the dull atmosphere of St. Stephen's.

The days of the dandies were not quite over when he resolved to have a 'regular try' for a lengthened notice in debate; and on a sultry evening after Whitsuntide he appeared in what Disraeli called the unusual splendour of a striking costume, with impressive-looking moustache, and equally impressive papers and blue-books in hand to discuss a subject nobody else was thinking of—to Mr. Speaker's dismay. In the first five minutes he had thinned the back benches on both sides of all who longed for the Park, and in the next five of not a few more sober-minded listeners whom his inarticulate utterances failed to engage.

Disraeli himself then, hat in hand, sauntered to the door, where his anxious Whip muttered in his ear as he passed: 'Too bad; here's a fine fellow likely to come over to us, and you—the leader of the party—turn your back and walk out without waiting to hear even what he has to say.'

The inculpated chief put on a certain look of penitence, and then said quietly: 'Yes, I own it is very wrong; but there are some things human nature cannot stand, and one of them is to sit here, on an evening like this, to hear a Saracen's Head creaking in the wind.'

But perhaps the best remembered of his audacities was that in which, after his opponents had brought forward their most important measures and thought it sufficient to rely upon those of a less prominent or contentious nature, he described their condition as one that reminded him of the high-peaked Andes seen from a vessel not too far out at sea, and whose aspiring summits, clad in snow, slept in the sunshine as being a range of exhausted volcanoes. Journalism made merry at the extravagant badinage, which was not yet forgotten when parties met again at Westminster, when the subordinates of the Ministry were heard to complain in the lobby of the ill-bred license that sought to hold up their chiefs to ridicule on the platform with metaphors and phrases that would not be ventured on in the House.

In a mingled group who were recounting the jokes of the recess regardless of one another's expense, Lord Elcho sardonically asked a Junior Lord of the Treasury why nobody had answered geologically the picturesque survey of the Andes taken from the sea. 'Because,' he said sullenly, 'no one could tell what was really meant; probably not even the jester himself.' 'Why can't you explain it to him?' said the noble questioner to an Irish wag who stood by. 'I can tell you: Dizzy meant to call you "used-up *craturs*"'—an alternative version which the author laughed at heartily when told it.

Ireland has not very often chosen statisticians as her representatives; but beside Spring Rice and Sherman Crawford there have occasionally been useful contributories from the other side of the Channel to the common stock of knowledge in the shape of arithmetic, who have sacrificed their chance of popularity in debate for the sake of giving Parliament lessons in the policy of Irish taxation and rating, arterial drainage, and outdoor relief.

One of the worthiest, if not the wisest, of these national monitors was given to boring the two front benches with supplies of useless knowledge, when, the audience being thinned down to the verge of a count-out, the few who felt bound to remain to finish Committee of Supply affected to listen in civil silence, without prolonging the dreary interlude by comment or reply.

The Leader of Opposition, weary of endurance, asked an Ulster member behind him, in a tone of well-feigned resignation: 'What is this fellow at home?' On being told that he was a rich and respectable trader, who never went to the Castle or to an aggregate meeting, but employed many people and gave to the sick poor—all which would not keep his seat for him next time—Disraeli said: 'I have generally found the Irish members either witty and well-bred gentlemen *or* scamps of the other sort—and this fellow's neither.'

Since the news of the Indian Mutiny, the public mind had not been stirred so deeply by resentful anger as it was by the correspondence from Bulgaria in August, 1876, recounting the cruelties and crimes of the Bashi-Bazouks employed by the Porte to repress the disaffection caused by oppressive taxation. Mr. Gladstone undertook during the following month to organize and stimulate popular feeling against the Turkish Government, and all whom he charged with abetting or palliating their misrule; and the Premier, believing that the inevitable tendency of irresponsible agitation was not merely to evoke sympathy for the victims of a lawless soldiery at comparatively obscure places on the Danube, but to compel the abandonment of Turkey to her fate, and to pave the way for the hitherto delayed advance of Russia to the Bosphorus, was tempted to indulge in expressions of ridicule at what he treated as newspaper exaggeration unworthy of literal belief.

During the autumn the country was moved from end to end with the recital of Turkish atrocities, and eloquent invocation of the public wrath befitting a Christian State unhappily entangled in alliance with an incorrigibly barbarous Power, inveterate in its enmity to the Cross.

Few of his former colleagues took an active part in the agitation, sustained by Mr. Gladstone with extraordinary energy and eloquence; but in every large constituency the contagion of the novel excitement spread, and Members of Parliament were everywhere called upon to endorse without reserve the tragic denunciation put forth in every variety of form from day to day. Many, of whom I was one, abstained from taking part as political witnesses to facts frequently disputed, and as often treated as exaggeration.

I had myself a painful recollection of delusions, practised, no doubt with the best intentions, on the public mind, regarding the excesses said to have been committed during the Sepoy Revolt, and the reckless encouragement thereby given to undiscriminating vengeance. For a considerable time, however, no expostulation would be listened to, and, in point of fact, no limitation of Hindoo or Mahomedan outrage would be believed.

I had also a painfully vivid recollection of the sanguinary details of merciless repression of rebellion in Ireland, which I had heard from the lips of living witnesses in my youth, but which no author of eminence or repute ventured to record fifty years after the events took place.

Mr. Forster, who had left England in August for a visit to the troubled regions of the Danube, and personally gathered from politicians of all creeds and races at Stamboul their varying versions of late events, told his constituents on his return in October that he was against any armed interference to extort permanent emancipation for Bulgaria, and he was satisfied the best practical course to adopt would be a joint representation of European Powers, which would compel the Porte to grant local autonomy to its oppressed provinces.

The same line of policy was advocated in a despatch by Lord Derby as at once indicating the renunciation of a responsible and exclusive rule by the Porte of its Christian dependencies in Europe, which the local independence obtained by Greece, Hungary, and Servia foreshadowed as inevitable, but which England wished to see effected without needless Moslem extirpation. It did not require the coincidence of view thus expressed by the Conservative Minister to render that of the Member for Bradford unpopular with his former Radical friends. He was held up to suspicion as a trimmer, who was always lurching for a compromise, and thenceforth the cry was incessantly reiterated that the Turks must be driven bag and baggage out of Europe.

This palpably beckoned Muscovite ambition to the Bosphorus. In every inflexion of diplomatic protest, Count Schuvaloff deprecated the imputation that the Czar wanted or even wished to have Constantinople; but as head of the Eastern Church it was his duty, at any risk and cost, to avenge the sufferings of the Christians, and to take material guarantees against their recurrence.

The New Year opened in prevailing anxieties and apprehensions regarding the existence of the Ottoman Empire. Misrule and extravagance had disappointed the hopes of timely retrenchment and reform which inspired the Black Sea Treaty. Administrative cruelties in the subject provinces, unatoned for and unguaranteed against in future, had combined Christian Europe in protest and warning, and a conference of the six Powers sat for many weeks at Constantinople to induce the Porte to adopt changes of system and locally protective institutions while there was yet time to avert impending war.

Midhat Pasha, who had lately been in England, was the only Moslem to raise his voice in counselling such concessions.

Almost in despair, the European delegates attenuated their requisitions to two essential points — demanded, as they unanimously said, by humanity and civilization. But the dignitaries and ulemas of the Empire, with two exceptions only, voted that Turkey wanted only to be left free to maintain her independence, and that her chiefs and people were ready to defy the insidious interference and the open threats of Russia.

Before the end of January it was known in England that Abdul Hamid had accepted their fatal advice, and by the end of April Prince Ignatieff quitted the Embassy at the Porte, and the following day war was declared.

Lord Salisbury declared, on behalf of the Government, that this decision fell nothing short of infatuation, and accounted for it only by the belief, sedulously spread, that Russia was too weak and divided to embark in a struggle wherein the Great Powers were likely to range themselves on opposite sides. But this delusion was soon dispelled. Armenia and Roumania were both invaded by hosts long collecting on the frontier, and Prince Gortschakoff, in a circular note, announced that the Czar would henceforth take means to enforce the demands on behalf of the oppressed subjects of the Sultan, which had been refused consideration at the instance of the Great Powers.

Lord Derby, as Foreign Secretary, addressed forthwith the regret of the British Government at this renunciation of a common accord. France, Germany and Italy showed no disposition to take any further method of intervention, and opinion in England gravitated obviously towards the policy of waiting events.

Admiral Slade, who had commanded the Turkish fleet for many years, and was now living in retirement, keeping up his close correspondence with the scenes of his earlier service, clung to the belief that the Turks would make a better fight for national life than our press and politicians supposed, and partial successes that from time to time proved the courage and endurance of the Ottoman garrisons seemed to justify the supposition. My friend would not believe that any great body of invaders could make their way across the Danube without a sanguinary conflict; but when the news came early in July, 1877, that 60,000 men had passed the great barrier stream, his faith gave way, and I seldom recollect his hazarding afterwards a favourable forecast of the campaign.

Plevna was taken by surprise, retaken by Osman Pasha, and then for many weeks held by him against encompassing hosts, until at last the remnant of his gallant soldiery, attempting to cut their way out of the lines, were overpowered, and many thousands taken prisoners.

The governing motive which withheld most of the Cabinets from interposing in the quarrel was the common apprehension of territorial disturbance that might ensue from any rupture of the general peace. Each and all of the Great Powers sedulously disclaimed ambition, but they all distrusted one another, and hardly took the trouble to conceal their *paulopost* future misgivings. Austria and Holland were especially sensitive, and their Ministers were disposed to be communicative on the subject; while the great statesman of Germany, as was his wont, took occasion to be tentative, if not tantalizing, on the subject.

Count Beust in conversation told me that not long ago M. Bylandts, the Dutch Minister here, told him that Prince Bismarck had somewhat abruptly asked him, 'Why do people persist in fancying that Germany wants Holland? Our system is founded on unity of language and ideas. What could we do with an old nation speaking another tongue, and wholly given to other pursuits, with its independent traditions and habits of self-rule? If the northern provinces of Austria were obtainable, that would be quite another affair.'

Not very long after Beust met him at Ems, and he observed casually, 'Why do your people often suspect us of coveting territory from you? What would we do with a Sclave element? It would never assimilate with our life. Denmark and Holland would be quite another thing. In race, religion, and much else they would commingle and combine much more readily than Posen and Galicia.' And so he talks whatever is necessary or suggestive.

With regard to Russia and the Porte, I said to M. Beust all thinking men amongst us felt that the great interests of England and Austria were one, and if the progress of the war threatened any permanent extension of Muscovite power on the Danube, there would be a decided manifestation of hostility in the influential portion of our community.

He said a thorough understanding between the two Governments regarding possible eventualities was not a matter of treaty, but was a thing to be done, and he was glad to hear one speak so confidently of the ultimate tendency of opinion in England regarding the present struggle.

Vehement appeals were made in the press and at public meetings to Government for the relief of Kars, and its gallant commander became the hero of popular assemblies at the time. But as the autumn wore on, and point after point of advantage was gained by the invaders, the Porte, in its distress, appealed to Europe against the impending effacement of one of the Powers acknowledged in every treaty down to that of Paris as essential to general stability and peace.

No interchange of confidential notes between the Western and Central Cabinets thawed appreciably the frost of fear whereby they continued bound, lest the participation of strife on their part should prove the irrestrainable letting out of waters.

In the last days of the year M. Missouris presented an urgent Note, by the desire of his master, invoking the interposition of England. Ministers were divided in opinion, some recurring to the belief of Mr. Gladstone, that the Czar had no design of permanently occupying the Euxine provinces or the capital of Turkey. But his army, being prepared to cross the Balkans, and all reasonable dreams of the capability of the *Redif* to resist the disciplined legions of the victor being at an end, the First Lord of the Treasury proposed that a British *corps d'armée* should be sent to the Dardanelles to protect Constantinople. After long and anxious debate, the Cabinet divided, and the proposition was over-ruled; and one who knew him well was known to have said that Lord Beaconsfield never seemed the same afterwards.

In a few weeks the Muscovite army passed the Balkans without losing a man, Sofia was occupied and Adrianople abandoned. An armistice having been concluded, the British fleet was thereupon ordered to the Bosphorus to protect British interests, on which Prince Gortschakoff issued a circular, declaring that his Government were compelled to advance a portion of their troops to Constantinople. The fleet then, being refused permission to ascend the Straits, retired to Besika Bay. The Grand-Duke Michael having taken up his quarters at San Stefano, a treaty was signed which suspended hostilities. The Russian army, however, still lingered within sight of Constantinople.

Count Schuvaloff to the last tried to affect airs of forbearance, almost of indifference, on the part of his Court, to Byzantine acquisition. His predecessor in the Embassy ventured once, making the same disclaimer, to remind an English Minister that in climate, creed, language, and occupation, Stamboul was the very antithesis of St. Petersburg, and the least fitted to be a Muscovite capital. 'Just so,' said Lord Palmerston; 'but that is no reason why Russia should have both.'

If the same was not said now, it was resolved; and Sir Stafford Northcote, without disguise, told the House of Commons that Government could not be responsible for the peace of Europe or the maintenance of our commercial position in the Levant unless furnished with the means of peremptorily arresting the tide of Cossack aggression. If Parliament had confidence in the sincerity and ability of Ministers, it would place in their hands forthwith a credit of six millions.

The demand evoked mingled expressions of feeling in contending parties. There were those on the Ministerial side who shrank instinctively at what they deemed the opening of the flood-gates of wasting and depressing war, while a majority of their colleagues broke forth in triumphant cheers at the recognition at last of their oft-repeated prognostics. On the opposite side like division of opinion was unconcealable. Many, if not a majority, declared against a step which all regarded as irretrievable. The Turks were never so unpopular out of doors for their sins of imbecility and oppression, and more than one eminent statesman leant to Mr. Bright's doctrine—that, whatever the faults of the Russian Government might be, we had no business to interpose. Peace at any price was not generally avowed; but the only policy to which it could lead was practically supported, in and out of Parliament, as it had been in 1854, and the losses and sufferings of the conflict in the Crimea, and the failure of the Porte to redeem its promises of amendment in its ways of rule, were relied on as justifying a refusal of what was asked.

But the weakness and irresolution of Lord Aberdeen's Cabinet, and the miserable consequences to which it led, had taught some of us another lesson. Palmerston was dead and Russell no longer amongst us; but the spirit that in questions of national exigency animated them still lived; and, in the painful conviction that the crisis had come, most of the Whigs and many of the Radicals were impelled to state openly that, if they were forced to choose, the traditional honour of the country was paramount to the claims of Party.

A right honourable friend who sat next me urged me to add a few words to what had been better said by others in this sense. They were necessarily few: 'I am speaking for a laborious and heavily-rated community. I own having listened with regret to the demand of Ministers; but believing as I do that the liberty of Europe is at stake, and in that liberty is involved the safety and prosperity of the realm, whatever the responsible advisers of the Crown publicly declare to be indispensable shall have my vote, be it six or sixteen millions.'

I need not say what contrary expressions such sentiments called forth. Sneers, frowns, and threats were abundant; but I cannot say that I had any cause to regret the part thus taken, though I have little doubt it was made contributory in after-years to the work of the supplanter.

Not long before James Clay, who had never relinquished the privilege of early companionship of saying what he thought without regard to diplomatic etiquette or party convenience, for neither of which he cared a jot, asked Disraeli 'why, if Russia's designs of territorial extension looked as formidable through the diplomatic telescope as they did to the naked eye—why something was not done in speech or writing to waken and warn the public mind to the impending danger.'

'Because,' said Disraeli, 'the subject is too serious for gasconade or profane swearing; and because letting off steam every now and then is rather a sign of not being ready to put to sea. Chatham thought our only rival worth watching was France, and long after Waterloo the Duke of Wellington thought so too; but times are changed, and for the rest of this century our only competitors for power are Russia and America. Both are ripening for the day of outburst, against which it would be useless and pitiful in us to rail. What we have to do is to prepare steadily to resist the shock of battle when it comes—a matter of grave anxiety and difficulty, but which cannot be lessened or mended by any amount of platform or Parliamentary rhetoric, or any display of red lights or blue rockets in the press. If the youth of the country are not brought up to recognise the price of envy we must always be liable to be called on to pay for national greatness, we shall never be secure.

'When we might have resisted the intrusion of

the Cossack into Central Europe, short-sighted selfishness shrugged its shoulders and allowed Poland to be partitioned and Sweden to be mutilated; and England, with the conquest of Canada, the capture of Gibraltar, and the rape of India, among national vaunts, has no pretence for railing at Cossack or Yankee lust of territorial power. We only make fools of ourselves by babbling about territorial covetousness and dishonesty, and the sooner the drivelling hypocrisy is given over the better. But that is no reason why we should not prepare to hold our own, and to redeem the time, seeing that the days are evil.'

An impression long existed in the minds of those who took the liberty of thinking as well as voting on questions touching national as contradistinguished from party interests, that the colonial policies of the two great Parliamentary rivals differed essentially in aim and tendency.

The addition to the Queen's title as Empress of India, and the summoning of Oriental troops to defend Constantinople against Russian attack, were confessedly meant by Disraeli as demonstrations that we must henceforth be regarded as an Asiatic as well as a European Power, and the acceptance of Canadian and Australian contingents to do garrison duty in England on the threatened outbreak of war wrought conviction in the public mind that the old country was glad of the opportunity of showing reliance on the fidelity of the communities sprung from her womb.

Cynical critics scoffed at what they called theatrical and fantastic policy, but it appealed to the pride and pluck of the nation, and painted in perspective future quietness and inviolability.

A few days after the announcement that the Ghoorka regiments were on their way to Suez, I happened unexpectedly to encounter Disraeli in Grosvenor Square. He asked me what was said of the news, and what I thought of it. I said I agreed with an eminent Whig friend, that the summons of a corps from India was like the act of a man who wished to show a wanton assailant that he had a left as well as a right arm. 'That's it exactly,' he rejoined, 'and that's what I mean to say. My hope and object is not only to keep the Empire together in drowsy times of peace, but to quicken a common feeling of duty and ambition in time of war.'

On the other hand, indications were from time to time interpreted to mean on behalf of his illustrious opponent that he considered enough had been done by the parent State for the colonies, and that, as they arrived at maturity, if they sought independence, we could do very well without them.

When this feeling was attributed by Sir Robert

Torrens, who sat for Cambridge, and by Mr. Jenkins, who represented Dundee, to the occupants of the front Opposition bench, it was not openly repudiated; and Sir George Grey, the distinguished ex-Governor of New Zealand and the Cape, openly averred that there were two antagonistic policies among them, of which the friends of unity of Empire ought to beware.

A striking verification of his view is disclosed in the biography of Mr. W. E. Forster. In a private letter of November 12, 1878, he said: 'You know I have always thought Gladstone and Lowe two docile scholars of the old Manchester school. I always contended against their disparagement of the colonies and of India as wrong in itself, and sure to become unpopular. Now, Disraeli is, as regards India, going much too far in the other direction.' But he adds: 'I expect to have to contend against a strong desire to cut the cable and get rid of the dependency.'*

The event amply justified the policy pursued. Within sight of the coveted City of the Blind, the Russian armies fell back, and a truce was agreed to which ended in their once more recrossing the Danube, local autonomy being secured to the long ill-used Christian provinces.

Non-intervention in the domestic affairs of

* To the Duchess of Manchester.

other States was one of the traditions in which I had been brought up, and one of the maxims which, throughout political life, I had without faltering or wavering striven to cling to. Remonstrance against barbarizing rigour and expostulation against desolating exaction were not only compatible, obviously, with international abstinence, but oftentimes appeared to be the duty of the British Cabinet.

And the stipulations of the Black Sea Treaty, under which the Porte covenanted to reform its provincial institutions, warranted the Conservative Cabinet in proposing a conference at Constantinople of all the signatories to that memorable compact, and pressing for certain definite ameliorations and improvements which they unanimously concurred in representing as calculated to underpin the tottering edifice of Ottoman rule; but until the refusal of any reform so suggested had gone beyond discussion, and the Russian Government betrayed their speciously repudiated purpose of territorial annexation by withdrawing formally from the European concert of advice, England would not have been justified in lending or offering to lend armed support to the Sultan.

I took no part, accordingly, in the animated controversy which for months prevailed throughout the country, and in which, undoubtedly, the rising tide of popular opinion was against the

Crescent, and in sympathy with the self-appointed protectors of the Cross.

Ignorant and reckless partisans called on one continually to take part on the side of humanity, and against its incorrigible oppressors; but, knowing what had happened not long before in Poland, Hungary, and the Caucasus, I could not be persuaded that humanity was likely to be the gainer by the Imperial substitution of Government by the Knout for that of the Bastinado; and until the mask was dropped, and the deformed championship of mercy was palpably transformed into exultant progress to the realization of the Czarina Catherine's dream of sovereignty from the Northern to the Southern Archipelago, no justification appeared to men like myself for halloaing on invasion or contributing to overturn the international balance of Europe.

The rubicon passed, our condition and our duty were metamorphosed. We could not hope to unconvert the frenzy of the day out-of-doors, or to silence its threats of deposition and displacement; but in Parliament and in the press we were bound in patience to possess our souls, and to bide the time until this tyranny of demagoguism should be overpassed.

It became known ere the Session of 1876 closed that the Prime Minister would appear in his old place no more, and surmise was busy as to the difference it would make in the tone, as well as the aspect, of the future legislative scene. Could he, with a lengthened rein, control or guide the majority in the Commons that had thus far drawn so well together? In case of unexpected difficulty, how was the arbiter to be consulted to whom varying opinions had hitherto deferred? What could be his motive for going to the Lords, and what title would he take? Every surmise proved erroneous; and when an old friend was asked the question in the lobby by a private correspondent of a great provincial journal, he told him gravely, in strict confidence, that the title would obviously record the fateful fact, being no other than Lord Dis-a-peer. Stafford Northcote took his place as Leader, and, despite his singular unlikeness, was generally accepted as always well-informed, always good-tempered, and always dependable.

I had frequently been asked by old friends who remembered Lord Melbourne, and some of whom, like myself, had served under him, to preserve as far as in my memory lay the characteristics of his share in the politics of his time not to be found in Hansard. No one was more careful of his memory, or more full of illustrative traits regarding him, than my old chief, Lord Taunton, and from him and from Speaker Denison I derived many of the anecdotes that eventually appeared in his 'Memoirs.' But I had, beside, the advantage of intimacy with one who, though a long way his junior, had peculiar opportunities of knowing incidents in the latter portion of his career which few others possessed.

Richard B. Sheridan not only expressed satisfaction on being told that I contemplated writing Melbourne's life, but introduced me to his sister with reference to the subject. Mrs. Norton was then a great invalid, and only at intervals able to recur to the period about which I wished to inquire.

One of the incidents I had frequently heard mentioned, but with provoking indistinctness, was that of her invitation to Mr. Disraeli, while still chiefly known as a successful novelist and prominent leader of the dandies, to meet the Whig Premier at her table. She told me the story with so much graphic point, not untinged with a certain satiric humour, that I felt I ought not to meddle with the affair in print without acquainting him of my purpose, and hearing whatever he had to say about it.

He was then living in Whitehall Gardens, where, by appointment, I called on him and spent most of an autumn afternoon. His father had been, he said, an early intimate of Thomas Sheridan, whom he tried in vain to inspire with public ambition, and occasionally had to warn off dangerous ground into which some caprice of the hour would have betrayed him into wandering. 'I do not remember having, in the days of "Vivian Grey," ever seen Mrs. Norton, except at a ball or the opera, but I knew her brother Charles, who was the handsomest creature that God ever made, and through him I became one of her acquaintances, and, I believe I may say, her friends. You remember the small house in Birdcage Walk, where that wretched husband of hers chose to live, and where the menage was on such a limited footing that I remember to have seen a difficulty about knives and forks, though the number of guests was necessarily small. Lord Melbourne, from the Home Office, kept us waiting half an hour, nothing uncommon with him, for in everything unimportant he was the most easy-going, dilatory, beg-your-pardon sort of man; and before we sat down my good hostess presented me with great *empressement* to him. The table was not long, but he was, of course, at the top of it, and I was at the bottom; and when our frugal feast was ended, he said to me, *à propos* of nothing: "Well, youngster, what are you up to?" I hesitated for a moment to reply, and he added: "What do you want to be?" This, of course, stirred me up, and I replied: "I want to be Prime Minister."' 'Then,' I said, interrupting my informant, 'you really did condescend to prophesy, as we are told? What did the Minister say?' 'He looked grave, and said, quite in a business tone: "Ah, that will never do. You had much better lay your account for some reasonable position when your friends come in, if they ever do, and qualify accordingly; but as for the lead, if you were in Parliament you would see that the succession is already fixed inevitably for the rest of our time in the Peels and Derbies." We had some quiet and agreeable conversation afterwards, and I met him once or twice in the same delightful company; but I don't think he thought much of me, and I was not thrown into collision with him, except at Taunton, where Lyndhurst advised me to stand against your old chief, Labouchere.'

I asked if he remembered his wrangle with a butcher at the hustings, who, looking up at him, after a florid passage on the Constitution, exclaimed: 'Well, there's one thing you can't deny: you're an author—you know you're an author.' 'Yes,' he rejoined; 'it is quite true. And I told the fellow it was, adding that if my opponent could tell me the name of any book he had written that had been translated into five foreign languages I would retire on the spot.'

Ten years later, when the defeated candidate had become the unrivalled satirist of opposition, and began to be looked upon as the successor of Sir Robert Peel in Tory lead, Melbourne, who had never forgotten the dialogue at Birdcage Walk, was overheard muttering to himself: 'By Jove! I believe he'll do it, after all.'

When the work appeared I received a letter of many pages criticising in characteristic fashion the memories it was designed to preserve: 'I had no idea you would have been able to accumulate so much new and authentic biographic material. All your remarks on the conduct and motives of public men indicate that they proceed from one practised in public life. It is a rare advantage for the political historian, and in which the usual treaters of such subjects are generally, and painfully, deficient.'*

Other critics who knew and remembered Melbourne were equally friendly in their appreciation. Even Mr. Hayward, who seldom missed an opportunity in private or in print of disparagement (not from any personal quarrel, for we had none, but in keeping with his prejudices as a partisan), tried to be impartial and just in the *Quarterly*; but the effort was too great to be consistently maintained.

His infallibility as a *raconteur* might be questioned if he tacitly acquiesced in the version I had given of the scene at Storey's Gate, and of the earlier family intimacies that had led the fair hostess to make the acquaintance of 'Vivian Grey.' I must have drawn, he cynically observed, upon my imagination in supposing that Isaac Disraeli and Tom Sheridan were friends, which, besides being improbable, he happened to know was out of the question; and he proceeded to tell the story authoritatively in another way.

* December 31, 1879.

Had this been the only error he affected to note, I should not, perhaps, have taken the trouble to correct or disprove it; but in his jealousy of the assumed rights of oracle he sarcastically contradicted another and wholly different incident of Parliamentary life, about which I felt that the mistake was his, not mine.

He rashly assumed, in the latter instance, that Melbourne put aside with a jest Evelyn Denison's complaint at the Home Office of some clauses in the new Poor Law Bill, and that his levity was indulged in with reference to the paupers. It was easy to show, by reference to dates, that the new Poor Law Bill was not carried or introduced until after George Lamb had ceased to live, and that Melbourne's jest could not, therefore, have referred to it, but to clauses in the Education Bill.

I called the attention of Mrs. Norton's brother to the subject, and in reply to my inquiry as to his recollection of earlier days, he wrote: 'Hayward is not right in his remark respecting the elder Disraeli. I am proud to say he *was* a friend of my father's, as the enclosed letter will show.'*

The enclosure was an autograph letter of some length from Isaac Disraeli to Thomas Sheridan, advising him for various reasons confidentially to lay aside a design on which he had consulted him of an elaborate work in defence of boxing: 'The

* From Frampton Court, January 31, 1881.

dissertation on prize combats you have so ingeniously projected may gratify the national taste, and the luxuriance of your imagination may supply matter to give the charm of truth to the novelty of paradox. If a Sheridan will bestow the talents he inherits on academical bruisers, doubtless he can convert *the Chicken* into Achilles and Gully into the wise Ulysses. Seriously, does not this science entirely depend on a kind of skill unconnected with the intellect, and in hardness of bone which the brave man needs not? If your heroes are those of the mob and nothing more, the philosopher will resign them to the gentle grapplers of Bow Street. I never saw a boxing match, and it is now so long since I have undergone a dry beating that I have no distinct conception of the whole operation.'*

A few days after the change of Government in 1867, the new Lord Chancellor had laid before the Lords a Bill which had been left in the Foreign Office, regarding the evidence obtained abroad against foreigners in this country, on which a magistrate might be called upon to issue a warrant of detention until the accused should be surrendered as no longer entitled to claim our hospitality.

The French Government complained that extradition was frequently refused because oral testimony had not been furnished confirmatory of

* King's Road, Bloomsbury, September 13, 1808.

the depositions made before a French magistrate and authenticated by judicial seal as genuine, in the same manner as was deemed sufficient in civil cases, and if no means were found to alter the magisterial practice in England they would give notice to denounce the treaty.

Lord Chelmsford concurred with his predecessor in thinking the request not unreasonable, and to allay misgivings that might be entertained respecting the use that might be made of the proposed facility for obtaining the surrender of political fugitives, he stated that by the code of Napoleon a refugee acquitted of an ordinary offence could not be put upon his trial for sedition until he had been restored to his former place of asylum.

The Chancellor could not allege that similar provisions existed in the laws of other countries, but he explained that Sir Thomas Henry, who presided at Bow Street, and whose decisions were entitled to the greatest respect, could not be expected to give up a prisoner on the production of documents which would not be sufficient without corroborative testimony *primâ facie* of guilt against a British subject.

The Bill was read without discussion and sent down to the Commons, where it was set down for second reading on August 3. It was difficult to make or keep a House for any purpose, and it seemed almost hopeless to obtain attention on a subject which during the long official rule of Palmerston had been practically suffered to sleep. But to those who sympathized with the apprehensions of not a few distinguished exiles hitherto dwelling, as they supposed, in safety within the four seas, it seemed that an effort ought to be made to stay the farther progress of a measure that, if it became law, would irreparably compromise their position.

If the principle of undiscriminating justice were waived in the case of France, it could not be maintained where the Russian or Austrian Governments made similar demands for rendition; and the few experienced friends who remained in town, whom I thought it necessary to consult, agreed in thinking that an attempt should be made to have the legislative question postponed at least until there should have been time for its public discussion.

In an almost empty House I made, accordingly, an appeal to Lord Stanley not to commit the country to a statutable change so important after Parliament might be said to have left town. Thanking him for having produced the diplomatic correspondence of the last six months, which had led to the construction of the Bill, and rejecting as untenable the colourable excuse that it was only a subordinate modification of the law of evidence, I ventured to contend that we should leave the law of the land where Sir Robert Peel's

Administration had left it in 1843, and where Lord Russell, Lord Aberdeen, and Lord Palmerston had preserved it to the present time. We asked now for no more, but we could be content with no less, than the maintenance of the traditional policy towards strangers which reflected our daily practice towards our own people.

Why had not the principle, invariably reiterated in our statutes, as regulating the conduct of magistrates, where friendless and often destitute foreigners were brought before them, been objected to by the United States or Denmark, and only by Imperial France?

The Duc d'Auvergne, writing to Lord Clarendon, frankly owned that what was wanted was not a modification of the procedure at Bow Street, not a trumpery concession as to the mode of taking evidence, but that a French warrant should run in Middlesex, and that when a man had been convicted in France, even in his absence, we should give him up—in point of fact, that the magistrates should cease to be independent judges, and that they should become agents of the French police.

He replied that no Government in this country would venture to ask Parliament for such concessions; but, unfortunately, the present Bill, by its obvious construction, practically yielded the first and worst of these concessions. It would be a source of genuine regret to all who loved peace and good neighbourhood that we could not agree to what was sought by France, but we could not with consistency or dignity give up all *vivâ-voce* proof, and deliver up foreign offenders upon nothing but documentary evidence. It was clear that, if we made these concessions, no Frenchman in England would be safe from the possibility of arrest.

The French Government said they had obtained prisoners from America on a simple *mandat d'arrêt* without proof. This was so startling that I wrote to the American Minister in Paris on that point, and Mr. Bigelow replied with an unqualified negative. He said: 'To procure a warrant of extradition under any of our treaties, it is necessary to produce, not only the *mandat d'arrêt*, but certified copies of the depositions upon which the warrant has been granted, attested by the oath (*parole*) to be true copies,' the witness being subject to cross-examination. Mr. Bigelow further said that an American magistrate must have that kind of evidence which satisfied *him* that the offence had been committed which would justify him in committing his own countrymen for trial.

I said, Stick to that, and we would be content. They would never persuade the people of England that, when they made themselves the jackals of a foreign despotism, they were dealing with the helpless foreigners they gave up in the same way as they would deal with Englishmen.

The principle of English law was that an accused person was to be deemed innocent until his guilt was proved. The avowed principle of the French code was that he was to be considered guilty until he had proved his innocence.

When a similar Bill was moved by Lord Malmesbury in 1852, Lord Campbell vetoed it in the outset, and said he never could consent to it. Why should we now be asked to consent to what the House of Lords in 1852 had declared to be unconstitutional?

M. Louis Blanc, one of the Provisional Government in 1848, and since its supersession by that of the Emperor a distinguished and respected denizen of our country, had written me a letter on the subject, part of which I quote: 'To form a correct idea of the dangerous and mischievous character of this Bill, it is necessary to bear in mind that in France justice has always been much more or less subservient to the purposes of the ruling power. To pass the present Bill would be, to a great extent, to make the right of asylum a snare, to forge a weapon not unlikely to be used against innocent persons, and to incur the accusation of having surrendered to a foreign despotic power the dignity of a free nation.' Pass this pettifogging Act, and by-and-by we should be called upon to take further steps in humiliation.

The Foreign Secretary denied that any such were reserved, but with my own ears I had heard the Keeper of the Great Seal declare from the Woolsack that he hoped it would lead ere long to a great expansion of the schedule of crimes that might reciprocally be prosecuted and punished. What if we were now, when half asleep, setting a precedent for exile-hunting at the bidding of the Kaiser or the Czar?

The Attorney-General relied on the terms of the provision requiring that the *mandat d'arrêt* should set forth descriptively the nature of the offence for which extradition was sought, and the circumstances under which it was said to have been committed, and argued generally that the proposal involved no essential change of judicial practice or national policy.

J. Stuart Mill said he had never met any enlightened Frenchman who did not say that the worst part of the French code was the law of criminal procedure, and that the mode in which the preliminary evidence was taken was the worst part even of that. The depositions taken preparatory to a criminal trial were taken in secret, and not in the presence of the accused. It was the easiest thing in the world, therefore, to get up a false charge, if there was any sufficient motive for doing so.

But argument availed little, and the Bill was read a second time by a large majority. The candour and good sense of the Foreign Secretary was not unimpressed, however, by the drift of the discussion, and the duration of the measure was limited to twelve months only. This afforded opportunity for further inquiry, and discussion in the press abroad and at home.

The leading members of the French Bar, MM. Jules Favre, Cremieux, Becker, and Jules Ferry, looked upon the insidious change demanded with grave apprehension. With many grateful expressions for the efforts made in Parliament by myself and others, M. Ferry, then at the zenith of his reputation as an advocate and jurist, wrote: 'Had I the honour to be an English subject, I should prefer to be cut in pieces rather than accept the impertinent derogations which in the name of a criminal procedure, at which France ought to blush, our Government seek to introduce by secret doors into the protecting armoury of the British Constitution. Comparing the Bill with the Convention of 1843, you will see the new arrangement has the effect of suppressing oral debate in the proceedings of extradition, and to introduce into English justice the French *mandat d'arrêt* as an equivalent to the open and audible procedure which is an honour to our neighbours. That convention required that the English judge should find in the affair submitted to him elements of suspicion and a presumption sufficient, according to English views, to justify the offender being sent for trial. The *mandat d'arrêt* only declares in the most concise terms the deed for which it is issued, and the law which decides that this deed is a crime. Mr. Torrens asks, not without reason, if the accused there finds any guarantee that the accusation shall not be modified or turned away from its first form. There is nothing in our laws to render this impossible. In fact, the qualification of crime only becomes defined by the decree of the Chambre de Mise en Accusation. Thus, delivered up by extradition on an accusation of a non-political crime, the accused may be acquitted and released on that head, and retaken upon another accusation, even political. The necessity of oral debate previous to the extradition ought to be maintained. This would be to oblige the French Government to prove the crime before the English magistrate, to exact that it should proceed as in England before the Grand Jury. There ought to be a clause stipulating expressly that an accused person, surrendered on a demand for extradition, shall not be troubled on any other protest, the extradition being annulled if the accusation is modified in any way.'*

Lord Aberdeen, in 1846, had confessed that to satisfy the French Government a new Act of Parliament and a new convention were necessary, and that the clause requiring that French

* Letter of M. Jules Ferry to Louis Blanc.

subjects should not be delivered up unless the evidence of their guilt was such as to warrant their commitment for trial by our law ought to be altogether omitted.

The Convention of 1862 unconditionally excluded accusations of a political kind as justifying extradition, and stipulated for the liberation of a person who had been brought to trial notwithstanding; but the convention unfortunately did not forbid the trial of a person for a second ordinary offence, and it was obvious that in Poland a man might be held in durance without limit under such a practice.

The Procureur du Roi in 1841 had issued a circular to judges of first instance inhibiting the sinister practice; but while the injunction had been observed under the government of Louis Philippe, it was reasonably argued that it could not be held equivalent to a law under another *régime*.

In accordance with a pledge given by Lord Stanley in the previous Session, a Select Committee was appointed early in 1868 to inquire into existing relations with foreign States regarding extradition, with a view to the adoption of a more permanent and uniform policy on the subject. The expediency of the legislative change we had contended for was thus acknowledged, and the competency of the tribunal to which the question was referred could not be doubted.

Mr. Walpole, the Solicitor-General, Mr. Egerton, Mr. Gorst, Mr. Graves, Mr. Schreiber, Mr. P. Wyndham, and Mr. Thomas Baring were supposed to represent the cautious disposition of the Government in the matter; while Mr. E. P. Bouverie, Sir R. Collier, Mr. J. S. Mill, Sir F. Goldsmid, Mr. Neate, Mr. W. E. Forster, Mr. Baxter, Mr. Layard, Mr. Stansfeld, and myself made up the number.

I willingly waived the precedence generally given to the mover of a Committee, and proposed that Mr. Bouverie should take the chair. A good deal of evidence, oral and documentary, was produced in support of varying views, and the proceedings were protracted until July. The most important witness was Sir Thomas Henry, Chief Magistrate at Bow Street, whose long experience deservedly gave the greatest weight to his opinions, and these were in the main identical with the desire expressed for a general and more equitable system.

After much consideration, the Committee reported in favour of a permanent statute on the subject being passed, within the margin of whose provisions all treaties with foreign States regarding the surrender of accused persons should be strictly framed in order that divergences and anomalies in judicial diplomacy might be thenceforth avoided.

Having moved for the Committee, I submitted

clauses, carefully framed, to secure the right of every fugitive demanded to his release if he could prove to the satisfaction of the magistrate or the Court before whom he was brought, or to the Secretary of State, that the requisition for his surrender had been made with a view to try or punish him for a political offence; that if acquitted of one offence he should not be tried for another until he had been restored to the country whence he was taken; that in any case he should not be surrendered within fifteen days; and that the committing magistrate should warn him that he had a right to apply for a writ of habeas corpus within that time. The magistrate was directed to hear and adjudicate in every respect on such evidence as would apply to the case of a British subject.

All these guarantees, for which we had contended in debate, were adopted by the Committee, and were finally embodied in the Act of 1870, the distinctive value of which was acknowledged by Sir Robert Collier, then Attorney-General. The Government, he said, had felt it their duty to take the responsibility of carrying the measure through both Houses, but—turning to the Member for Finsbury—he said: 'This is your Bill.'

The Act of 1870, though carefully avoiding in terms the claim to be a new departure from international usage, was in reality, and was felt to be, the casting of anchor in a shoal of conflicting decisions whereby Ministers might in future ride out either despotic or revolutionary outbreaks of complaint that England was not true to the profession of constitutional neutrality.

It provided for the first time a clear and consistent rule to be observed by the Foreign Office under all circumstances, and when understood by foreign Governments the effect in common was better than many of us had ventured to hope for.

In the course of the next few years every European Court except that of Russia and of Spain, and every Democratic Republic of consequence save that of the United States, agreed to extraditional engagements on this uniform basis; and the hesitation of America was understood to arise on special and technical grounds, which happily have since been removed, while Spain has recently conformed to the established practice.

As was, perhaps, inevitable, grumblings arose occasionally at an imputed want of complete reciprocity in unprecedented cases, and, yielding somewhat unaccountably to murmurs that had really no echo of importance in the public mind, the Cabinet in 1877 appointed a Royal Commission to inquire into the working and effect of the law of extradition, and of the treaties recently contracted under it.

Lord Chief Justice Cockburn was appointed chairman, and several of the most distinguished members of the judicial bench consented to act upon the inquiry. I should have gladly been omitted from the list of members, but, for reasons which were more obvious, perhaps, to others than to me, I agreed to be named with Sir John Rose, who in England, as Resident Commissioner, represented Canada, where it was, I believe, presumed there was a general coincidence of opinion.

We met early in the ensuing winter, and much pains were devoted to retrospective examination of what had been done in former reigns, and careful comparison of recent circumstances that were said to call for legislative reconsideration and revision.

The Chairman's draft report appeared to embody the conclusions of the great majority, by whom, after more than one day's consultation, it was agreed to. The seventh section raised the question whether, if a person be surrendered in respect of one extradition offence, he should, when transferred to the country claiming him, be liable to be tried for another.

Political and local reasons being excepted, they saw no reason why he should not. There seemed no reason why a foreign Government should act disingenuously towards ours if it were to put the person surrendered on his trial in respect of a crime which was not the ground of extradition in the particular instance. It might be discovered after the surrender that the party surrendered had committed some other offence deserving of punishment.

They saw no reason why, under such circumstances, the offender should escape with impunity. What possible interest should we have in what became of him? We should not be warranted in assuming that he would be dealt with in the foreign country otherwise than according to justice and right.

They therefore recommended the repeal of that portion of the existing Act which forbade trial for any offence other than that for which extradi tion was granted.

From this recommendation, and the reasoning on which it rested, I could not but dissent. To repeal this provision would be a waiver by statute of our primary jurisdiction in the matter, and would be practically an invitation to a foreign Government to deprive its subjects of the right of asylum which time out of mind all our neighbours had enjoyed, irrespective of creed, race, or local institutions. Had we to deal with countries only whose jurisprudence rests upon what England deems the principles of social and political civilization, there would, perhaps, be little risk in the concession.

Criminal justice, as our people understand it,

and as our laws and Courts interpret it, implies publicity of arraignment, confronting with the accuser, and the weighing of evidence by an irremovable judge indifferent to the frown of power. It implies the verdict of a fair jury, a record open to legal scrutiny, and the fearless criticism of an unfettered press.

The fear entertained by those who were jealous of any lessening of the present safeguards mainly rested upon the possibility of a person, when acquitted of one extradition offence, being detained in custody for an indefinite period on the imputation of one or more offences, none of which may have in them any political or religious character. Parliament could not affect ignorance of the disparity of foreign laws, and the repugnance to our own of the principles upon which criminal justice is frequently administered under them.*

With the citation of several instances of the evil and injustice deprecated, I submitted my separate report, which was in due time laid before both Houses. But on its becoming known that unanimity had not prevailed, I was requested by the Chancellor to acquaint him with the considerations that had driven me reluctantly to formulate my reasons for dissent. Lord Cairns had been a law adviser of the Government when the second

* Reasons for dissenting to Section vii., appended to report of Royal Commission, May 30, 1878.

debate arose upon the subject ten years before, and naturally recalled the varying opinions which it drew forth. The fact that many foreign Governments, including that of France, had actually ratified treaties embodying the principles of international law for which I contended, and the knowledge that no complaint had in the interval been preferred to our Foreign Office on the subject, weighed, no doubt, materially in his mind; but I am bound to add that no one could express more lucidly or candidly the paramount sense of duty which he owed as keeper of the conscience of the Crown, and no terms of mere compliment or acknowledgment could have been to me so grateful as those in which he intimated his conviction that no amendment of the statute was required, and that none was likely to be undertaken.

Fourteen years have passed, and Ministers entertaining various political opinions have since then held the seal of the Foreign Department. But no attempt has been made to break down the humane and equitable statute of 1870, and I rejoice to think that no indication has appeared of any disposition to do so.

As the report of the Commission was likely to direct attention in both Houses to the questions raised in controversy regarding the Statute of Extradition, I wished Lord Beaconsfield to be aware of the conditions on which I had told Lord

Cross I could consent to serve on the inquiry; and that it would be impossible for those who thought as I did on the subject to profess acquiescence in the recommendation of an altered policy embodied in the report.

I did not feel justified in asking if the Cabinet had come to any legislative decision. He volunteered a negative, but said his 'individual opinions were generally embodied in Lord Derby's despatch of the 26th of June, 1876' (to the United States), 'but that since that more pressing subjects had occupied his mind, and he had not looked particularly into what had since transpired.'

I rejoiced that the principles there laid down fully satisfied those who had induced Parliament to pass the Act of 1870, as establishing firmly the basis of extraditional freedom; and that, believing no essential difference in feeling or conviction prevailed between this country and America, we should cheerfully support any accommodation of diplomatic forms that would bring the two Governments into unison in reciprocal practice. If, unfortunately, the difficulty raised at Washington were allowed to prove insuperable, there was too much ground to fear that Russia, and perhaps other States, might seek to be treated on an equally retrograde footing, and after two or three wars on the Continent, the mutual right of asylum we had hoped for would be gone. I instanced the cases actually pending of the fugitive Archbishops of Posen and Cologne, neither of whom, if now given up, could be certain of obtaining liberation from imprisonment under a penal law. He said he was disposed to think very much in the same way of the matter, but that he had added my name to the Commission because he knew the attention I had given to the question, and that he would mention all I had said to Lord Derby. He thought it not impossible that we might one day have to face another attempt like that of Napoleon upon the liberties of Europe.

The conversation turned to other topics, including the discussion between Gladstone and Lowe regarding the county franchise, and he said, laughing, that it was a curious occupation for leaders of Opposition to be proving one another to be wrong on the most important subjects.

Before leaving I mentioned having seen Angeli's portrait of him at Colnaghi's. 'Oh!' he exclaimed, 'is it not hideous?—and so like. But he is a favourite at Court, and the Queen has sent me her own portrait by the same hand. What a wonderful fellow Gladstone is, after all! He had a dreadful passage, I hear, coming back from Ireland, and the moment he got on shore he began to make a speech to the Welshmen, telling them "they were all right and to keep so."'

In 1870 there passed away a class-fellow and cotemporary who for several years led in Parliament a majority of the Irish members under the banner of Home Rule. Isaac Butt was in many respects a remarkable man. Brought up at the feet of Gamaliel, he was known in his youth and prime as an advocate of Toryism of a type the most pronounced. His easy and good-natured disposition spared him the pain of making personal enemies, while he never failed to indulge in specious and showy rhetoric in praise of the tenets and doctrines in which he had been brought up. I remember having seen him wearing the Orange insignia after he was called to the Bar, and in the first elected corporation for Dublin he led the minority against the Whig and Catholic majority, who chose O'Connell for the first popular Lord Mayor. For some reason that I never understood, he was viewed with disfavour by the influential Irish Tories, and, despairing of their help to obtain a seat in Parliament, he accepted, in 1852, the reversion of a vacancy at Harwich.

His maiden speech at St. Stephen's was professedly impromptu, and I have often heard him say that he believed he could always do better without preparation, for his flow of dignified and vigorous language was upon all subjects inexhaustible, while his critical acumen made him feel conscious how much there was unknown, because unread, upon any question of general importance. An early dissolution bereft him of the opportunity of distinction, which was the day-dream of his life; and gaining no little popularity in Ireland by several forensic efforts on behalf of the Fenians, he gradually made up his mind to take sides with the National Party, by whom he was returned, in 1871, for the city of Limerick. Thenceforth he devoted his chief energies to the development of a scheme of domestic legislation, in which many concurred who had never agreed before in any proposed remedies for Celtic poverty and discontent. He asked me on one occasion to sign the declaration in favour of constituting a local legislature for the transaction of local affairs, to the reasonableness of which he persuaded himself that not a few English and Scotch members would be ready to assent, and, upon being questioned how far such a concession would secure contentment, and on what he relied for its preserving loyal independence, he said, laughing, 'Are we wiser than Grattan? and, though he failed in his day, why should we not have better luck next time? for we don't profess to stop short of resuscitating the Parliament.'

It was not, perhaps, surprising that under the circumstances he should have preferred indulging in plausible generalities to entering into explicit details of the great change he had undertaken to advocate. Did he really believe in the possibility of reconstituting two separate and legislatively co-equal assemblies in Ireland, like those which bore the name of Grattan's Parliament? A friend of mine, not indisposed to concession, pressed him on the point, and could only extract a laughing assent, with the responsive question of 'Why not?' 'Because,' was the rejoinder, 'the brief attempt of 1782, to realize the dreams of legislative independence, without an Executive subject to local Parliamentary control, proved signally abortive, and because in less than seven years the policy of the English Parliament on matters of vital importance, constitutional and commercial, was deliberately rejected by that of Ireland, there being no means of arbitrating their differences known to the law, or apparently attainable by the ablest and best men of the day.'

In time of peace the divergence seemed to the greater Power intolerable, in time of war too grave to be suffered to exist; and no Minister in our day would undertake the responsibility of defending both islands from foreign attack without unity of Parliamentary support. If Butt could induce his followers to be content with a thorough incorporation of the three kingdoms, leaving all local offices and appointments as in Scotland to be enjoyed by the natives of each country, while in the Imperial Executive Irishmen as well as Scotchmen should have a proportionate place, and with a criminal code identical throughout the realm, he might hope to succeed in redeeming Mr. Pitt's Act of Union from the reproach so long attached to it. But if he held out expectations in Ireland that the Parliament of the Volunteers of 1782 could be recalled to existence, he was deceiving either himself or them.

Knowing the inveterate versatility of the man, I felt that it would be mere trifling to inquire if he would bind himself not to make use of any concession that might be made to nationalism as a means of stimulating further agitation: and I knew too well that it was not in his power to stay the instability of convictions that had been his besetting weakness through life. But I asked, if federalism in any shape were offered, what assurance would be forthcoming that the Celtic majority would not, after two or three bad harvests, call on their representatives to denounce the treaty of compromise as unworthy and insufficient?

He thereupon recited, with infinite rhetorical force and persuasability, the answer he was prepared to give if interrogated on the point by the Prime Minister, and which would no doubt have overwhelmed with satisfaction all who were disposed to be satisfied before. The movement about which he was sanguine, however, came to nothing. Several of his supporters fell away from misgivings as to his firmness of purpose, and before his death in 1879 there were strong indications of his losing his power of suasion and position of ascendancy among those he had sacrificed many professional advantages to retain.

In a former Parliament my learned friend, as I reminded him, had voted with the best men of both parties after a long debate for a motion of mine deferring the abolition of the Irish Vice-royalty until Government were prepared to establish in its stead a distinct Secretaryship of State. It was a protest on practical grounds, which a great majority of the House felt I had made clear, that the existing form of the Irish Executive, however it might be deemed out of date, ought not to be changed until something more in harmony with the improved spirit of the time was ready to be put in its place.

While a separate Parliament existed, on whose yearly votes the provincial revenue depended, the presence of a Lord-Deputy at the opening of each Session to ask for supplies and to recommend taxes or loans was perhaps necessary: for a Sovereign hardly ever appeared in the appendant realm, Dublin Castle was far from Windsor, and a stormy sea took days and sometimes weeks to cross. But steam had shortened distance, the Union had put an end to a separate Exchequer, and royalty was no longer personally unknown in Ireland.

Taxation, wherever levied and expended, had to be accounted for at Westminster, and accountability could most duly and directly be exacted from a member of the Cabinet. If the laws and institutions which prevailed in the two countries were the same as persons who had never been in office imagined, the Minister for the Home Department might be tempted to try whether, in addition to his other labours, he might not undertake the daily affairs of another six millions of people.

This seemed to be, in fact, the supposition of Mr. Roebuck, who asked the House of Commons, by resolution, to 'abolish the Lord-Lieutenancy of Ireland, and to make her what he said she ought to be—a fractional part of the great kingdom to which she belonged'—but without suggesting how the change was to be carried into effect, or recognising the hourly difficulties of administering two systems of statute law essentially different by the same hand. 'I have always been of opinion,' said Lord J. Russell when Prime Minister, 'that Ireland is a great loser by not having a Minister in the Cabinet to explain the interests of that country, and to enforce the course which he might recommend. I do not believe that the Home Secretary could efficiently discharge the additional duties which would be thrown upon him if the two offices were united. I believe it would be better upon the whole to keep the Lord-Lieutenancy than to attempt to throw this immense mass of business into an office already sufficiently, if not over loaded with business of the State.'

I knew the desire of Lord John to do administrative justice to Ireland, because I had had opportunities both officially and privately of estimating the comprehensiveness of his views and the far-sightedness of his policy. He had studied, as few of his colleagues had done, the historic concatenation of blunders and oppressions that had alienated the heart of the country, and the cure of no one or any half dozen of which could be relied on summarily to restore popular health or content. He was himself a landed proprietor in Leinster, and an aristocrat to the core; but, consistently with true pride in his order, and true loyalty to the Empire, he was for employing Irishmen of rank and property like English nobles and proprietors in the business of their common country irrespective of creed or faction; and he had proved his readiness to share Executive office between men of ability whether born on the east or west of the Channel as had never been done before in our time.

I heard him blame Sir Robert Peel for the opposite course in the formation of his Government in 1841, when possessing a majority that virtually rendered his duration absolute. When he himself in 1846 was invested with the same responsibility, without anything like the same Parliamentary strength, he did not hesitate to make a great resident peer Viceroy, and a member of the local bar Chancellor; to entrust various secondary offices abroad and at home to Irish representatives; to propose, as he told me himself, to put Mr. Shiel in the Cabinet, and, when difficulties came in the way of that intention, to make him Master of the Mint and subsequently Minister to Florence.

How little soever these concessions availed to mitigate popular discontent during the dreadful days of famine, the acute miseries of which neither he nor anyone else dreamt of their being able to allay, he adhered to the opinion in which I knew Lord Lansdowne, then President of the Council, thoroughly sympathized, that the peaceful permanency of the Union could only be maintained by making all classes and creeds in Ireland feel a sense of co-partnership in the benefits and distinctions of empire; and I cannot doubt that under either of them, as head of the Government, Dublin Castle would ere this have been transformed from a minor theatre for the performance of the mimic shows of power, into a business-like centre of native administrative rule.

In consonance with these views, Lord Russell had brought in a Bill to abrogate the functions of Viceroy, and to enable her Majesty, when so advised, to create a fourth Secretary of State. It evoked little objection, until the latter condition seemed about to be withdrawn or left undecided. To most of those with whom I was in the habit of acting, the proposal thus lamed tended to weaken and worsen the authority of Government, rather than to presage or to pave the way for reciprocal and equal incorporation.

A deputation consisting of influential men of both sides deprecated the mutilated change, and pressed for an assurance that a distinct department should, under all circumstances, be maintained.

The Premier did not affect to have modified his own opinions on the subject; but we had reason to believe that he had been dissuaded from insisting upon them by the Ministerial jealousy with which the constitution of the Cabinet would fain be kept among a privileged few. Ambiguous words in one of the clauses of the Bill appeared to save the noble lord's consistency, but they failed to satisfy his remonstrance; and we declined in consequence to vote for the second reading.

In the House of Lords the Bill was denounced by the Duke of Wellington as indefensible in detail and unworkable in practice, and its author, baffled in his original design, agreed to its being withdrawn.

The uncompleted scheme of union left the Viceregal Government a water-logged and drifting raft in the trough of angry seas—not the three-decker it was meant by its author to prove in defence of the Empire. Generations were suffered to pass away without its initiatory promises being fulfilled, and a whole library of separate statutes had been persistently piled up for provincial government, which at best required the undistracted attention and local care that a discontented dependency needed.

I undertook in 1857 to make it clear to the House that, until junior partnership were conceded or something like identity of legislation agreed to, the Executive ought to be confided to a distinct department, confidentially related to that at Whitehall, but avowedly and mainly devoted to the wants and the welfare of a country too long perplexed by being told to halt between two authorities—that of exceptional enactments supposed to be suited to a community of Colonists and Celts, and that of a constitutional code fitted to secure the happiness of Scotchmen and Saxons.

Every year numerous Acts were passed, no matter who sat on the Treasury bench, with a stereotyped provision, 'not to extend to Ireland,' or *vice versâ;* but all were bundled together to the Queen's printer and bound together in the same annual volume, with the illegible motto, 'Let him that heareth understand, if he can.'

There being still no indication of any change of this tantalizing system of dissimilar rule, I asked Lord Palmerston if he would support the *Previous Question* as most likely to combine convergent shades of opinion against an inconsiderate motion; and on receiving his assent I prepared to cite in detail the discrepant and divergent statutes passed in our own time for the separate portions of the ill-United Kingdom, not as local or temporary, but as permanent and general Acts.

My hon. and learned friend said he wished to see Irish counties and parishes the same as English counties and parishes, and he spoke as if a chart of the realm were spread on the floor, on which we had nothing to do but to trace parallel lines of law. But our business in Parliament was not to deal with unresisting maps, but with restless men.

'Let anyone look into the index of his copy of the statutes for a few years back, without party fear, favour or affection, and what would he find? Forty years before a Constabulary force of many thousand men enlisted and drilled, armed and officered, under Government had been organized by Sir Robert Peel as Chief Secretary, and strengthened by his successors in office as the best and most reliable guarantee for peace and order.

'Would any English member rise in his place and propose that a duplicate force of the kind should be established in Great Britain? or did anyone forget what befell a small water-colour of that original when timidly presented there?

'Five-and-twenty years before an elaborate system of primary instruction on neutral principles with regard to sect had been devised by Lord Derby and decreed by Parliament, at a cost to the Treasury of half a million a year, which no one had ever since seriously proposed to abrogate in Ireland, and nobody gravely argued should in its essential features be adopted in England. Twenty years before tithes had been swept away in the one country, while they were still maintained in the other; and ten years before a court of inquisition without precedent into the solvency of Irish landlords, and the sale, without reserve, of their encumbered estates, was created, the like of which it was never whispered that any Minister, Whig or Tory, had thought of setting up in Great Britain.

'Were hon. gentlemen aware that the whole frame and scope of criminal judicature in Ireland was different; that, instead of voluntary prosecutions, all indictments were laid before the jury by legal officers appointed and removable by the crown; and that summary jurisdiction at Quarter Sessions was administered by public functionaries, paid by the State, and permanently appointed? Could it be necessary to point out the essential differences between the systems of poor relief firmly established on opposite sides of the Channel, or of sick relief in dispensary and home? Beside all these, there were scores of specific Acts on every variety of subject which were not binding on the two communities in common; and of which it might be literally said that the same thing was virtue in the one that in the other was a sin.

'Within the previous seven years no fewer than one hundred and twenty Acts had been passed applicable exclusively to the step-sister kingdom. All this might be thought right or considered wrong; but until the day of fusion came, or at least until its dawn, it would surely be safer, juster, and more consonant with the life-giving precept of doing as we would be done by, to suffer distinct methods of government by distinctively responsible statesmen.'

When I sat down, Sir James Graham turned to me and said, 'There is no answering this; I will go away.'

The debate proceeded for some hours, and at its close my amendment was carried by 266 to 115, and since then the proposal has not been renewed.

Far from repudiating his vote of 1857, the Member for Limerick, as he had become by acclamation, was ready to defend the retention of the Lord-Lieutenancy, which he wished to see conferred on a royal Prince or on one of the territorial magnates whose names were associated with the annals of the country. He had outlived traditional party and sectarian prejudices, and had won no inconsiderable popularity by reviving the demand for a separate Parliament under the name of Home Rule. What he would have done with it had any unforeseen concurrence of events, as in 1781, presented the opportunity, I do not know, and I never could persuade him distinctly to tell. The last ten years of his life were devoted to painting in vivid and versatile colours the happier condition of things before the Union, in extolling the genius and patriotism of the patriots and politicians of that day, and endeavouring to persuade Ulster that it might confidingly embrace Munster, that Protestant nobles and gentry had nothing to fear from Catholic tenant-right, and that historical and social enmities would be forgotten in an independent Parliament, the question of Church Establishment once out of the way. But though he practically gave up his lucrative profession to promulgate these sanguine views, and was met with out-of-door welcome and applause wherever he came, failure to rally to the cause any notable support of any conspicuous adherents of the rival denominations saddened his declining days. The ambition of younger and more impetuous men cavilled, and at length quarrelled, with his ceremonious adherence to constitutional terms and methods; and ere long the reins of agitation were grasped and firmly held for several years by one who, in most respects, was of a signally different nature.

O'Connell was accustomed to sway the multitude alternately by his eloquence and his humour. Charles Parnell possessed neither. His delivery and choice of language when he first began to address the House were alike unfurnished and unfitted for purposes of leadership; but he had the rare talisman of being in earnest, and the gift (no one could say exactly how or why) of impressing his hearers with being so.

A cold but keen critic who sat near me during one of his efforts to extort attention to his uncaptivating but uncapitulating views, repeated when he sat down what was said at first of Robespierre: 'Il ira loin, il croit.' And far he went ere long. The pressure of the confidence his daring and his diligence gathered round him, and the impressiveness of the contrast between him and the good-humoured, easy-going, unmatter-of-fact aspirants to popularity amongst whom he moved, steadily but rapidly made for him a position wholly unlike that of any other democratic leader of our time.

When standing at the table to take the oath of admission, Bright, who sat near him on the front bench, was struck by his look, that had so much of craft and so little of time-serving in it, and—turning to the colleague who sat beside him—he muttered through clenched teeth, as was his way: 'He has the eye of a madman.'

His unexplained reserve, which every day grew, if possible, more intense, at first repelled and then perplexed, but ultimately fascinated, the Celts; and it became at last one of the spells that few of those near him ventured to make free with, far less to question.

The contrast between him and O'Connell in this respect was curious. Instead of rebuking or frowning off a too familiar questioner, 'Dan,' as he loved to be called (every day in the week except Sunday), parried the interrogatory with a jest or a sarcasm that made its repetition impossible. A friend of mine—knowing that he thought it expedient to prolong his attendance at Westminster between the verdict of the jury against him in the Queen's Bench and the deferred sentence, while every week he wrote to the expectant association in Dublin to say he would return in a few days—met him in the hall of the Reform Club, and, after propitiatory inquiries about his health, abruptly asked him: 'When are you going to Ireland?' Without hesitation, he gave the best and briefest answer the language afforded—'Yes.'

I have often been asked, when telling the story in what is called good society, to explain—what did he mean? But I must say that in Ireland I never knew the anecdote miss fire. Parnell was seldom, if ever, chargeable with a joke, but an impassive stare served him instead for defence against intrusion.

Every year his influence grew, and with it not only his facility of expression, but his power of marshalling complicated and often cumbrous facts, which came to be received by all sides with attention, and which, without platitude or exaggeration, he condensed at the end into the demand he had undertaken to make. Those who at first heeded him least, and at last hated him most as a dangerous foe of the existing order of things, were the freest to acknowledge his growing ability, and the strength, as it seemed, of his singular position. One thing only I disbelieved in his ever obtaining – namely, the confidence of the Catholic clergy, whom, though careful not to offend, he could not dissuade from silently distrusting him. I remember, after his fall, asking how they could have so long appeared to rely on him. The answer I received was: 'Well, no doubt, he had to be got rid of.'

Bright entertained a high opinion of Parnell's ability, but did not mince phrases in denouncing his aims as dangerous. Those who knew him did not infer animosity or ill-will therefrom. It was his way, and he gave himself the benefit of its license unto the end.

His own relative, having renounced the tenets in which they had been both brought up, and become a Catholic, suddenly outran him in popularity on the other side of the Channel, founded a successful journal, and was chosen member for one of the Midland counties. Bright was mortified by his secession, and could not resist the temptation of accosting him at the opening of

Parliament with, 'Well, Frederick, how is your new superstition?' Lucas was not a man to be daunted, and on the instant replied, 'Better, John, I think, than the old hypocrisy.'

Bright had long enjoyed great popularity in Ireland by reason of the part he had taken on the Church and land questions, but he told me that he did not see his way respecting Home Rule. The precedents of Switzerland and America had led many Irish Liberals, no doubt, from time to time to favour the idea of a local legislature for local objects; and many English Liberals were free from any insuperable prejudice in the direction of Federalism, if that would do. But the notion of setting up a House of Lords at Dublin, which O'Connell sometimes talked of, and Butt dreamt of as possible, made few converts; and the language held more recently by Parnell in Ireland convinced him, he said, that, given a State Legislature, it would be used when opportunity came for separation.'

The experiment, he believed, would fail. If momentarily successful, as in 1782, owing to defeat abroad, it would insure incessant collision between the two Parliaments, and end, as it had done before, in the weaker competitor being bought up by the stronger. As for two separate Administrations, responsible to two separate Parliaments, and removable by each respectively, the thing was out of the question. The example of Hungary and Austria was not to the point. Count Beust, the author of the existing system, always said that his arbitrament was between contending national claims, neither of which could be appeased except by compromise; and he had often expressed the opinion that the case between Great Britain and Ireland was in no respect identical. Austria *without* an autonomous Hungary must have ceased to be a first-rate Power; England *with* an autonomous Ireland could not long remain so.

Were Cobden living, he would certainly refuse to support any measure that incurred the risk of dismemberment. During the civil war in America, he had never yielded to the plea advanced in favour of secession. Bright said he had urged him, on the eve of the notable banquet at Newcastle, to dissuade Gladstone from lending any countenance there to the aspirations of the South for independence, and Cobden declined only because he knew that the attempt would be fruitless. When the memorable declaration of the then Chancellor of the Exchequer appeared, that the Confederate States had made themselves a nation, his colleague, Sir George Lewis, lost not an hour in repudiating publicly the inference that the British Government were prepared to recognise separation.

Among the veterans who fell out on the long Parliamentary march, few were better known or liked than the Member for Waterford. The Major, as he was familiarly called, had served many years abroad, and exfoliated a good many of the political prejudices and social traditions in which he had been brought up. There was little in common between him and the Home Rule leader but their love of jovial society and the indulgence of bantering humour, which all true Celts encourage and enjoy. The memory of neither can be credited with any of the sarcasms or *bons-mots* of Curran, Shiel, or O'Connell; but they claimed the national right to make fun of friends to their faces, with or without the prefix that they meant no harm, and with readiness in reserve to beg a dear fellow's pardon for saying anything that could have offended him.

Major O'Gorman would have taken it ill had anyone questioned the sincerity of his belief in the Church, but he made no profession of being what is called a practical Catholic, and the occasions were not rare, in or out of Lent, when he forgot, towards sundown, the day of the week. On one very hot afternoon, when he had been faithfully sitting, if not standing, up for the neglected rights of Ireland, he relapsed into a doze, during which the House adjourned, and he found himself without a comrade in political battle, driven to the alternative of seeking at his club, or in the precincts of the Parliamentary dining-room, for the renewal of the strength whereof he was not a little proud. Choosing the latter as the readier resource, he called for the *carte*, which an Irish waiter was prompt to lay before him. In a somewhat dissatisfied tone he said, 'No, not the fish; give me the other.' The attendant muttered unobtrusively, but loud enough to be heard, 'This is Friday, sir'; but the Major was obdurate, and, looking down the *menu*, pointed to a grilled fowl, which he desired to have with a pint of madeira. He had not long been engaged with the appropriation of the savoury viand, when the waiter approached, tendering him a visiting-card which bore the name of the priest of the parish that had done most to return him. For a moment he hesitated, and then exclaimed, 'Well, take away the devil, and show in the priest.' Capricious or wayward partizans of the old type were not to the mind of Parnell, and at next election O'Gorman was discarded. The party, to make itself felt as an effective force, must be reorganized on a different basis. To be regarded as national it must be representative of something more than the personal pluck and social good-nature that for fourscore years had alternately scoffed at the Union and scolded its authors without apparently making any impression on its stability.

Monster meetings and midnight clubs, seditious speeches in Ireland, and temporizing votes in the lobby, did little to disturb supercilious imperialism.

Whigs and Tories went and came; but in the composition of Cabinets Irishmen were seldom if ever found. Political ambition seemed to have died out in the peerage and gentry of Ireland; but if men of family and fortune would rally to Home Rule, they would be welcome as county candidates, and the reproach of religious exclusion must be diligently effaced. On the other hand, the farming and trading classes must be practically convinced of the share they would have in a College Green Parliament by men from their ranks being chosen to represent them at Westminster. One condition only was indispensable, that all should vote together.

Meanwhile circumstances unforeseen were rapidly tending to change essentially the nature and scope of the design. A succession of bad harvests had rendered the payment of high rents difficult, while the spread of railways in America and Russia, and the consequent influx of foreign produce, made them impossible. In the reality of agricultural distress, political sentiment and speculation would have been forgotten had not Parnell seized the opportunity of combining them as they had never been combined before.

Home Rule was thenceforth held out as the new way, and the only way, to pay old debts, and agrarian revolt became the order of the day. The provisions of Lord Ashbourne's Act, enabling tenants by means of advances from the Treasury to purchase their holdings, solved the riddle of existence between owners and occupiers in certain districts; and had they been sanctioned ten years earlier, they would no doubt have averted much mischief and misery. A comparatively few wealthy proprietors made important reductions of rent; but the majority of the landlords being heavily encumbered were not in a position to do so, and the winter of 1879 was in two-thirds of the country one of despair.

THE PARLIAMENT OF 1880.

Returned for Finsbury a Fourth Time—Compensation for Disturbance—Growth of Obstruction—A. M. Sullivan—Flogging in the Army—Emigration—W. E. Forster—Arrest of Parnell—Spencer Viceroy—Assassination of Cavendish—Coercion Act—Reform of Procedure—Bradlaugh—The Oaths Bill—Committee of Remonstrance—Majority of Three—Workmen's Dwellings—Government of London—Water Rate Bill—Expense of Elections—Local Dissensions.

THE Dissolution being announced on March 8, the next three weeks were everywhere spent in preparations for the coming fray. Lord Beaconsfield's manifesto spoke confidently of a renewed lease of power, denounced the policy of withdrawing troops from the colonies, which he described as the first step to Imperial disintegration, and reproached the advocates of Home Rule in Ireland with consciously promoting that purpose.

This was undoubtedly an electioneering exaggeration. Many excellent men, sincere in their loyalty to the Constitution, believed that local affairs would be better cared for by a domestic but subordinate Legislature, and were content to use the indefinite phrase of Home Rule, confident that the restoration of Grattan's Parliament was not within the sphere of practical politics, and that the Fenian promise of separation was an idle dream.

Lord Ramsay, who had been spoken of for some time as the coming representative of Finsbury, had been induced in January to stand for Liverpool, where he sought to win the Irish vote by the adoption of the elastic term tolerated, if not trusted, in Ireland, but which he found by experience was neither trusted nor tolerated on the eastern side of the Channel; and, having been defeated at the poll, he was said to be ready to resume his place as my antagonist.

The Patriotic Club were sanguine and loud on his behalf, and the Conservatives were busily canvassed by Colonel Duncan, who, in the supposed inevitable schism among Liberals, expected to win a seat for Ministers.

My experience of what might be attempted in case four candidates went to the poll led me to ask Mr. Adam, the Opposition Whip, whether it was intended to support Lord Ramsay and my old colleague, Alderman Lusk. Whom he may have consulted before answering I did not know, but his reply was distinctly in the negative, and next day a deputation from the extremists were told that on due consideration his lordship had decided not to stand. Thenceforth I was practically at ease.

Without canvass or committee I resolved to abide the fourth appeal to the judgment of the constituency, whose registered numbers, after allowance made for misnomer, absence, sickness, and death, considerably exceeded forty thousand. Many old friends doubted to the last whether the virulence of the factions, personal and political, might not prove successful in dissuading or deterring enough of old supporters from voting to allow the moderate and plausible stranger to win.

I did not pretend to answer their misgivings by numerical arguments, for which I owned that positive data were wanting, or by reference to multiplied acknowledgments of useful work done without discrimination of sect, class, or party in past years.

In each of the previous contests I was glad and grateful for Conservative support, but I had never played for it or paltered to secure it. I had from my youth upwards unswervingly advocated every civil privilege which Dissenters and Catholics had obtained, and if they cast me aside because I adhered to the Church, and refused any pledge for its overthrow, I thought their doing so would be unwise and unjust, but I would not juggle or trim.

When the testing-time came, somewhere about two-thirds of the eligible community recorded their suffrages, and about the middle of the following day I received the significant note from my leading agent in the Returning Officer's room, from which all but the officials and clerks had been excluded, 'Come at once'; and as I entered without interrupting the buzz of legal reckoning that was going on, he said in a low tone: 'You cannot be beaten now.'

Few audible words were spoken during the next hour: then the result showed that I had been returned by 15,247 votes, being nearly double the number polled for me ten years before.

Mr. Gladstone was returned for Leeds and subsequently for Midlothian, where the issue of the struggle was watched from afar with exceptional interest. The total result of the General Election was 360 Liberals, 246 Conservatives, and above 60 Home Rulers of various shades of opinion. The Caucus claimed a gain of 60 seats to the credit of their organization.

The absence of the Queen abroad delayed for some days the change of Ministers; but on resigning office on April 21, Lord Beaconsfield advised her Majesty to send for Lord Hartington, who, in concert with Lord Granville, recommended her Majesty to confide the task of forming an administration to Mr. Gladstone.

At the Academy dinner the following week he was frank in acknowledging without reserve the manner in which his former colleagues had acted in ceding to him a pre-eminence each might have justly claimed for Parliamentary services rendered during the five years he had enjoyed comparative leisure. Both resumed office with him; Lord Cowper was named Viceroy of Ireland. Lord Northbrook, Sir William Harcourt, and Mr. Chamberlain entered the Cabinet, which for the first time since the days of Addington included no Irish commoner or Irish peer. The omission excited more feeling at the time from the choice of Mr. Forster as Secretary for Ireland.

When discontent with the halting system of rule initiated by Pitt was yet unorganized, or had lapsed into slumber, it was not deemed prudent to provoke invidious comparison with the habitual treatment of Scotland, and to those who understood popular susceptibilities it seemed strange that the return of sixty Home Rulers for Ireland should have been chosen for this unfortunate experiment in administrative exclusion.

Mr. Perceval made Sir Arthur Wellesley Chief Secretary notwithstanding his recent election for Tralee; Lord Liverpool appointed Marquis Wellesley Viceroy in spite of his having been born in the City of Dublin; and Lord Grey equally disregarded the disqualification of nativity. Lord Granville found room for three great Irish proprietors in his Cabinet, and Lord Melbourne for two prominent Irish members of the House of Commons.

The victor of Waterloo had himself been Prime Minister, and when afterwards waiving official precedency to Sir R. Peel, continued to sit in his Cabinet to its close. Lord Russell's reliance in 1846 was upon three great Irish nobles as his colleagues, and upon Lord Bessborough as chief of the Irish Executive, with Sir W. Somerville as Secretary; and Palmerston, when placed at the head of affairs, laughed at the cavils that were raised at his sharing Ministerial distinction with members of the Irish nobility.

Was it meant, critics asked, to ignore henceforth such traditions, and to commit the peace and safety of an excitable community to one who was practically a stranger to all their ways of life and feeling? The Member for Bradford was not unconscious of the difficulties that beset his acceptance of a post to which he felt that 'there were strong reasons why, if possible, an Irishman should be appointed.'*

To one who in a time of unexampled exigency had had daily opportunities of knowing what the duties of that office required, it was a matter of genuine regret to see a man of Mr. Forster's energy and courage so misplaced. Without pretending to more foresight than others, I could not help fearing more painfully than they the aggravation of public mischief that was likely to ensue.

* Private letter to an Irish gentleman before accepting office, April, 1880.

In a bureau at Whitehall, his untiring industry, zest for information, freedom from petty prejudice, and shrewdness in appropriating suggestion of detail, would have had unquestioned scope for useful exercise. His bluntness in private colloquy, and his needless snubbing of deputations, would have signified little there; his reticence towards subordinates and his arrogance of tone with strangers who thought they knew much better the perplexities that had to be dealt with would have easily been forgotten. But to deal with a people, or rather with two jealous and suspicious communities engaged in life-and-death grapple, the lack of amenity, courtesy, and lightness of touch added undoubtedly to the fret and fever of the hour.

Still, so long as he could deceive himself into imagining that agrarianism could be checked by Quaker lectures on the superiority of hard work, obedience to law, and improved measures of agriculture, Irish peers and Irish peasants took little heed of him whom the Dublin mob called the Right Hon. Robinson Crusoe. It was not until his luckless attempt to gain popularity with the latter at the expense of the former, by giving tenants compensation when evicted for non-payment of rent, that Forster became the object of personal distrust by the propertied classes without gaining the confidence of the multitude.

A succession of bad harvests had caused an

accumulation of arrears of rent, especially in Munster and Connaught; and evictions, which had been previously but five hundred in the whole of Ireland, were multiplied, till in the first six months of 1880 they reached double that number, each serving as a threatening notice to every occupier in the neighbourhood.

The low fever of fear and discontent betrayed every day the tendency to delirium, social and political. The Secretary for Ireland became convinced that if nothing was done to quiet the apprehensions of the people, it would be difficult to avert dangerous disorder during the later months of the year, and he persuaded the Cabinet, though not without hesitation and misgiving, to sanction a Bill, to which he gave the title of Compensation for Disturbance, whereby the County Court Judge was enabled, at his discretion, to extend the benefit of the Land Act to cases where excessive rent could not be proved, and where heavy arrears were due. The title sounded like an alarm bell of general confiscation to come, and though the second reading was carried by 295 to 217, fifty English Liberals abstained from voting, and twenty voted against it.

In Committee the Irish Attorney General moved an amendment denying the outgoing tenant's claim to compensation where he had had permission to sell his interest in the holding.

Endless debate arose as to whether this would practically work as a reasonable limitation, and Mr. Parnell thenceforth declared his hostility to the measure.

The worst feature in the controversy was the utter uncertainty it disclosed as to what the effect would be, and I remember taking some pains to convince one of the Government that one of the greatest miseries and mischiefs in Ireland was the enactment of laws about which neither lawyers nor laymen could honestly agree. But with Mr. Forster success in his first essay at restorative legislation was a test of his being entrusted with the confidence and power for which he had stipulated as Proconsul.

Mr. Law's amendment was eventually withdrawn, substituting for it some vague terms about the offer of a 'reasonable alternative.' The prolonged efforts at modification—some with the view to expansion, and others to circumscription—had not changed the prevailing conflict of opinion on the principle of the measure, which its authors repudiated as setting a precedent, and its opponents spurned as being left-handed and deceptive. The Irish members abstained from voting either way on the third reading.

In the Upper House the Duke of Argyll vindicated his resignation of the Privy Seal on account of the measure; while Lord Derby, though endorsing his criticism, characteristically asked the

Peers, for the sake of peace, to waive their antipathy to even a temporary departure from what they deemed safe and just, and to try whether it could not be amended in Committee.

Lord Beaconsfield, on the contrary, declared that he could not agree to any of the three proposals to which they were asked to assent, and the second reading was rejected by more than two to one. The Peers likewise refused to consider a Registration Bill for Ireland, intended to assimilate the practice in all parts of the United Kingdom, upon the ground that, having been sent up late, they had not time for its consideration.

The Irish Secretary did not scruple to avow in his place his vexation and resentment at this summary rejection of both his measures of conciliation, and to anticipate the dangerous effect in the distressed and disturbed districts during the coming winter, which might lead to the adoption of much stronger measures, both of concession and coercion, than Government had hitherto attempted.

In response to this untimely prognostic of agrarian anarchy, Mr. Parnell, in addressing a great multitude at Ennis in September, enunciated the plan, already designated boycotting, whereby every man who took an evicted farm, and everyone who aided or abetted eviction, should be shunned as a leper in the fair, refused custom or sale in the market, and treated as an intruder at the altar.

Before the year was out, the contagion of this revolutionary scheme had wrapped two-thirds of the island in its paralyzing spell, and the courts established by the Land League publicly heard and determined the merits of each case as it arose.

The signal for acts of summary violence was set by the fate of Lord Mountmorres, who had incurred popular dislike by his conduct as a rigorous magistrate, and was put to death on the highway near his own home in open daylight.

Forster early proposed to suspend the Habeas Corpus Act, and to prosecute the prominent movers of the agitation. Mr. Gladstone clung to the hope that the friends of law and order would combine to suppress the tendencies to outrage, and wished to defer as long as possible the suspension of constitutional freedom; but ere Parliament reassembled in 1881, the progress of social disintegration had become more painful and palpable, and the Cabinet reluctantly authorized the introduction of a measure for the protection of life and property, whereby any person suspected of countenancing lawless proceedings might be arrested and imprisoned without trial, on the warrant of the Viceroy and the Chief Secretary.

Twenty-two nights were spent in debating its details, at the end of which it was passed by an overwhelming majority comprising Ministerialists,

Radicals, and Conservatives. But the obstruction systematically offered to repressive legislation provoked at last Speaker Brand to assert a discretionary power of terminating debate, which he had long resisted importunity to exercise, and which led to the introduction of the change of procedure of which the most prominent measure was the *clôture*.

From a seedling in the garden of Conservative schism, an object rather of curiosity to party opponents than of serious concern, obstruction spread gradually into different but receptive soil. Like the exotic bramble that, at first neglected as of no account, grew apace in some of our outlying provinces till it became difficult to know what to do with its noxious usurpation of space properly devotable to useful things, it assumed year by year more and more vexatious dimensions. The dignity of Government could not bring itself easily to take steps for its extirpation, and preferred the air of rebuke and admonition, encouraging independent surveyors of the field of business to treat its presumption with ridicule, and chop the head of its budding wherever it appeared.

No apter wit for aid of this kind was to be found among Whig Radicals than that of my valued and lamented friend the member for Southwark, who was ever ready at shortest notice to turn, without spite or malice, a mischievous proposal inside out by a happy, humorous phrase.

One night, when we had been kept out of bed till two or three o'clock by the use of the primitive expedient of alternate motions to adjourn debate, or that the Speaker do leave the chair, a young member, who had dropped in late after a long revel, not very clear in apprehension of the grave constitutional issue said to be at stake, was impressed as a fresh recruit to make the next formal motion, and being exceedingly drowsy, he could not get through the half-dozen needful words without a piteous yawn. Locke was at once on his feet, and with irresistible gravity exclaimed, 'Sir, I put it to you, and to every honourable gentleman of right feeling on either side of the House, whether the honourable gentleman is not an awful example of what a man may be brought to for want of sleep?' Within ten minutes we were all on our way home.

I cannot help recalling here another and equally effective *mot* of my learned friend. Coming in before midnight from a City dinner, where he had spent an inspiring evening, while we for our sins had to perform the protracted duty of intermittently listening to statistical sermons on the evils of alcohol, he asked me as he sat down what we were about; and seeing that from incredulity he became indignant at learning that the members for Wales had got Mr. Peter Rylands to make a vehement speech in favour of shutting up public-houses altogether. I said to him in fun that I was sure the House expected him, as the known protector of the interest of the brewers, to say a word on the other side.

Up he got, and after stating how he had spent the preceding recess in the Principality, and that in a more drunken country he never was in his life, he addressed the worthy member who had just sat down in tones of affected reproach for his new-born zeal in the cause of compulsory abstinence: 'for I declare,' he said, 'I have with my own eyes seen that honourable member within the precincts of this House—the better for drink.'

Locke used always to say, however, that no expression of his or of anyone else of his sort on the fertile theme in question compared, in the mirth it excited, with the explosion of mercantile wrath by a well-known representative of the spirit trade in one of the Munster counties. By dint of greater thrift and larger capital, Scotch distillers had found their way to compete with native rivals in various parts of Ireland; and he undertook to convince the Chancellor of the Exchequer that in his Budget he ought to impose a differential duty on whisky made on the eastern side of the Channel to protect the national producers of the article; and to persuade the House of Commons that this should be done not so much for the sake of any manufacturing profit as to guard his unsuspicious countrymen from the deleterious effects of a most deleterious compound.

The laughter with which this exposition of views and motives was received, far from daunting the mover, spurred him only to louder and more eloquent denunciation; and, rising in vehemence as he went on, he exclaimed: 'I solemnly declare that if anyone who hears me was, without thinking, to take a mouthful of that poisonous Scotch fluid, he would feel as if a torchlight procession was going down his throat.'

A. M. Sullivan, whose early loss the best men of his party most deplored, shrunk at times from the tactics of obstruction carried too far; but he felt and deprecated not the less earnestly the discourtesy they provoked. Unprofessedly, though often egregiously, it assumed the form of conversational interruption; not very loud, but when prolonged completely baffling every effort to obtain a consecutive hearing.

A recent recruit in the Celtic corps, when resolutely trying to make the grievances of his constituents known, was persistently foiled by the buzz of inattention, and especially by the chat and laughter of a noble lord and gallant gentleman sitting right opposite, who evidently thought the opportunity propitious for the interchange of social anecdote and jest.

Vainly the youthful member begged to be heard,

but the higher he raised his key the more confused became the din. At last, during a despairing pause, Sullivan rose to order and gravely asked the Speaker 'whether his honourable but inexperienced friend behind him was justified in thus persistently seeking to interrupt the conversation of the two honourable members opposite.' A general laugh and ringing cheer announced the success of his appeal, and the House was recalled to considerate good humour.

Among the various specifics for the prevalent epidemic of garrulity was a simple-looking one of a standing order, that nobody but a Minister should be allowed to make more than one motion or one speech on the same day. The babblers, of course, declared it was poison meant to destroy the life of debate; but many dumb sufferers, tired of being whipped night after night from sleep or amusement for no practical purpose, thought it a remedy well worth trying, as certain to allay the irritation caused by the same identical bores.

Being asked by Speaker Brand how I thought it would work, I observed that after all the greater number of those who abetted obstruction troubled the House very seldom, and that the offenders were a comparative few chosen for their known facility of talk to be the mouthpieces of real or supposed grievances, and some of whom, perhaps, would often be glad of an excuse to sit still.

In illustration I gave the following incident.

One evening when all but the requisite quorum were at dinner, I met in one of the corridors the Member for ——, with whose monotonous maunderings we were all too familiar, looking miserably dull and dejected, after the failure of a motion on which he had delivered 'what he called his mind' by the space of thirty-five minutes or more. In reply to a civil expression of hope that there was nothing serious the matter, he told me in plaintive tones that he was unfortunately obliged to wait until number three, and four, and perhaps five in the list came on, for he was expected to speak on every question. In general he did not mind it; but just then he was very unhappy, because he felt quite unfit for it. I could hardly help asking why, and I shall never forget his mournful answer: 'Well, indeed, for two reasons: I've lost my wife, and I have the toothache.' I owned it was a grave defect in our constitutional system that an amiable man like him, ambitious of fame, should be put in such a false position, but I could think of no other solace than the Chiltern Hundreds.

A struggle had long been waged at intervals, and with varied fortune, by men of genuine spirit and consistency, against the degrading practice that still lingered, under the sanction of the Mutiny Act, of corporal punishment in the army. Constitutional Government, sometimes supposed to have come mature into the world on the change of dynasty at the Revolution, had in reality been of slow growth in many important respects, not only in the treatment of dependencies, but in that of unequal and dissimilar classes of our own people. Government by Parliament had taken over the functions and privileges of prerogative in 1689 without defining strictly their limits or statutably ordaining how they should be exercised, and there consequently arose during the reigns of William and Anne various anomalies regarding the defensive forces of the realm by land and sea.

When withdrawn from historical inquiries into the character and influence of administrative rule by Cabinet in the last century to take part in active political life, I felt strongly impelled to promise help whenever possible to those who sought the abolition of corporal punishment in the army. The gradual abatement that had taken place in the degrading and demoralizing practice served only to confirm my disbelief in its alleged indispensability, and my hope that ere long we should see its final abandonment.

So long as the safety of the realm depended on militia, train-bands, and volunteer corps, discipline was left to the discretion of their respective officers, and summary resort to the lash was recognised as the readiest and cheapest way of enforcing subordination, as well as for checking license too apt to occur in arbitrary quarterings, onerous billetings, and requisitions of food or forage. But while these grew less than of yore, and the conditions of enlistment were gradually changed, liability of the soldier to capricious and often cruel ill usage seems to have been worsened rather than improved.

Rigorous penalties for insults or excesses were endured from fellow-countrymen without murmur or complaint; but it was otherwise when foreigners in the pay of the Crown might work their wanton will, or gratify their greed of exaction, among an unarmed people. On the other hand, discipline in garrison or camp was, after all, said to be the best security for the safety of the town; no distinction of origin could be made in military law: summary punishment for secondary offences, it was contended, was the truest humanity, and its exemplary infliction the surest guarantee of public order.

Parliament after the Revolution felt the necessity of sanctioning the power to try by courts-martial cases of mutiny or desertion within the realm; but, even in the critical state of affairs then existing, they refrained from granting any jurisdiction to military tribunals superseding the authority of the courts of law, by which all men, whether officers or soldiers, were entitled time out of mind to the judgment of their fellow-men. No one under the rank of captain was competent to sit on a court-martial formed to try a capital charge; no man on the muster-roll was to be held exempted from obedience to the ordinary tribunals, and liability to the new jurisdiction extended only to the regular army, which consisted largely of foreign troops.

The statute was passed at first for six months, but it was re-enacted every Session until the 10th of Anne without alteration. Other provisions were added with regard to mustering, billeting, impressment, and transport; but no essential change in the jurisdiction affecting the rank and file was proposed. The number of troops in pay having continued to increase, Parliament had reiterated rather than enforced its jealousy of a standing army by specifically reciting the number of officers and men whom it consented each year to arm and pay, and the practice ever since has been punctiliously observed.

In national recognition of the valour and devotion of the hosts led to victory by Marlborough from Blenheim to Bouchain, the penalty of death for disobedience to orders or neglect of duty in time of peace was struck out of the military code; but in 1716, the Cabinet affecting to ascribe to this leniency desertions to the Pretender, the merciful provision was repealed.

In 1717 the Mutiny Bill brought in by Ministers differed from all that had preceded it. 'The system of discipline became in effect a source of rigour theretofore unknown.'* New articles of

* Clode, 'Military and Martial Law,' p. 49.

war might be made from time to time under the sign-manual, to which courts-martial in future should give effect; and provisions were introduced which it has been truly said 'stamped upon our military code that penal character which made it a reproach to an Englishman to be a soldier.' Capital punishment was authorized for every act of disobedience or neglect of duty, with discretion to award such other punishment as a court might deem fit.*

A general court-martial was to have for a president a field-officer, and was to consist of none but those who held commissions; and where the offence was punishable by death, they were to be sworn, the concurrence of a majority not less than nine being required to give validity to the sentence. Private soldiers were to be still subject to the civil tribunals. It was not directly proposed to do away with amenability to the ordinary courts of the realm; but when anyone was acquitted by court-martial, before civil proceedings could take effect, the acquittal might be pleaded in bar. Other conditions were introduced for the first time expanding materially the scope of military law. Subordinate offences not involving punishment affecting life or limb—immoralities, misbehaviour, or neglect of duty—were made punishable at the discretion of courts whose members need not be sworn, or hold

* Clode, 'Military and Martial Law,' p. 51.

higher rank than that of ensign, and its jurisdiction was extended by anticipation to whatever might be included in additional Articles of War.

This was, in effect, to establish in time of peace a summary power to inflict corporal punishment without limit on the rank and file for offences often incapable of definition; and to exonerate all those who might be acquitted by such tribunals from liability to be sued in courts of common law.

The change thus introduced took away hitherto unquestioned rights from freemen of the humbler ranks in life, and fixed a deep gulf of caste between them and the privileged few bearing arms. Objecting, as many men of conscience did, to large and permanent additions to the standing army for what they called Hanoverian purposes, they organized resistance to the measure that well-nigh sealed its fate.

Walpole, dwelling on the proposed increase of corporal and capital punishment when there was neither invasion nor insurrection to be feared, exclaimed, with passionate energy, 'Those that will have blood must have blood!' and Shippen lamented his Majesty's unacquaintance with the language and principles of the constitution, which led him to sanction claims of executive power suitable for the meridian of Germany, not of England.

When the cry was raised, 'To the Tower!'

Walpole would have made a way of escape for his Tory ally by an ingenious explanation of his words. But Shippen refused to equivocate or retract, and was sent to spend the rest of the Session in the recognised prison of politicians. Two hundred and forty-seven supported Ministers, while two hundred and twenty-nine sided against them.

In the Upper House eminent men of both parties objected that by conferring an unlimited right of adding to the Articles of War, the power of the Executive was greatly increased without control, to which it was answered that the Articles might be inserted in the Bill; and, if thereafter extended, they could be inserted on the renewal of the statute from year to year. Devonshire, Townshend, and Argyll, Oxford, Harcourt, and Strafford, urged that no man should suffer any punishment except for offences explicitly named in the statute. But this limitation was not inserted until 1748, under the advice of Lord Hardwicke.

An objection of still wider scope was raised to the constitution of regimental or summary courts-martial in time of peace, for the trial of misdemeanours or breaches of discipline. In these tribunals subaltern officers were declared capable of acting without being sworn, while an unlimited power of corporal punishment, imprisonment, or other penalties was given them.

Offences against person or property of either soldier or civilian were made cognizable by courts-martial, unless civil proceedings were taken within eight days, and obvious facilities were created for screening delinquents until the time had expired wherein they could be made amenable to the civil power. Clauses were introduced subjecting any officer to be cashiered for refusing to surrender a culprit to the civil magistrate; but, on the other hand, acquittal by court-martial was in all cases made a bar to proceedings before the ordinary tribunals.*

Plausible assurances were given by Sunderland and Stanhope that no fear need be entertained that tyrannical additions to the Articles of War would ever be suggested by so wise or benign a Prince as George I., or that sentences needlessly severe would be sanctioned by him. But the question was in reality not so much of danger from despotic temper on the part of the Crown, but of overbearing or oppressive treatment of the soldiery by inexperienced and ill-conditioned officers of a different rank and class in life clothed with arbitrary power, and called upon casually to exercise it without appeal or responsibility.

No verbal amendments in Committee silenced independent opposition, and when carried by 91 to 77 votes, a protest against the measure was subscribed by Devonshire, Argyll, Rutland,

* 5 George I.

Oxford, Archbishop Dawes, Harcourt, Strafford, Belhaven, Townshend, Dartmouth, Guilford, Willoughby de Broke, Anglesea, Scarsdale, Boyle, Northampton, Islay, Bishops Robinson, Trelawney, Bisse, Atterbury, and Smallridge, and twenty other peers: 'because the exercise of martial law in time of peace, with power to inflict punishment in life and limb, not only for mutiny or desertion, but for ordinary misdemeanour and immorality, has never been in any previous reign without special consent of Parliament, but has always been opposed and condemned as repugnant to Magna Charta and the fundamental rights of a free people.'*

The unlimited discretion in the infliction of secondary punishments for sins and shortcomings by the rank and file, once adopted in the form of an annual Act, soon came to be regarded as inevitable. Despite the pledges given, new offences, actual or colourable, were from time to time added to those said to be indispensable for the maintenance of subordination.

The inequality of sentences according to the temper of more or less inexperienced judges, and according to the equally certain inequality of physical capacity to endure torture, became the normal and accepted condition of things. It was, unfortunately, but the exaggerated reflection of the anomalous state of the criminal law under

* Lords' Journals.

an uncodified multitude of statutes, each of which was passed to put down, as was said, a particular crime growing prevalent, without regard to what else in the name of law existed already.

Before the close of the century crapulous cruelty or ruthless youth indulged in the privilege on the magisterial bench, or in the barrack-room, of what one of the greatest commanders of our own time has branded as the 'ferocity of punishment.'

In 1792, Sergeant Grant, who had borne an excellent character as a man and a soldier, was sentenced to a thousand lashes for the good-natured though inexcusable fault of assisting two drummers to enlist in the East India Company's service for better pay; and when appeal was made to the Court of Common Pleas to interpose, Chief Justice Loughborough pronounced no censure or regret at the enormity in refusing the application as beyond the function of the Court.

The plea always urged for resort to the lash for offences against discipline was the reckless and often desperate character of men in the rank and file. Enlistment for a long term of years, with liability to be sent on foreign service, was generally unpopular. Youths respectably brought up were not easily caught by the licentious talk of the crimp, but, confused and ashamed at having got into a scrape, the resource that readily suggested itself was to go for a soldier.

To a great extent, the recruiting sergeant relied upon making up the number wanted from inmates of the gaol, who were glad to change their unlucky plight for a red coat and a knapsack.

And hardly any attempt was made during the remainder of the century to mitigate the hardships of the soldier's condition by modifying the terms of the Mutiny Act. Increased severity of punishment was vindicated by the example of foreign armies, and as there was no compulsory enlistment, it was continually said that the renegade or the poacher knew what he was incurring as liability when he took the King's shilling.

Sir Charles Napier, in his admirable work on Military Law, recounted the scenes he had witnessed during his earlier days of service: 'I then frequently saw six, seven, eight, nine hundred and even a thousand lashes ordered by regimental courts-martial, and generally every lash inflicted, and I often saw the unhappy victim of such barbarous work brought out from the hospital three and four times to receive the remainder of his punishment—too severe to be borne, without danger of death, at one flogging.'

At length the conscience of the community awoke to a certain sense of shame and remorse. With the consummation of victory, there came a sense of mercy, if not compunction, over the popular mind.

The habitual resort to the lash as an essential

means of education had brought most of those who sat in either House to regard with a shrug of indifference tales of the barrack or the camp. But in 1811 Sir Francis Burdett, then representing Westminster, drew attention to the instance of a private in the Lancashire militia who had been flogged for complaining of the quality of the bread served out to the regiment, and for writing a song, and detailed numerous instances of cruelty in the name of military discipline under the Mutiny Act, which he moved the Commons to address the Crown to prevent in future. He found but ten supporters, and repeated his proposal in the following session.

The Duke of York, then Commanding-in-Chief, thereupon issued a memorandum to restrain the immoderate use of the cat. A soldier in garrison at Dinapore was sentenced in 1825 to 1,900 lashes, notwithstanding. But in 1829 district courts-martial were restrained from ordering more than 300; and in 1832 regimental courts were restricted to 200. In 1849 the number capable of being inflicted by any court-martial was reduced to fifty; but in the colonies and India the progress of mitigation was more tardy.

In the Parliament of 1865, my friend Sir Arthur Otway, seconded by Major Anson, had carried by a majority of one a resolution for its entire cessation in time of peace; but on the following day Sir John Pakington, then Secretary for War, told us that the Government could not submit to a decision come to by so small a preponderance of votes, and that they would persist in Committee in retaining the clause of the annual Act to which we objected.

We failed to induce the leaders of Opposition to take issue on the point, and our sanguine anticipations were for the time doomed to disappointment, that the degrading and deterring system of punishment for all manner of offences, whether serious or trivial, should be maintained in our military code after it had been abandoned by most of the States of Christendom.

My friend Neate was particularly impatient that what he justly deemed public opinion should be thus over-ruled at the instigation of one who possessed such little weight even with his own party in legislative matters, and whose ambition to shine as an exquisite of fashion provoked, if it did not justify, my friend in dubbing him 'that gilt-edged and diamond edition of man.'

But the honourable and gallant Member for Chatham was neither daunted nor discouraged, and, regardless of the changes of party, he persisted in putting what might be called probing questions to each successive head of the War Office.

Meanwhile, a new trouble in Parliamentary procedure arose, in the shape of persistent obstruction to the necessary Bills of the year when in Committee. Mr. Parnell and his friends availed themselves of the tempting opportunity, and became the inappeasable propagandists for the abolition of the lash.

Memories were still too fresh with them of the hateful use that had been made, not only unlawfully, but according to law, of that barbarous weapon of power in Ireland, and they readily sought for sympathy and approval in a wider circle for their assertion day by day of the principles and the policy of reform in military discipline.

Officialism on either side of the table scoffed at the pretended humanity of the 'political roughs' below the gangway, and every jackanapes and toady of the Horse Guards might be heard declaiming against the suspected Fenianism that would render all subordination in the army impossible.

It would have been the merest affectation in those who, ten years before, had for an hour snatched the cat-o'-nine-tails from the grasp of the drummer, and who ever since had hoped against hope that the maximum of forty-nine strokes to which the punishment was said to have been reduced would be wholly swept away, silently or unmoved to note the unexpected support of their cause; but while they doubted to what the new movement would tend, fear crept into Council, Ministers began to mutter, and by degrees to articulate that they were disposed to reconsider the whole subject. Lord Hartington moved that 'no Bill for the discipline or regulation of the army will be satisfactory to the House which provides for the retention of corporal punishment for military offences.'

This was the knell of doom to the dear old system of flagellation, and when, in the next Session, the Gladstone Cabinet had been restored, our leader on the question, Sir A. Otway, pressed the new Secretary at War, Mr. Childers, whether effect was to be given to the resolution, the answer was that it was intended to bring in a Bill, then in course of preparation, on the subject which would be acceptable to Parliament and the country.

It was no secret that the Government had a good deal to contend against in the shape of Horse Guards prejudice against the change, and that high authorities declared it would prove fatal to the discipline of the army. But it was legitimately deemed right, on the part of independent members of the House who had been its advocates, to accept as a pledge what had been stated of Ministerial intentions, and the result fully justified the confidence thus shown.

After a few months, during which the odious practice was held in abeyance within the United Kingdom, an end was put by statute to its resuscitation in time of peace. And if something was left unascertained and unasserted with reference to military penalties in Crown colonies or garrisons, one may safely trust to the progress of humaner sentiments proving ere long operative there also.

Those of us who cherished the hope that analogous tendencies to indulge in the arbitrary infliction of bodily pain as the penalty of dulness, idleness, or indecorum in reformatories, public schools, and gaols had been stunned by what we had done have been warned of late that an attempt to revive the condemned system is about being made in different directions.

The difficulties of maintaining discipline are doubtless great, and those of effectually deterring by example from the commission of petty offences against property or public order are confessedly greater. But nothing can justify in the mind of those who helped to snatch the instrument of torture from military hands a recurrence to the maxims and practices of the last century, or to the resistance offered to the reasoning for their abrogation.

So long as the tyrannical sense of power can be gratified at will by its brutal exercise, public law and public opinion will have need to keep a firm rein upon its neck.

The history of all races in all times attests the miserable truth that the irresponsible infliction of pain on the weak and helpless is a sensual instinct, disguised though it may be under the ceremonies and the words of duty, to which Parliament and the press ought to show no toleration. Classic and ecclesiastical annals are full of boastful triumphs of irresponsible rigour; but who will supply the record of wanton or wrongful sufferings inflicted, and for which, from the very nature of things, no *amende* has ever been made or compensation rendered?

Years have passed since it was my good fortune to aid in obtaining the obliteration from our military code of a practice which, to the last, the highest authorities declared indispensable; but while I have never ceased to look back with satisfaction on the change thus effected from a civilian's or a jurist's point of view, I deem it a great pleasure to have recently learned, from the lips of one who stands so high in national confidence as Lord Wolseley, that the army is in a variety of ways more amenable to discipline and better conducted than it was under the government of the lash.

At a dinner given by Count Vicelli at the Orleans Club to Prince Czartoryski, M. Gavard, Professor Birkbeck, and others, the life of the company was Monckton Milnes, who recalled how Bishop Wilberforce used to heap reproach on the way in which Palmerston dispensed Church patronage: 'If he had lived long enough he would have made Jowett a Bishop, then some friend of Satan, and then one of the Cowpers.'

Arthur Kinnaird, who was present, laughed, but protested, and asked if he thought Melbourne did better. Milnes disclaimed being a judge of ecclesiastical merits, and said he did not know what the Bishop of Winchester might have thought of their comparative orthodoxy. 'But I happen to know,' he said, 'of a proof given by Melbourne of resistance to extreme pressure, both political and personal, in favour of a most distinguished adherent, whom he refused to make a Bishop on the ground of having flogged excessively one of his pupils for an offence which it was afterwards discovered he had never committed.'

He was at the head of a great school, and in private the friend of several of the most distinguished and influential Whigs at a very critical time; and when the question was asked several years later why he had never obtained a mitre, the cause was stated to a Select Committee of the Lords in circumstantial terms.

Lord Clarendon, who had never heard of the incident before, pooh-poohed the story as incredible; 'whereupon,' said Milnes, 'I said, "There is present one who cannot be mistaken about the fact, and who may, if he will, verify the statement."'

A Most Reverend member of the Committee thus appealed to expressed his regret that the affair had not been allowed to pass into oblivion, but he could not deny that on the complaint of the parent of the ill-used boy the mastership of the institution had been changed by the trustees.

In Committee on the Irish Land Bill in 1881, a clause enabling commissioners to facilitate and aid emigration of families from overcrowded districts gave rise to much discussion. Lord Randolph Churchill criticised its terms as too vague for practical application, and said it would be contemned by the public at large as a mere blind to conceal infirmity of purpose.

Mr. O'Donnell and Mr. Biggar denounced the purpose of the clause as committing the House once more to the error of supposing that Ireland was over-peopled, and Mr. Healy feared that if by such means the population were perceptibly reduced, a pretext would be afforded for diminishing the representation of Ireland at Westminster. In previous years the subject of an organized system for enabling families to exchange their rack-rented farms at home for farms of virgin land at a mere nominal rent in the colonies had engaged much of my attention; but I shared the views of men of experience in more than one of our dependencies, that without some recognised centre at home where accurate information could from time to time be had regarding the varying conditions of employment and trade in places widely remote from one another, it would be vain to expect that heads of families, or even venturous young men, would invest their little savings in so hazardous an enterprise as the abandonment of home without any reasonable certainty of being able to find a living at the other side of the globe.

The wise and humane provision of an information office established by Lord Russell when Secretary of State had, through short-sighted parsimony, been suppressed. Until it was revived, I was persuaded that nothing effectual could be hoped for in the direction indicated in the Bill.

Far from assenting to the suggestion that whatever sum Government might contemplate giving as a grant in aid ought to be placed at the disposal of the Poor Law Department, and doled out at its discretion to such Boards of Guardians as came to it deferentially for help, I made free to tell the House what had befallen a former blunder on the same lines some years before.

When some of us had, in a time of exceptional want of work, urged the Government to subsidize cheap trains of emigrant ships across the ocean, the head of the department was so ill-advised as to issue a circular to Boards of Guardians making the offer in question.

I confessed to having been one of the Colonial Institute who, not having the fear of Gwydyr House before our eyes, felt it to be an imperative duty to issue forthwith a counter-manifesto, warning the local authorities not to be lured into acting as recommended, for the best of all possible reasons—that we had actual and absolute knowledge that if they sent their poor, debilitated, or damaged people across the sea, in order that local rates at home might be relieved of the cost of their maintenance, the unhappy creatures would everywhere be refused and sent back as unfit and inadmissible in the character of settlers, coming, as they would do, with the brand of pauperism upon them, and that, without any fault of their own, their last state would be worse than the first. Red-tape might exclaim, How presumptuous and disloyal to centralized infallibility such a proceeding! but our broadside silenced that of the office, for within a fortnight the misleading circular was withdrawn.

Mr. Forster did not hesitate to accept substantially the recommendations contained in my amendment, and later on I had the satisfaction of voting in supply once more for a modest but sufficient charge to provide and maintain an information office, where intending emigrants are now able to learn what the rate of wages and the price of food and the letting value of land are in every quarter of the world.

A cessation of boycotting and violence followed the passing of the Protection Act, and for some weeks its author cherished the hope that the fear of its enforcement would permanently check the tendency to crime. The provisions of the promised Land Bill, though still undefined, must, it was thought, tend in the same direction. But agitation recovered its spirits and opposition its energy, when week after week and month after month the powers of arrest and imprisonment without trial granted as indispensable were held in reserve, while the peasantry gradually became impressed with the belief that they were only meant as threats and warnings, and would not actually be used at all.

The local struggle between owners and occupiers began afresh, and the constabulary often confessed their inability to detect the instruments or the sources of instigation. Prædial terrorism muttered within its teeth, and injuries to cattle, attacks on isolated houses and assaults on defenceless individuals on the highway, were followed by open resistance to legal proceedings for distraint or dispossession. To avert the loss of life too likely to ensue in these affrays, the police were enjoined not to use their arms except in self-defence, and even then to load with small shot instead of ball-cartridge. The suggestion was ascribed to the Chief Secretary, and drew upon him the spiteful nickname of *Buckshot* Forster.

I happened during the autumn to have before me for the purposes of historical research letters of Lord Wellesley in 1823 and 1824, describing confidentially the deplorable state of things then existing in many parts of Ireland, arising out of quarrels about tithes and rent; and it filled one with despondency, almost with despair, to recognise the similarity, if not identity, of the miserable details after half a century of legislative changes, meant for the most part well, but marred continually by being yielded, not given.

To avert civil war emancipation had been avowedly surrendered at discretion: educational, municipal, and electoral equality had bit by bit been extorted, and finally the Anglican Establishment had been swept away at the sound of the explosion at Clerkenwell.

When an ignorant Jack-in-office once affected to recount some of what he called splendid proofs of justice and generosity, I heard an eloquent son of Curran exclaim in a paroxysm of impatience, 'You never granted even emancipation; you dropped it with a curse!' And the curse of unwilling, bit by bit, and always too late yielding has unhappily clung on to Ministry after Ministry, and from one generation to another.

At the end of June agrarian crimes in the quarter had risen to 961, as against 245 in the corresponding period of the previous year; and the Protection Act, notwithstanding the arrest of Mr. Dillon and of certain obscure agents of the League, was confessedly about to prove a failure unless the entire scope of its operation were changed.

The passing of the second Land Act in July,

which empowered judicial commissioners to review and revise contracts between landlord and tenant and to reduce rents that, with reference to current prices, seemed too high, was not achieved without difficulty; but a belief which I confess I shared, that not only the great landlords, but the bulk of the resident gentry, deprecated its rejection, gave the Government a great majority in the Commons, and led the Lords to refrain from materially altering its tenor. Another but brief lull ensued, and it was not until October that, at the instance of Mr. Parnell, the truce between contending forces was brought to an end.

The Member for Cork took occasion at a great assembly in Dublin to set its statutable menaces at defiance. The agrarian movement became every day more formidable, and the idea seemed to have struck root, even in Ulster, that, if long enough sustained, it would end in what was significantly termed the disestablishment of rent. This consummation in prospect furnished for the first time a commissariat of the most practical and complete nature to the political organization for a repeal of the Union.

The popular leaders, saying they could not be sure of the practical working of the Land Act, and not choosing to bank down the fire of agitation, but for the lurid glare of which it never would have been seen, advised their followers not to become claimants in the new courts until test suits proved what the course of decisions would be, and meanwhile to maintain their former attitude in all respects.

Forster was incensed at this attempt to exercise a suspensive veto on the new law, and he began to look for further powers of despotic repression. The Quaker-Cromwell was no doubt bent, if possible, on stifling without bloodshed all open questioning of authority, but he was determined, come what might, to put resistance down wherever its threats were heard or violence was seen.

Would the Land Act beat the Land League, and save Government from more stringent coercion? He had little, almost no, hope that it would; but it might be well to wait a fortnight longer, when the Land Courts would be at work. He did not think they could wait longer, if they were to act at all.

If Parliament were called together to pass a new Bill suppressing the Land League, and declaring illegal any combination to resist a legal debt, [English] Radicals and working men would resist the passing of any such statute; the delay would be great, and, if passed, no jury would convict under it. The League would change its name, members would address their constituents, all political meetings would have to be prevented, and the orders to boycott would be given and obeyed without meetings.

A renewed struggle for rent in November was impending, and if Ministers were to paralyze the Land League at all, they must do it before then.*

Of these perplexities the public could but surmise the nature; but an unusual assembling of the Cabinet justified the solicitude with which every letter from Ireland was laden. The forces contending for mastery seemed to await a signal for decisive encounter, and the bravest held his breath for a time.

Unconscious of what was awaiting him, Mr. Parnell, by a speech in Dublin, exceeding in bitterness of reproach and insult all he had previously uttered, palpably, in the judgment of the law officers of the Crown, furnished incitement to disorder and sedition.

The Commander of the Forces was alone consulted by the Chief Secretary as to the means of striking a sudden and stunning blow; and having obtained the sanction of the Cabinet,† he telegraphed to Sir Thomas Steele the pre-arranged word 'Proceed.'

In a few hours several of the leaders were arrested and committed to Kilmainham Prison;‡ and the fact was announced by the Premier at a great dinner in the City as the proof of his pledge that 'the resources of civilization were not exhausted.'

On the morrow the press and the public

* To Mr. Gladstone, October 2, 1881.

† October 12, 1881. ‡ October 13, 1881.

hastened to the conclusion that the anti-social movement was paralyzed, if not crushed. But in a few days there appeared the memorable 'No Rent' manifesto, which rendered the quarrel more inveterate than ever.

Without waiting for another meeting of the Cabinet, Forster issued a proclamation suppressing the Land League, whose treasurer, Mr. Egan, with his books and funds, made his escape to France. The incarcerated members were exempted from all the ordinary penalties of imprisonment. They were suffered to confer, to receive visitors, write to their friends, and Mr. Parnell was allowed to attend the obsequies of a relative on his parole. But in proportion as public agitation was suppressed, secret societies became more active.

Towards the end of April rumours prevailed that the Cabinet generally desired once more to try what could be done by conciliation in Ireland and a mitigation of coercion. Lord Cowper was known to be weary of his thankless task, but Mr. Forster affected no disposition to relax the system he had arrogantly insisted upon as indispensable. Negotiations had been opened with the imprisoned members through Captain O'Shea, who led Mr. Chamberlain and others to depend upon their using their personal influence to repress agrarian violence on their being set at liberty.

The details of the singular affair have been

variously given, and need not be recounted; but it is evident that by degrees Mr. Forster became aware that his advice no longer swayed his colleagues as to what should be done, and when Mr. Parnell offered that a well-known agent of the League named Sheridan, hitherto believed to be engaged in conspiracy to outrage, should be employed for the purpose of restraining crime, he determined to resign.

On the Home Secretary's announcement that Mr. Davitt had been a second time released from Portland, the question was pointedly asked whether the 'No Rent' manifesto had been withdrawn; but to this Mr. Gladstone refused to give any other answer than that important information had been received as to the future intentions of the Land League.

Forster had turned down the straight collar of a Friend when combating the cause of the North against Gladstone, and had conformed in many things he never learned to like when first in office; but in the main he was inconvertible. Two years of what ought to have been experience of the difficulties of Irish government had untaught him none of his old invincible prejudices that extreme poverty was the foundation of the agitation wherewith he had failed to cope. He might as well have believed, and acted on the belief, that the seaweed left to perish on the strand was the real cause of the storm.

Talking once to O'Connell about the misery and shame of agrarianism, which in his heart he loathed, though he dared not upbraid, I dropped some expression indicative of a similar error, and he replied, with a melancholy smile: 'There is no danger in poverty; it is the snug, saucy, and venturous youth of the farmer class that plot and perpetrate all the prædial mischief.'

But all Forster's belongings and his bringing up led him to measure physical good and evil by the one standard of money, and he clung to the last to the conviction that if he could only feed enough of the pauperised, and fine enough of those he called 'village ruffians,' the troubled land would subside into prosperity. He had had his opportunity, and had used it with an ineffable egotism, which had concentrated upon him a degree of hatred which his executive colleagues at Dublin hardly shared. Hence in no slight degree the versatile implacability with which his life was sought by the Invincible Brotherhood, and hence the anxiety of his Ministerial colleagues to let him drop as a broken staff, lest it should pierce their hands.

Lord Cowper, tired of being ignored, asked to be relieved from his thankless office, and on the 1st of May, Forster, becoming painfully conscious that what he called his policy of repression was about to be relaxed, if not reversed, requested to be relieved of his charge. The House was crowded on the 4th of May to hear his explanation, for the details of which, at his discretion, the Queen had granted leave. I happened to sit near him, and marked, I cannot say with sympathy, but with intense interest, his attempt to justify himself without impeaching his late colleagues. He bore himself, I must say, with manliness and dignity, confessing that he had been—he did not say warped or wheedled, but that was what he evidently meant, into recognising the preliminaries of the Kilmainham Treaty; and when he came to the point where he must acknowledge or repudiate reliance on lawbreakers without any pledge that they would in future obey the law, he urged the Government not to buy obedience, nor to attempt any blackmail arrangement. A majority on both sides quivered with emotion as he recounted the three conditions upon which he would have agreed to the liberation of the suspects, who were detained for public safety, not for personal punishment: That they would not again set up their own law against the law of the realm; restoration of general order and quiet; and fresh powers of repression given to the Government. But none of these was attainable; and when he was required to recognise the active participation of Sheridan, a notorious conspirator, who for some time had in various disguises been eluding the police, and whose aid was now to be relied on to repress what he had theretofore been employed in blowing into flame, he owned that he regretted having ever seemed to sanction the negotiation.

With the reappointment of Lord Spencer as Viceroy, with Lord Frederick Cavendish for his Secretary, the belief spread that a new chapter was about to open in the troubled history of Ireland, and that with the operation of the Land Courts peace was about to be restored. On Friday evening, when the House adjourned, this was the prevalent feeling with most of us; and next day having been fixed for the re-opening of Epping Forest, a great many were glad of an excuse so loyal for a long day's enjoyment out of politics and in fresh air.

The morning came, and unusual crowds thronged every approach to the ancient wood, which, having been allowed to fall somewhat into decay, had been cleared and brightened by every art and phantasy of arboriculture, and rendered in every way a fitting scene for the first out-of-door ceremonial the widowed Sovereign had been induced to take part in. The weather was signally propitious. Everyone seemed to partake of the enjoyment, and the sanguine whispered one to another, 'Surely the winter of our discontent is passed.'

Before sundown, those of us who had reached town heard at the clubs that the telegraph from

Dublin announced the reception of the new Lord-Lieutenant as having been one of unbroken welcome.

There was a dinner at the Admiralty, and a numerous assembly after. Forster, accompanied by his daughter, had hardly reached the anteroom when a dreadful whisper reached him of the tragedy that an hour before had been enacted within eyeshot of the windows of the Viceregal residence in the Phœnix Park, and Sir W. Harcourt, taking Lord Hartington aside, communicated to him the contents of the telegram just received, that his brother and the Under-Secretary, Mr. Burke, had been assassinated.

Amid the grief and horror that ensued, the Cabinet hastened to reverse their immature policy of compromise; and, denying technically that any treaty had been made the basis of releasing the Kilmainham prisoners, they proceeded to fill up the vacated posts and to bring in an extension of the Coercion Act, with additionally stringent clauses. The subsequent discussion of the provisions of the Prevention Act occupied many weeks, and ended in a sitting of thirty hours, during which the Chairman of Ways and Means, Mr. Playfair, named and reported twenty-five Irish members as guilty of persistent obstruction, for which they were suspended for the day. In thirty-one divisions there was never a minority exceeding forty, and seldom above half that number.

Mr. Bright and Mr. Chamberlain, addressing their constituents, took their full share of Ministerial responsibility for what had been done; but the inevitable rebound of agrarian discontent followed the repressive blow which for a brief gasp was supposed to be effectual. Outrage of every description increased, and the failure of the Protection Act, as administered by Mr. Forster, grew obvious.

The Premier, at Hawarden, dwelt chiefly on the embarrassment to progress caused by obstruction. Like disorder in Ireland, it had been scotched, not killed, by resort to methods hitherto regarded as outside the pale of constitutionalism; and Speaker Brand told his constituents at Lewes that he did not himself fear the old liberty of speech being compromised by the adoption of reasonable modifications of debate.

During the last days of the year the *Times* published three letters of mine on the reform of procedure, which, when republished as a volume, were dedicated by permission to the Speaker. Without seeking party support or provoking party suspicion, it seemed to me possible to suggest changes for the devolution of legislative work to great committees chosen at the beginning of each Session, with due reference to the person and place, capacity and business.

Instead of the one old engine groaning and toiling, and often failing to do an overgrown amount of work, we might have five or six simultaneously and proportionately occupied in weaving and clipping, tinting and finishing, what were termed laws. The judges were loud in their complaints of the hurried, clumsy, and obscure wording of each annual batch of statutes. Was it not time to try a more methodical and intelligible way of Act-of-Parliament-making?

When England was but a parish realm, and Parliament met only now and then for a few weeks, there might have been no harm in the rule that every line of every clause of every Bill should be put to the vote of the whole House in Committee, not because half the members came at nine in the forenoon and sat till three in order to perform this duty, but that a sufficient number (small enough sometimes) could generally be got together for the purpose. But now when three kingdoms, with five-and-thirty millions of people, most of them wanting something done to make their condition happier—to say nothing of half of Asia for a possession, colonies without stint, and an undeveloped empire somewhere, as Voltaire said, in the direction of the North Pole—every year demanded legislative care, it was a mere superstition to talk of the indispensable necessity of carrying every measure through Committee of the whole House.

Not once in the week did St. Stephen's contain for an hour the bulk, or the half, or the quarter of its members when engaged in that most unsatisfactory and generally unintelligible business. But let each member have a chance of understanding and voting on one-sixth of the work in which his constituents were concerned, and exempt him from the liability of being drawn or driven into voting on the other five-sixths about which he knew nothing whatever, and we should, by the mere rule of the distribution of labour, be able to give a better account of ourselves at the end of each Session. And then as to obstruction, even a Parnellite or a member of the Fourth Party could not, after all, be in more than one place at a time, so that his factious capacities would be cut down by five-sixths, while the total output of Parliamentary hewing and clearing would be essentially improved.

I had no end of letters, complimentary and encouraging, about my plan, but it only found favour so far in the eyes of our rulers that two Grand Committees, one for trade and one for law, were resolved on by way of experiment; and because, I suppose, each of them succeeded admirably, the expedient has been allowed no further to go, and we are again said to be entering into the cloud of obstruction.

The *clôture* had attractions which no other expedient had for those who had often felt the burden of getting through the business of the year, or the vexation of having to abandon for want of time half that they had hoped to carry; and after much debate the resource, borrowed from the United States and France, was carried by 318 to 279, among whom were a few Liberals.

When Parliament met in 1880, Mr. Bradlaugh had presented himself, and in a written claim desired to be allowed to affirm instead of taking the oath of allegiance, which certain Dissenters were by statute permitted to do. Speaker Brand declined to determine the question, and referred it to the judgment of the House. Lord F. Cavendish, as Secretary to the Treasury, moved for a Select Committee to examine the statutes and precedents and to report their interpretation to the House. By a majority of one they decided that the junior Member for Northampton, not professing himself a member of any Nonconformist communion, could not claim the benefit of the exceptional Acts.

Next day Mr. Bradlaugh came to the table and offered to take the oath, notwithstanding the decision of a judge in a recent trial at law that, in consequence of his public disavowal of any religious sense of obligation, he could not in legal proceedings be allowed to do so, and his letter in the *Times* of the same day volunteering the notice that he felt no religious obligation involved by complying with the traditional form. Sir Drummond Wolff moved that Parliament should act in accordance with this decision, and refuse to permit him to go through a form which he had publicly declared was not binding on his conscience.

Mr. Gladstone advised instead the appointment of a Committee to inquire into the competency of the House on the subject, and, the amendment being carried, the Committee reiterated the ruling of the court of law. Mr. Labouchere then moved that his colleague be allowed to affirm, and was defeated on an amendment of Sir Hardinge Giffard by 275 to 230, 30 Liberals voting in the majority. Mr. Bradlaugh took his seat, notwithstanding, the following day within the bar, and on being ordered by the Speaker to withdraw, refused until removed by force.

The business of the House having been greatly retarded by the frequent recurrence of the controversy, the Prime Minister carried a resolution to the effect that everyone returned as duly elected should be allowed to affirm, subject to any liability he might incur by statute.

Next Session Mr. Bradlaugh spoke and voted frequently, and suits were brought to recover the penalties thus incurred, amounting to £45,000. On appeal, Judges Baggallay, Lush, and Bramwell affirmed the decision of the court below against him. A new writ was moved for Northampton, and Mr. Bradlaugh was again returned. He then presented himself at the table to take the oath, and in defence of his claim was permitted to address the House from the bar.

After some hours' debate it was resolved, by 208 against 175, that he could not be sworn.

Mr. Gladstone, when subsequently appealed to, threw the responsibility of advising the House on the Leader of the Opposition, on the ground that, having been himself outvoted on a question of procedure, he could not be expected to undertake to guide the majority as Leader.

In one of the subsequent attempts in 1882 to induce the House to admit him, Mr. Bradlaugh repeated from a written copy the terms of the oath, and kissed a Testament which he took from his pocket. Sir Stafford Northcote, treating this as an insult to the dignity of the House, carried a resolution that he should in future be excluded from its precincts. Regardless of this inhibition, he insisted on sitting and voting in a division on February 22, when 291 against 83 ordered his expulsion, and a new writ was issued accordingly. Lord Hartington, Sir H. James, Sir T. Brassey, and Mr. Goschen voted in the majority. Mr. Gladstone, Mr. Fawcett, and Mr. Childers did not vote. The Irish members, both Radical and Tory, were for exclusion. Bradlaugh was again re-elected.

The Speaker having ruled, on a question asked regarding the previous vote of expulsion, that its efficacy had expired in consequence of the fresh re-election, Sir S. Northcote, to prevent a renewal of the disorderly scene, moved that the Member for Northampton be refused access to the House during the remainder of the Parliament. The Premier objected that this was an aggressive, not a defensive act, for which he could not vote; but on Mr. Labouchere offering an assurance that his colleague would not renew his former attempt in the hope that Government would bring in a Bill to put an end to the controversy, Mr. Gladstone intimated the willingness of Government to consider how such a measure could be framed. The prohibitory resolution was then carried by a majority of fifteen.

At the commencement of the Session of 1883 the Member for Northampton offered through his colleague, Mr. Labouchere, to take the affirmation in the form that Dissenters were allowed to take it in certain cases: and thereupon a Bill was proposed by Government to substitute a general affirmation in all cases, instead of an oath.

In the debate which arose on the motion for leave to bring in the Bill,* I stated at some length the reasons which obliged many men of opposite politics to refuse their assent.

The Bill of the Attorney-General, consisting of a single clause, offered to everyone entering the Legislature the option of making an affirmation instead of taking an oath, and would, if construed retrospectively, have made good Mr. Bradlaugh's claim.

* March 20, 1883. Bill thrown out May 3.

Sir Henry James offered to bring up a clause in Committee denying its applicability *ex post facto*, and stating as precedent the section in the Catholic Emancipation Act of 1829 which refused Mr. O'Connell the seat for Clare to which he had been elected the year before.

The technical analogy was strictly correct, but in all other respects the contrast was remarkable.

The great tribune was a great actor, and often said and did for rhetorical effect what he subsequently refused to be literally bound by; and knowing how fickle are the whims of politicians' consciences, and how recalcitrant the vows of administrative powers, he sometimes talked alternately in opposite ways.

Between his startling return for Clare against a Cabinet Minister and the introduction of the Relief Bill, there was much discussion as to what he really meant by standing, and whether he would really try to take his seat.

Chief Baron O'Grady—the wittiest Celt of his time—when asked his opinion on the agitating question, said, 'I think he will, although he said he would.'

But how worthily he bore himself in that memorable transaction, after all! Heard at the bar in the striking personification of a long disqualified race, he never thought of gulping the anti-Catholic oath, thenceforth about to be abolished. Whatever his faults or errors, he would neither juggle with the terms nor bully about the substance. 'I do not speak,' I said, 'at second-hand or at random; for I knew him well, and everyone who did must recollect how unwavering under all circumstances was his fidelity to the faith in which he lived and died.'

Men who were known to be unbelievers in the religious sanctity of an oath, and many who were supposed to be sceptical regarding its binding efficacy on conscience, acquiesced in the traditional observance without hesitation or the avowal of any scruple.

Mr. John Stuart Mill, whose philosophic opinions were well known, did not ask to be allowed to affirm instead of swearing when taking his seat for Westminster; and in 1869 he justified his doing so in terms that could hardly be mistaken: regretting the continuance of the ceremony, but repudiating the claim to set it at nought as a political grievance.

'With regard to taking an oath, I conceive that when a bad law has made that a condition to the performance of a public duty, it may be taken without dishonesty by a person who acknowledges no binding force in the religious part of the formality, unless he has made it the special and peculiar work of his life to testify against such formalities and against the belief with which they are connected.'*

* Letter to G. J. Holyoake, published in the *Daily News*, April 25, 1882.

Practically not a few members of each House concurred in the conclusion acted on by the metaphysician, though they did not agree in his abstract reasoning. Their sense of public propriety was wounded, not by Mr. Bradlaugh's offering to take the oath, but by his attempt to turn the belief in God into a gratuitous and ostentatious jest. They did not see that they were warranted by abetting an act of buffoonery to offend the religious convictions of their fellow-legislators by abrogating a law hallowed by usage, and which individually they did not feel had done them any harm, merely at the bidding of one wilful and wayward man.

Submitting to his demand to be allowed to affirm as if he had religious scruples such as those contemplated by the statute of 1866, passed for the easement of certain pious Nonconformists, would be to play the fool.

Beside these non-contents, who practically stood neutral, many devout and earnest men were not unwilling that, either by legislation or deliberate conference between both Houses, the initiatory ritual of admission to membership should be considered with a view to the future; but they could not become parties to a change in the law framed and brought forward at the angry bidding of an avowed foe of Christianity.

His colleague openly proposed a truce in his attack upon the dignity and consistency of Parliament, if Ministers would undertake to carry a resolution or bring in a Bill that would suit his purpose: and although the condition was not formally or audibly accepted, with the Speaker in the chair, everybody believed that the compact had been agreed to in general terms, and that during the recess provisions would be framed that would entitle Mr. Bradlaugh and his friends to say that they had swept the relics of a national faith from the Order Book of the Legislature.

A Committee of independent Peers and Commoners had sought to combine, irrespective of party differences, men of acknowledged weight and influence in a grave remonstrance against the apprehended change. I consented to act as chairman, and to conduct the correspondence rendered necessary, in order to ascertain how far members of different religious communions and representatives of different orders of society throughout the United Kingdom concurred in deprecating what we deemed a waiver by Parliament of a time-honoured profession of national faith.

From the days of Elizabeth Anglicans and Catholics, Presbyterians and Episcopalians, prelates of the Church of England and of the Church of Rome in Ireland, had never signed the same declaration of public policy. What if we could, without platform rhetoric, or resort to the aid of agitation in the press, afford them the opportunity of expostulating in concert against giving way to demands so unreasonable?

Inducements we had none to offer. Our appeal was simply to the coincident opinions or to the open minds of those to whom our circular was addressed.

Though adhesions of undoubted weight and influence daily came in, it was felt that, without the approval of the Primate, that of the episcopate in the Upper House could hardly be expected; and the desire he expressed seemed reasonable and wise, that, before giving his decision, he should be fully informed of the purpose the Committee had in view in taking a course so exceptional and so encompassed with difficulty as that of combining in one religious act the clergy and laity of different persuasions.

The opportunity was afforded by an invitation of Professor Birkbeck and myself to Addington; and we were directed by our colleagues to lay before his Grace unreservedly the grounds of our hopes and fears.

Illness prevented my learned friend from fulfilling the engagement, and I was left to act alone. The duty was not free from anxiety lest I should fail through any oversight or misreading of the varied considerations that might determine the Prelate to give, or to defer until next Session, his judgment on the policy we ventured to recommend.

From the outset he stated his entire sympathy in the object proposed, and warm approval of the terms of the declaration. But what if it drew forth only the protest of a minority, respectable perhaps in number and dignity, but not strong enough to counteract the force of public opinion that would be said, however sophistically, to be united against them?

I did my best to show that we might depend not merely on the cordial support of the clergy and the best of the laity of the Church, but of the bulk of the Presbyterian community in the United Kingdom, and likewise of the Roman Catholics. I told the Archbishop that Cardinal Manning was ready to append his signature, and said he only delayed it lest it should tend to deter those whose names it would be more important to obtain, but that we had his permission to affix it whenever it might be deemed to be most useful. 'Then I think I cannot do better than to leave the matter—at all events, for the present—in your hands, confiding to Lord Harrowby, Professor Birkbeck, and yourself the discretion to annex or withhold my signature as time goes on.'

Without hesitation I respectfully declined to accept of the trust, with which, under any other circumstances, I should have felt much honoured. But I was sure that my noble and my learned colleague would agree with me in feeling that the public sanction of Canterbury must never be exercised on a question touching the Christian character of our Legislature save by the Primate himself.

But that I should not seem to be either importunate or unhopeful, I asked leave to consult certain leading Churchmen, representative of different ecclesiastical views, as to whether it would be for the interest of the Church that the declaration should appear with the Archbishop's name. Having his permission, this was done, and in due time the answers, which were all in the affirmative, were transmitted to Lambeth.

We had the satisfaction of reporting the adhesion of a great number of additional Peers and Commoners, and the signature of Canterbury was placed at their head.

Five nights' debate, fluctuating through many changes of temperature and time, came to an end at last by daybreak on May 4, and, amid a scene of rare excitement, the numbers for it appeared to be 289, and against 292, 17 English and Irish Liberals voting in the majority, and 36 Home Rulers. Eighteen English and Scotch Liberals were absent, and 22 Irish, and but 2 Conservatives without pairs. It was a curious coincidence that the same majority of three, and composed very much of the same proportions, had defeated the Irish University Bill ten years before.

The Artisans' Dwellings Act had in many districts effected the difficult but necessarily gradual good contemplated, while in other places it had not been put into operation at all. Some of the London vestries responded to the humane intentions of the Legislature by enforcing thorough repair of dilapidated and insalubrious homes; and in many instances, when the neglectful owners were impecunious or absentee, demolition, as the statutable penalty, followed. But in other places, where rates were already burthensome, employment slack, and several industries depressed or desponding, the local authorities shrank from carrying the Act into execution. Even with the promised aid of the Treasury, vast slums remained unredeemed, and gigantic rookeries in several of the centres of the town continued to set at naught the hope of improvement.

In 1875 Home Secretary Cross brought in an alternative scheme for opening overcrowded districts to the benefits of light and air by the combined action of the Executive and the Metropolitan Board of Works. He would drive much-needed thoroughfares through these jungles of disease and death, promising, with the best intention, doubtless, but with too sanguine reliance on remedial possibilities, to provide habitable dwellings for the multitudes to be displaced.

It was, in short, an attempt to grapple with an evil at the other end, and on a wholly different theory of habitation reform from that which had been tried, and whose progress was tantalizing and tardy. I did not affect to be convinced of error or to despair regarding the ultimate benefit of persistence in the gradual policy Parliament had sanctioned seven years before; but, where the need was so urgent for stringent remedies of some kind, I felt it would have been worse than invidious to object to the alternative plan proposed. It would tend to improve the aspect and respiration of the town, if it did nothing more: the practical change it would make in the local plight of the people, whether for the better or the worse, no one could tell. While, therefore, giving the Minister ungrudgingly credit for the munificent aid he guaranteed for the working out of the scheme, and acknowledging frankly the disappointment that often waylaid the promise of bit by bit amelioration, I reminded the House that 'overcrowding could not be put an end to merely by destroying the houses in which the very poor herded together for shelter. The evil had been created by legislation, and by the changes in the law of settlement, which had led all men who were out of work to come to London and other large towns, where they remained to prey on each other.'

If wholesale dilapidation were to take place because the wretched courts and alleys swarmed with waged labour and famished poverty, striking society as it passed with the sense of disgust or shame, the terrible question must importunately be asked, Whither were the evicted to go? The first requisite of labour, whether skilled or unskilled, was to be within reach of its work, for to find some easy resting-place afar off was a grim and dangerous mockery.

Inevitably, the first result would be to spread the taint of contagion over the hitherto decent neighbourhoods more nearly contiguous, and, in plain but irrefutable language, to spread the sphere of slum: or, what might be thought in many respects more dangerous, to compel the cast-out multitudes to swarm more than ever in what would be called workmen's quarters.

Parliament would do well to remember what had come of improvement elsewhere. Communism was hardly heard of in Paris, and was little feared till M. Haussmann had rendered its West End the wonder and delight of its neighbours, and I implored the Government previsionally to take into consideration these things while there was time. At all events, let it be clearly understood that the enormous cost of wholesale demolition and displacement would impose an automatic check to the use of this alternative, while in nine cases out of ten, if any good were to be wrought, it must be by the comparatively slow and unpretentious process of bit by bit reform.

The measure passed rapidly through both Houses, and the efficacy of the wholesale clearance and rebuilding can best be appreciated by a visit to the piles of six and seven story buildings that have been reared in certain districts. But inquirers will ask, What has become of the evicted population?—scarce a resemblance to whom can be found in the tidy, cleanly, snug, and airy tenements, with cut-stone basements and spacious staircases, before them. As was said long ago, and cannot be too frequently reiterated as a warning to thoughtless benevolence: ''Tis not quite so easy to do widespread good as those may imagine who never tried.'

Five years later, the two systems being experimentally found not only not conflicting or incompatible, but in a certain sense mutually supplementary, the provisions of the Act of 1868 and those of 1875 were combined in one statute, which, with some additions, was, on the recommendation of a Royal Commission of inquiry, re-enacted, and is now the law.

Great relief has been found from the aggravation of pressure in the central districts of the town in the extension of tramways to the suburbs and the consequent abatement of fares in third-class trains on several of the principal railways. Without these auxiliary aids to the enjoyment of the first necessary of life—open air—I know not what the Metropolis would by this time have come to, and it is with grief I cannot adequately express that I see the beneficial effect of this enlargement of the sphere of working-men's residence already countervailed to a great extent by the erection of whole villages, one had almost said towns, all round to meet the effluent demand without any adequate regard to the conditions of house-building essential to health.

Long rows of two-story cottages, without under-stories, or even air-draughts under the ground-flooring, built without any genuine mortar in the walls or weather-tight roofing, have risen year by year, and are still rising to tempt the working men into tenancy at nominally moderate, but practically extortionate, rents.

In other words, the slums are getting transplanted, and Metropolitan authorities look on, caring for none of these things. This is not the place to discuss how a bridle could be put in the mouth of speculative rapacity. In common with old friends of better dwellings, I have tried, but in vain, to persuade Government to interfere; and after five-and-twenty years' experience I am forced to the conclusion, expressed by Lord Shaftesbury in a letter already quoted, that nothing will be accomplished in the way of prevention until the local inspectors are appointed by the Executive and made irremovable by the local jobbers in municipal senate assembled, as practically they now are. I will frankly confess that, when politically young, I thought differently. I was enthusiastic for the increase of localism as a counterpoise to the corrupt influence of over-centralization;

and in many important respects I rejoice at the change that has in our time been brought about. But everything right has a wrong side, as everything bad has something good on its side; and I am firmly persuaded that most, if not all, humane and sensible men acquainted with the difficulties of the government of London would rejoice at seeing the inspectorate of dwellings taken out of infirm or apathetic local hands.

The steady overgrowth of London beyond its municipal raiment and housing had for some time engaged the attention of all Metropolitan clubs and callings. The Metropolitan Board of Works, after completing great and beneficial enterprises, had unfortunately become discredited through the malfeasance of some of its principal officials.

Many of the vestries of the large parishes had fallen into disrepute, not only for the toleration of jobbing now and then, but of unseemly brawling about local questions in which nobody took an interest outside the parochial confines. There was, in short, a weariness of the *status quo*, and a universal expectation of a more uniform and intelligible system of local rule being substituted by statute.

In 1831 the Metropolis of the census comprised 78,029 acres from Hampstead to Wandsworth, and from Stepney to Fulham, fifteen miles by twelve. In 1851, civic and suburban London contained 305,933 dwellings, and more than two millions of people, with rateable property assessed at £9,964,343 a year.

Since then the number of habitations had not, indeed, kept pace with that of property or population, but had increased twenty-five per cent., while these had more than doubled. Such an aggregation of intelligent and active communities, possessed of so much opulence, yet restless with so many wants, nowhere else existed in Christendom.

How comes it, then, that nowhere else is urban life so inorganic, that nowhere else are the thews and sinews of local rule developed so imperfectly? A quarter of a century has elapsed since the first attempt was made to reduce to anything like uniformity of system the local institutions of London.

Without the semblance of ground-plan, unity of design, or bond of cohesion, several great towns had grown up contiguously on either side of the Thames between Battersea and Blackwall. Westminster and Southwark had defined boundaries, having time out of mind sent representatives to Parliament.

By the Reform Act of 1832 five new boroughs were formed out of the remainder, and two representatives were assigned to each. The City alone possessed corporate privileges and civic organization, while outside its ambit lay a confused and anomalous wilderness of parochial jurisdictions and extra-parochial liberties, whimsically unequal in their scope and tenor, and frequently irreconcilable in their pretensions and powers.

The attempt to describe the chaos that prevailed reads now like an incredible fiction. Three hundred different bodies, under various appellations, and with the utmost diversity of functions, claimed the right by prescriptive usage, or by modern Acts passed from time to time, to impose local rates for various purposes. No fewer than 10,448 individuals as vestrymen, commissioners, guardians, members of manorial courts, and magistrates of quarter sessions, were engaged in daily contention, carried on at the public cost, about the right to do all that required to be locally done, and how *not* to do it. Streets were unpaved, rights of way were disputed, whole regions lay in darkness by night, unswept and unwatered by day.

Commissioners of sewers, many of them named *ex officio*, possessed but ill-defined jurisdiction, which they exercised in general so negligently, and at times so arbitrarily, that as a desperate remedy their number was reduced from upwards of a thousand to twenty-three, and subsequently to eleven. Their character for efficiency, however, did not mend, and parochial wags affected to believe that their real function was that of accumulation—not dispersion—of nuisances, especially in the article of debt.

Diversities in the mode of choosing vestrymen and requiting parochial officers naturally arose from the wide discrepancies of situation, ways of life, and other special circumstances in busy communities, practically remote from one another from want of leisure, curiosity, and facilities of cheap locomotion; and within reasonable bounds these disparities would have mattered little.

In Hackney no one was qualified who dwelt not in a house valued at £40 a year; and Bloomsbury was so genteel that no man, however good his trade, was allowed to serve if he let any part of his house in lodgings.

Shadwell, more dependent upon weekly wages, thought £10 a qualification high enough: while Poplar distrusted any whose respectability fell short of £30; but Mile End had confidence in the proof that £12 rental gave of integrity, and St. George's-in-the-East had faith in a rating of £1 4s. How far these amounts might be qualified or accounted for by dissimilarity in the standard of valuation which each parish formed for itself, it would puzzle an antiquary now to discover.

More serious was the mischief arising from the multiplication of paving and lighting boards, especially in parishes whose confines interlapped from ecclesiastical causes long forgotten. Seven different bodies belonging to St. Clement's, St. Mary's, the Savoy, and St. Martin's divided among them the duty of keeping open the highway from Charing Cross to Temple Bar, and by their neighbourly jealousies added in no slight degree to the impediments of the journey.

In Westminster the line of delimitation was generally drawn down the centre of the street, an infallible receipt for partial stoppage twice as often in the year as would otherwise have been avoidable. Sometimes the roadway belonged to one board, the pathway to another, and the lighting to a third; while, as a climax, the watering on the right hand was always done in the morning, and on the left hand after sunset, insuring to the inhabitants of both the benefit of dust throughout the day. It fared even worse with the inhabitants of large growing parishes in the suburbs.

As each additional estate was let on long lease for building, a local Act was promoted by the influential vendor, which nobody took the trouble to oppose; and its clauses invariably provided for the full autonomy of the new district, utterly regardless of how it might affect those that lay contiguous, or the luckless portions lying between.

In St. Pancras sixteen independent boards 'did the paving and lighting under, and by virtue of, the enactments in such cases duly made and provided'; and forasmuch as the said enactments took no cognizance of the adjacent or intervening localities, and conferred no right of taxing them, their inhabitants were left wholly unprovided for.

Combining in revolt, they made three attempts to obtain a general Act for the parish, but private rights and privileges proved too strong for them, and, after paying their costs, they succumbed in despair.

The aged and infirm poor were driven from the parish their labour had helped to enrich to some other that knew them not, forthwith to be bundled out again. To the generation that has come to maturity under a different state of things, that which some of us are old enough to remember seems almost inconceivable.

In June, 1852, a Royal Commission, consisting of Mr. Labouchere, Mr. Justice Patteson, and Sir G. Cornewall Lewis, was appointed to inquire into the state of the Corporation of the City.

By far the weightiest opinions given in evidence before the Commissioners were against the Metropolitan Council for the aggregate towns of the Thames, and 'in favour of reforming the old corporation, and giving a new corporation to each of the surrounding boroughs.'

To expand the existing central jurisdiction so as to embrace the whole of the urban and suburban area would, in the judgment of Mr. Samuel Morley, be very undesirable. 'It would be too large a body a great deal. Each corporation should be confined to the duties of its own locality.'

Mr. Thomson Hankey gave similar advice as to

the need of distributing the duties and localizing the functions of municipal rule; while both advocated the establishment by delegation of a Board of Works, carrying into effect improvements of exceptional nature and cost. The Commissioners reported unequivocally in confirmation of these views.

To advance the boundaries of the City so as to include the whole of the Metropolis 'would entirely alter the character of the Corporation of London, and would create a municipal body of unmanageable dimensions. We therefore advise that this course should not be adopted. A Metropolitan city requires for its own local purposes municipal institutions not less than other towns. We see no reason why the benefit of municipal institutions should not be extended to the rest of the Metropolis, by its division into districts, each possessing a municipal government of its own.

'We further suggest the creation of a Metropolitan Board of Works, to be composed of a very limited number of members, deputed to it from the council of each Metropolitan municipal body, including that of the City; and that the management of the public works in which all have a common interest should be conducted by this body; and we recommend the proceeds of the coal-tax be transferred to its administration; that the Board of Works should be empowered to levy a rate upon the entire Metropolis for any improvement of general utility, within a certain poundage, to be fixed by Act of Parliament.'

Regarding the great circumjacent expanse of urban life, the Commissioners were careful to avoid the lazy error of treating it as a single town. More correctly, as they say, 'London may be called a province covered with houses. Its diameter is so great that the persons living at its extremities have few interests in common. The inhabitants of opposite extremities are in general acquainted only with their own quarter, and have no minute knowledge of other parts of the town. Hence, the two first conditions for municipal government would be wanting if the whole of London were placed under a single corporation.'

Here, then, is the impartial and deliberate judgment of a Commission consisting of one of the best judges who ever sat on the common law bench, and two of the most respected Ministers who ever held the seals of Secretary of State—men thoroughly read in the constitutional history of their country, and thoroughly versed in the administration of its affairs.

Given habitually to deal with facts and necessities as they presented themselves, and deeply impressed with the conviction that the soundest legislation is that which recognises the natural developments of society and promotes its spontaneous tendencies to organization, they put aside with judicial gravity fantastical suggestions for erecting an unwieldy and ill-proportioned system, which they clearly saw would be unmunicipal in its very conception, and unmanageable (save by external influence) should it ever be set in motion.

They saw nothing to apprehend in the erection of as many corporations as there were boroughs in the Valley of the Thames; they saw everything to warn us against making the experiment of one.

In 1853 two millions of people seemed to them palpably too many to be fitly or safely represented in a single town council. What would they have said to the proposition of one municipality for four millions? To them rateable property to the extent of £9,964,318, diverse in every conceivable form and character, seemed infinitely too wide a field for corporate taxation. What would they have thought of giving over £25,055,674 of rateable property for an assembly in Guildhall or Whitehall to experimentalize upon?*

Besides the value I placed on the deliberate judgment of my own former chief in administration, I had from early infancy the greatest respect for the judgment of Sir G. C. Lewis. His patient and pondering mind, habitually devoted to historic studies and the comparative anatomy

* 'Government of London,' *Nineteenth Century*, 1880. W. M. Torrens.

of political institutions, fitted him specially to advise Parliament on the task it was called on to undertake. He thought the wisdom of the Legislature would best be shown by following a good precedent wherever it could be found, restoring what had been lost by decay or lapse; content to improve rather than eager to invent; to consolidate and elevate rather than startle by some new device; to underpin, enlarge, and copy with improvement, rather than subvert to make room for the transcript of some foreign design.

Unluckily the drawing of the Bill fell to others, and was dictated by the panic fear of disease, originating, it was believed, in the river having become gradually little better than an open sewer. For a system of thorough drainage, a Central Board, with power of imposing general rates, was deemed indispensable, and requirements in the *paulopost* future for the preservation and growth of social and municipal health were allowed to stand over till a more convenient season. The opportunity thus lost did not again recur until the Metropolitan Board of Works had ceased to command public confidence. But now the question pressed for solution. What else, or what better, could be done?

I thought it my duty to lay the case fairly before my constituents, and to ask their instructions as to what they desired me to do for the preservation of their distinctive individuality and local exemption from interference, exaction, or control, which could not command their confidence or respect. Among half a million of people, I could not anticipate absolute unanimity, even upon Finsbury affairs; but I had the satisfaction of finding a marvellous approximation towards unity of judgment on all the leading questions that seemed to be involved. And, consulting with the most experienced of my cotemporaries in the representation of the capital, Sir James Lawrence and Lord Mayor Fowler, I rejoiced to feel that there was substantially little difference of view amongst us on the vital alternative of centralization or district Home Rule. The perplexities of adequate water supply gave us most concern, but I think we all came to the conclusion that nothing could be less desirable than the scheme sometimes propounded on the score of economy for seeking in one distant, though it might be abundant, source the means of supplying that first necessary of life to the millions of people dwelling on both sides of the Thames We all thought, and for one I have never changed my opinion, that it would be infinitely safer, better, and more economical to let each independent municipality make its own drinking bargain with a separate company, *or*, if it so willed, assume the responsibility of bringing the requisite comfort of life to the doors of its people.

I felt sure that in this, as in most other things of importance, definite and actual knowledge of what was locally required, and direct and practical accountability in the method of finding and governing municipal demand and supply, could not be compensated for by any agglomeration of half-knowledge and interchangeable ignorance in any new device of centralization.

Sensible men in Marylebone shuddered at their affairs and rates being committed to the chances of a scratch vote by delegates from Wapping, Hackney, Battersea, and Camberwell, and sickened at the notion of being compensated by the correlative right being bestowed on their deputies to blunder or passively job in the case of Chelsea, West Ham, Woolwich, and Fulham.

The force of these reasonings was appreciated generally by the press, and the mediaeval magnificence of Guildhall was so much gratified at finding the case for intelligent localism as against central government on the sweepstakes principle put common-sensically by one who could not be suspected of being subject to its influence, that they ordered ten thousand copies of my article to be sown broadcast. But it mattered naught with the active organization in favour of joint-stock municipal monopoly, which had for some time been holding meetings and beguiling uneasy ratepayers to sign petitions for something bigger and better than the somewhat damaged authority of Spring

Gardens. The leaders of the Municipal Reform League revelled in every mistake made by that obstruction in their way, and held out everywhere to the ignorant and needy the prospect of adequate revenues for the support of a Metropolitan County Council from the expropriation of City endowments.

Few men of social or industrial influence lent their sanction to the agitation, whose chief spokesman, Mr. Firth, M.P. for Chelsea, at length persuaded Government to give ear to its importunities. In 1883 the Home Secretary stated that a measure had been prepared for the reform of the government of London, for which, if time could not be found in that Session, it would probably not be wanting in the next. Early in 1884, accordingly, Sir William Harcourt laid upon the table a Bill which hardly satisfied the cravings of the League, and which the West End, City Corporation, and suburbs concurred in deprecating. Numerous meetings assembled throughout the Metropolis to discuss the changes it proposed, and with comparatively few exceptions the existing local authorities, with a decided concurrence of opinion on the part of the great body of ratepayers, came to resolutions adverse to the centralizing policy of the measure.

It was not until July that its provisions came before the House for discussion. Mr. Ritchie moved as an amendment to the second reading that, while ready to consider the question of reform in the government of London, the House declined to assent to a proposal by which the control over the levying and expenditure of rates would be vested in one central body, 'to the practical extinction of the local self-government of the various cities and boroughs of the Metropolis.' There was hardly a member of that House, he thought, who really and honestly believed there was any real demand for it in the Metropolis. Its tendency, he would venture to say, would be practically the destruction of local self-government in the Metropolis, and the inauguration of a vast system of centralization which would not tend to good government in any way. Faults there were, no doubt, in the existing system. In what system were there none? But, whatever its shortcomings, under the administration they were asked to abolish London had been converted from a badly-paved, badly-lighted, badly-drained city, to the healthiest city in the world. It was, in fact, practically impossible to treat London as a whole.

Lord Algernon Percy seconded the amendment, expressing the disapproval of the people of Westminster, in which his colleague, Mr. W. H. Smith, fully concurred. The champion of centralism, Mr. Firth, relied on votes obtained at public meetings, which he professed to believe represented, without prejudice of class or occupation, the general desire for thorough organic reform. The fundamental flaw in the constitution of the Board of Works was its being dependent on indirect election—householders choosing vestrymen, and vestrymen choosing Metropolitan rulers. When Parliament had conceded household suffrage in the affairs of the Empire, it was idle to deny its capacity in affairs of the capital. He endeavoured to disarm the fear that the ancient city would be despoiled of its wealth or divested of its administrative privileges, noting with emphasis the absence of any provisions in the present Bill tending in either direction.

It fell to my lot to reply next day to these specious arguments. A system of municipal federalism had existed with the sanction of Parliament, which, though not perfect in several of its details, gave to the intelligent and frugal inhabitants of each great district the right to govern their own concerns, and to send to the central council whom it deemed best fitted to provide for the comparatively few though important works for common benefit thorough drainage, viaducts, open bridges, and embankments.

If it was now thought right to sweep this away, why not consult the feelings and wishes of the diverse groups of parishes and unions on which Parliamentary representation had been conferred by numerous statutes, so as still to preserve in modified form the same respect for modified rule which had been shown in every charter confirmed and in every new charter conferred on the great towns of the kingdom?

Was it because the four millions of people who dwelt in the ten Metropolitan boroughs were the most orderly and peaceable in the Empire, adding by their industry the greatest amount to its wealth, and requiring the least amount of civil or military force for the preservation of order, that they were, without their consent, or a pretence of their having been consulted, to be flung into one truckle-bed of centralization, and made liable, without limit, to be mulcted and fleeced to carry out experiments in municipal empiricism?

How was this new organization to do its work? Confessedly, by the substitution at first of a corps of well-paid officials, inevitably ere long to give place to an army of civic officers, without whose aid it must be impossible for the new County Council to perform its infinitely ramified duties; and eventually, no doubt, leading to the payment of the members of the body themselves.

A more corrupting and disintegrating change than this could not be conceived, nor one more contrary to the traditional spirit of English local life. Could anyone seriously believe that with all the army of inspectors and sub-inspectors, commissioners at high salaries, and assistants looking to advancement by jobs, clerks without number, and deputies without end, the work of Metropolitan administration would be better done under the control of a central council?

Experience would speedily prove that it could not be done at the same cost to the ratepayers, and even if it could it would be dear indeed at the money.

The pretence that in a central council of 240, triennially chosen, by party excitement and lavish expenditure on blue posters and brass bands, a superior class of men could be got to take charge of the multifarious concerns of ten great cities and towns, was no more than the unthinking chatter of West End clubs, whose idle members looked to the opening of a new career of social and political ambition.

And if it was said Parliament might overhaul even the unintentional blunders of ten metropolitan cities rolled into one, how would they ever get to bed? The House would soon be asked to sit upon Saturday, and one must tremble even for the observance of the Sabbath.

In the paroxysm of national madness in 1792 Paris was persuaded it ought to be one and indivisible. At every whirl of the revolutionary wind the civic machinery had been made subservient to purposes of confusion and convulsion; and such is the dread of the opportunity of mischief it affords, that down to the present day, even under a democratic republic, the Mayor of Paris is not allowed to be chosen by the people or their representatives, but is nominated by the head of the State.

Look at results. Notoriously the death-rate was very much higher in Paris than in any one of the cities of Surrey or Middlesex, and the rates greatly in excess.

New York was another signal example. There was centralization with a vengeance, and inordinate rates to match. At first the decline downwards might not be obvious, but to that it would come.

An American gentleman asked me not long ago if it were true that in London we were thinking of boiling down all our old independent ways of municipal life into one average mess. I said I hoped not, and asked how it fared with them on the banks of the Hudson. 'I take it,' he said, 'that the difference 'twixt you and us is just this: We are in the mud, and we have to get out of it; you have first to get into it, and then, if you can, to get out of it.'

Sir Charles Dilke undertook to defend the scheme, and laid much stress upon certain recent errors and eccentricities of vestrydom, which had lent itself to thwarting the operations of the Artisans' Dwellings Acts. He protested vehemently against the imputation of a desire to extinguish the existing bodies, which he said Ministers were preparing to reconstitute and reform as district councils. And to these amended and consolidated organizations the Legislature might secure all that it was feared was in danger of being lost.

It is unfortunate, however, that year after year has been suffered to pass without the realization of such an assurance, and that the central body, subsequently called into existence by another Administration, seems to be only unanimous in the desire to monopolize every species of municipal authority and power.

The Lord Mayor of London (Sir R. Fowler) and some others, having spoken, the House divided on the amendment, which was rejected by a majority of 70; but before the second reading could be formally put to the vote the Government announced that it was not intended to proceed further with the measure that Session. The measure was not again brought forward until the Government had changed, and Conservatives who had vehemently opposed Sir W. Harcourt's plan of municipal unification supported its reproduction *mutatis mutandis* by Mr. Ritchie.

Centralization in the affairs of empires is indispensable for unity and external action and defensive strength, but, misapplied and perverted in municipal affairs, is little more than a fine name for chartered monopoly. The pushing, placarding, palavering few undertake to supply at lessened cost some want of the community on a new and uniform system, provided they are allowed to clutch and part among them all the profits of the business, whatever they may be, and provided they are never to be held responsible for any blunder, neglect, or jobbing in the doing of it.

The legal power of extorting rates without limit for what are called improvements or experiments is the *sine quâ non* of the scheme; and the right of each contributory to vote or not to vote for one of his taxing masters out of several (most of whom he does not know anything about), is, he is told, an adequate protection against his being fleeced to the skin.

In small towns, and even in cities of moderate size, these mischiefs are kept in abeyance, because the expenditure is within bounds susceptible of scrutiny, and because the prominent municipal spendthrifts and their place-hunting hangers-on are easily recognised and brought to book. But when the traders in central jobbing contrive to take in and do for a number of distinct and dissimilar communities happening to lie within telegraphic or telephonic communication, in the multitude of councillors there is heard the whisper at first, and then the chuckle, of reciprocal irresponsibility all round.

Paris and New York have long ago found out this to their cost, and if anyone would only show their wearied and burthened citizens how to escape from the nightmare which oppresses them they would be too thankful.

But nobody would propose in our time what the late Sir Robert Peel and Mr. Gladstone wanted to do in Ireland—namely, to abolish municipal self-rule altogether, and hand over all the taxing, lighting, paving, watering, and rebuilding functions of towns to Commissioners appointed by the Home Office.

The inhabitants of New York and Paris would stand no nonsense of that kind, and what else to do they seem to know not. Yet the people of London, unwarned by their example, have suffered themselves to be driven into municipal centralism, under the plea of economy and uniformity and accountability. But six years' trial of the over-distended system has so disenchanted them that, at the second triennial election in March last, over 250,000 unhappy ratepayers refused positively to vote at all! Surely no sentence of repudiation like this was ever passed by a great industrial community.

The law of legitimate proportion observable in nature is not less true in social organization. Frankenstein, being a materialist philosopher, thought he could with impunity disregard such rules and limitations; he would make something bigger and better than ever existed before, and when complete his monster could only gape and grin at him, and prove that it was incapable of healthful action or length of days.

We who objected seven years ago to tumbling the whole affairs of the various and divers though contiguous cities of the Thames into one drag-net of central jobbing, dwelt specially on the disappointment and mischief likely to ensue if all the sources of water-supply and all the ramified details of its administration were vested in monopoly in a comparatively few hands. We did not insist that the eight water companies should be allowed to retain their profitable privileges to the detriment of the great body of consumers; and we thought Bills might be certainly framed by Government enabling public trustees to take over existing waterworks at their equitable value, and to take as tenants in different districts solvent companies to work the old sources of supply or to work new ones.

But we would have had such trustees with salaries to raise them above the suspicion of jobbing, without any temptation to clandestine plunder, and subject to inquiry by Parliament. Each board of trustees, three or five in number, should have a union of two or three of our great parishes to keep in health—that is, in plenty of fresh water. We would have each of them look for increased supply to districts hitherto untapped, in order that the people of London should never have cause to fear being overtaken by that greatest of calamities conceivable in urban life—a water famine; and each separate water trust would have every other as its legitimate competitor for the credit of economic management, scientific foresight, and just administration. But we were told by the centralizers, and every politician of their kind, that nothing would do but a complete assimilation of pipes and stop-cocks, basins and filter-beds, gathering grounds and snow-hid fountains, hundreds of miles by aqueduct from the thirsty lips of five millions of people.

Magnificent enterprises for making London look large, dependent upon remote mountains for drink from day to day, were obviously essential to the manufacture of gigantic fortunes by engineering or contract, employment and inspection. Nature, it was true, had in her primitive discretion been shedding her tears all over the world impartially, bidding her children husband the rainfall everywhere that everyone might have enough, and when they neglected it silently letting it percolate through her divine bosom to be preserved far down out of sight for time of need.

But our Brobdingnag inventors despised such suggestions of common-sense humility. Rainfall and river-flow are with them but the alternatives of semi-barbarism; everything must be artificial—perilously brittle or not does not matter—in the cosmogony of capital; and if in working out their plans municipal institutions must be bloated and gorged, and made unsteady by financial intoxicants, what does it matter? For my part, I think it matters a great deal, and I think that happily the means are still open to us in the Metropolis for countervailing some at least of the danger and demoralization that our French and American neighbours deplore.

Concomitantly with the project of establishing a Metropolitan Parliament, there were always held out promises and pledges of the reform and reconstitution of district councils, which should have large and comprehensive powers for the guidance of their own specific affairs. What has become of these encircling phantoms of local government? or why should not Marylebone and Kensington, St. Pancras and Islington, Lambeth and Brixton, West Ham and Stepney, with their respective neighbours, whose alliance they might seek to form, be given the opportunity to pronounce their separate and distinct judgments on the question of water-supply, and how they can best secure it?

Neither they nor their so-called representatives in the debating school at Spring Gardens have the slightest capacity for judging what any one of the other districts had better do. The aggregate of ignorance is a miserable burlesque on general wisdom, and long speeches (for the newspapers), stuffed with platitudes about 'the finest capital in the world' a poor consolation for annually rising rates, or for the vexation and worry of having the water cut off for days or weeks together in the humble home.

The craze for uniformity in civic matters is not less foolish and futile than it has always proved in matters of religion and trade. The wise instincts of our people have ever rebelled against presumptuous attempts to cramp their inventive facilities in manufacture, and the right of private judgment in points of belief. Wrong-headed men in nearly every Church have in turn boycotted, fined, imprisoned, and, where they could, burned alive or otherwise persecuted, seceders from their edicts and decrees, and every community in Christendom has come at last to put down this abominable and abortive method of caring for men's souls.

So likewise with industry: the archives of every country in Europe are full of laws and charters establishing monopolies for rigid rules of agriculture, manufacture, shipping, knife-grinding, importation of sugar, spinning and weaving of silk, etc., etc., without which none of these benefits of civilization could, it was said, be realized. The last of these numerous impositions which endured as an orthodox contrivance down to our own day was the undertaking by statute to guarantee a uniform price for corn, and prohibiting anyone to import breadstuff from the prolific world without heavy penalties in the shape of Customs duties.

I was myself one of the league that spent five years in agitating for its abolition; and who, with my honoured friends Messrs. Cobden and Bright, refused inexorably to be content with anything short of a total renunciation of the hateful pretence of uniformity in the market price of bread. Uniformity, like most other things in daily use, is capable of rendering cheap and easy service, or of doing an infinity of mischief. A fixed standard of coinage, a settled weight in the breakfast loaf, a maximum fare for cabs, a limit to the amount of water in milk, so many sacks and no less in a ton of coals, and a thousand other salutary applications of the rules of uniformity, are recognised by common consent, chiefly as a means of preventing fraud.

But does anyone propose that there should be only one form of promissory note or one set of bankers to issue these essentials of business life? Will anyone say that we should have a Government or a municipal bakery presided over by a set of fellows who may be up to their necks involved in the art and mystery of rolls and buns?

The difference between one mammoth company or corporation for water-find and water-sale, and the supply of that prime article of life by a number of separate and independent institutions—call them trust boards or district councils, what you will—is the vital difference between competitive management and stark-naked, monstrous, unwieldy, and irresponsible monopoly. A fixed price of drinking water, equivalent always and everywhere to the actual value of the article and no more, is simply a will-of-the-wisp. What we want is the greatest and best supplies of that precious necessary of life, and therefore the greatest diversity of resources for its procurement, and the most ingenious, constant, and reliable guarantees for its daily diffusion.

Pending a general change of system, it was thought needful to correct an abuse that had gradually arisen of charging the householder in London a water-rate upon a valuation arbitrarily fixed by each company, instead of according to the terms of the general valuation Acts.

For three centuries Parliament had allowed joint-stock companies to trade under charter in this first necessary of life, and in the main they had succeeded in quenching the daily thirst of the multitude, and enabled them decently to wash and be clean.

But the rapid increase of population and of manufactures of various kinds within the widening circle of the town rendered the task more difficult of performance, and the uprise of what may be called the science of public health caused numberless doubts to find credence as to the purity of supply, and the adequacy of the sources whence it was derived.

The companies continually asked for fresh powers to tap the neighbouring streams, and to exact payment for the subterranean disposal of what they had to sell.

So long as alternative sources universally existed in public fountains and private wells, the controversy between vendors and purchasers was hardly brought to issue.

The City made terms it thought sufficient with the New River Company, and took little heed of the comparative drought that occasionally befell outlying districts and growing suburbs, where householders were obliged to pay such water-rents as the different associations thought fit to impose; and when these were now and then represented to Parliament as capricious and excessive, Committees of Inquiry were appointed, and on their reports local Acts were passed, which stilled the popular grumbling for a time, but with any view to a permanent or general system of municipal equity established nothing.

On the outbreak of a fatal distemper, a hue and cry was raised that the drinking-wells were everywhere liable to be poisoned by land-drains from the cesspools then universally in use, and the Legislature, in a humane fright, passed an Act shutting up all the wells.

This made the companies apparently indispensable, there being then no essential municipality and no other local authorities strong enough to think of setting up in business for the sale of pure water.

The companies thenceforth asserted their vested right in the exclusive traffic, and, marvellous to say, they obtained from the Legislature what amounted to a practical ratification of their pretension and legal powers of enforcing a graduated scale of charge on the inverse ratio of wealth and poverty, whereby the rich were to be let off more lightly according to their wealth, and the poor charged more heavily according to their poverty.

In 1852 grievances such as always arise under an irresponsible system made so loud a moan that an expiring Parliament thought it really ought to do something to show sympathy, if it could not afford relief; and the companies having promoted Bills for the increase of their capital stock, the formation of more gigantic reservoirs, and other purposes, advantage was taken to refer all their demands to a Special Committee, who had no lack of broad hints given them that they ought to interpose with a firm hand in favour of the general safety.

I had the honour to be one of the five thus appointed, and for forty summer days we fasted and ruminated, and strove to grope our way to something like fixed principles of reasonable supply and demand. And at the end we laid down as conditions for granting what was asked that the dividends declared by the companies should never exceed ten per cent., and that houses under £10 rent should not pay more than eight shillings a year water-rent, those under £20 not more than twelve shillings, and so on in proportion upwards.

The companies of course declared they must throw up their Bills if we insisted, but on reflection they thought better of it, and we had hopes that we had really accomplished something; but after a few months they discovered that, by issuing new stock exclusively to the old proprietors, the ten per cent. maximum would prove but india-rubber, and gradually the limit of percentage on the rent which we had fixed for the benefit of the humbler classes was quietly made to depend on the ingenious assumption that the water-rate should be assessed on a private valuation made by each company, and not on the public valuation on which all local taxes were levied.

It took time, of course, to ripen the questions thus originated, and it was not until many years later that they were boldly faced in a court of law, and the issue plainly joined whether the water-rent could legally be charged upon the gross value of premises, or only upon the net value.

To my friend Mr. Dobbs is due the credit of having, in his own person, fought this question from Quarter Sessions to Queen's Bench, and from Queen's Bench to the Supreme Court of Appeal. The Lords unanimously decided in his favour, but it was still left by each aggrieved individual to waste his hours and his earnings in a little lawsuit against the wholesale water-merchants.

Many of my constituents asked me to try what could be done to induce Government to take the matter in hand, and in concert with other Metropolitan members I pressed the subject on the consideration of the Ministers. But their hands were already full, and we could get no assurance that anything would be attempted during the Session.

Under these circumstances, I undertook to frame an Act to amend existing statutes, and with the support most cordially and effectively given by a majority of my colleagues, we brought in and carried the measure known as the Water Rate Amendment Act, whereby the charge was thenceforth based on the public valuation of all parishes in the Metropolis by Mr. Goschen's Act of 1867.

It was hopeless, perhaps, to expect that among the 30,000 constituents differences should not arise from time to time regarding the conduct of their representatives, or that those who wished to ingratiate themselves with men in power should not rail at their lack of docility to Ministerial lead. I was frequently upbraided in the press and at club meetings for presuming to act in accordance with what I felt to be the prevailing opinion in the borough, and what I believed to be for the general interest; but as the great majority gave no indication of discontent, and from many quarters I continued to receive cordial expressions of approval. I was willing to let my critics have their say, and patiently to abide the issue at the next election.

A cry, however, was raised in 1884, that I should convene a general meeting (at which the bulk of the overgrown constituency would certainly not attend, and by whose decision, whatever it might be, they certainly would not be bound). I preferred instead to address the electors through the columns of the local journals, on past and future legislation, reminding them that the great increase in their numbers consequent on the outgrowth of the town, and the enfranchisement of every householder and lodger, made it less possible every year to gather into one place anything like a representative portion of the constituency.

It seemed to me clear that the flagrant disparity still existing between dwindling boroughs and rapidly expanding cities would call for legislative revision in another Parliament, and the inconsistency must be sooner or later remedied of allowing a £5 cottager or £10 lodger south of Highgate Arch to vote, but denying a similar claimant north of that imposing edifice the like privilege. In the random zest for fault-finding, I had been ignorantly accused of thwarting the transfer of election charges from candidates to constituencies with a view to keep the eligibility in the fewest hands, the fact being that in Committee on the Ballot Bill I had moved that, inasmuch as Parliament was called together for national purposes and objects, not to gratify local or personal ambitions, the legal expenses should be borne by the national revenue, instead of being paid for by individuals, some of whom did not care what they spent, while others were half ruined by an expenditure they could not afford. What I did object to was the blind injustice of casting the burthen on the local rates, for the manifest reason that in large constituencies the addition would hardly be felt, while in small, or even moderate, boroughs it would be a serious and odious aggravation and increase of liability.

The question of election expenses, overlooked in previous discussions on reform, had been revived in the public mind, especially in London, by the provisions in the Elementary Education Act for the triennial choice of members to serve upon the School Board. It was clear that much of the trouble and costs of Parliamentary contests might frequently be expected to arise under the new law, and in the thoughtless desire to secure opportunities of serving on the School Board to persons well qualified to take part in its proceedings from their previous experience, but who could not afford to compete with richer men in an expensive struggle, a cry was raised that the legal charges at elections generally should be limited by statute, and should be paid out of local rates. I thought the latter alternative altogether unjust in principle, and manifestly blundering in its proposed application; and at public meetings, and in conference with deputations, I deprecated the notion of saving the pockets of candidates by imposing an extra burthen upon struggling ratepayers. National education had come to be recognised as a national duty, not a parochial or personal benefit; and if so it ought to be borne out of the national resources.

The returning officers' charges at a general election varied from £80,000 to £90,000, and might, at the utmost, be put at £100,000 in future, an item which would be of little account in the annual Budget, but which, if broken up into three or four hundred separate local items, would form a most unequal and inequitable imposition. The overgrown size of the Metropolitan constituencies rendered the hardship upon their representatives peculiarly onerous, from which I for one should gladly be relieved; but I could not find it in my conscience to vote for transferring the burthen to my already heavily taxed constituents.

The same thing applied to School Board elections, and for both I hoped the Government intended to propose reasonable limitations. They had brought forward a Bill which set a maximum upon legal charges, but as it did not contain any provisions for making them a liability on the part of the Treasury, I moved an amendment to that effect, which found many supporters, and which, after twenty years' reflection, I continue to regret not having been adopted.

For some time there had been an insidious spread of a system of centralized interference, said to have been copied from that in vogue with the wirepullers in America. Mr. Forster at Bradford, Mr. Cowen at Newcastle, and several others of less note, had been long the objects of its depreciatory criticism and defamatory comment. Under the name of organizing for the purposes of registration, active committees were formed, widening slowly into societies of the idler and more fanatical members of the community, and assuming the pretentious names of Liberal Associations: all of them adapted and directed from a central seat of usurpation.

Mechanical ingenuity was applied to reduce the free spirit of party to unquestioning uniformity. At first the subordination of local claims and opinions to the silent inquisition of an irresponsible few was disowned; but gradually the mask was dropped, and everywhere it was said openly that the Caucus was a new power, that had to be dealt with privily and locally if politicians would keep their seats. Of those who resented and resisted the proposed yoke in the first instance, not a few were worried by the torment of incessant dropping of detraction into parley, negotiation, and, at last, reluctant surrender.

After the passing of the Education and the Ballot Acts, Mr. Forster believed himself strong enough to set the Caucus at defiance; but by degrees the instinct of expediency, which was strong within him, though sedulously kept out of notice by his bluntness of manner, prevailed, and, to the regret of all who respected him, he consented to be put up with others as a candidate at the next election, on the suppressed assurance that no attempt would be made in reality to oust him in favour of a stranger.

For some time a clique of politicians in Finsbury who had never said, written, or done anything worth remembering, had been busily caballing against my continuance in the representation. Awaiting the redistribution of the borough into seven electoral districts, each entitled to choose one member, they hatched their organizations accordingly.

The rules of each separate club were stereotyped impressions of those ordained at the central office of the Caucus, and furnished to those who would accept them in the various constituencies throughout the kingdom as dictates to thought and fetters of local action. For effect, each branch was authorized to boast of, say, 500 members, said to be chosen by ballot, to elect an executive council, with subordinate secretaries and agents, and at their discretion to correspond with persons supposed to be affording aid or advice in promotion of the general objects.

Where existing members could not be made amenable to the factious or fantastic tests dictated from headquarters, new candidates more compliant were introduced to unsuspecting notice in the local press, and by degrees at gatherings yclept meetings of the Liberal Association, where the old and influential party leaders seldom if ever appeared, and were never expected to appear. The presumption and petulance which characterized the progress of the scheme deterred the best men of all ranks from lending it their countenance. And as in Finsbury it was practically a reproduction of the cabals that had on former occasions threatened to usurp the free and deliberate functions of the constituency at large, I was continually urged to resist being drawn into any acknowledgment, direct or indirect, of such unconstitutional pretensions.

My refusal naturally affronted the vanity of petty agitators, and I was assured in various forms that, if for no other sin than that of declining the yoke of the Caucus, I should be vehemently opposed at the dissolution. I knew that elsewhere the same means were in course of employment to oust every man who had ever exercised a conscientious right of representative judgment on disputable subjects.

One of the most prominent topics of cavil was that which related to the conduct of the London School Board. Regarded generally as its founder (though in point of fact my original suggestion was that of three comprehensive Boards, not of one only), I could not but observe its early deviation from the course of frugality in expenditure we had been led to expect without sincere regret, and its apparent readiness to challenge wanton rivalry with voluntary schools without serious concern.

Its rapidly increasing expenditure, and the consequent excess of rates beyond the limit specifically promised when the Elementary Education Act was passed, gradually caused no little discontent throughout the Metropolis, and confirmed the suspicion among those who had founded and supported voluntary schools that the ultimate purpose of the measure was their absorption and effacement.

No pains had been spared to disarm religious misgiving, and no plausibilities of respect and gratitude omitted to win the acquiescence of Churchmen, Catholics, and Wesleyans in a scheme belittled by its Ministerial authors with the epithet of 'supplementary' to pre-existing institutions. Their personal predilections might, they imagined, have quenched such invidious fears, and if not, the positive assurances proffered, that the new local rate should never exceed threepence in the pound, ought, they said, to have quieted ungenerous distrust or groundless alarm.

It was not to work out philosophic or fantastic experiments in unusable knowledge among the children of the waged and well-to-do working-classes that additional buildings and additional teachers were to be provided, but to reach the forlorn offspring of the destitute and dissolute—the 'gutter children of the courts and alleys,' for whom Parliamentary instruction was intended; and how could such an unpretentious purpose be mistaken by thrifty ratepayers as ever likely to cost threepence in the pound? Yet no sooner was the legislative machinery set in motion than signs began to appear—at first that a little more, and then a good deal more, was contemplated than had been disclosed.

New schools on a larger and showier pattern than those already existing were decreed here and there, and then on improved models elsewhere. Year by year the school-rate rose by half-pence and pence to meet growing needs and claims it would be shabby to deny, until in the course of the first decade double the annual sum was reached that had been named as the original limit. Contracts for additional schools became a new branch of the building trade, and bargains for sites of previously doubtful value were known to have gladdened the hearts of not a few slum owners, and swelled the solicitors' bill of costs.

It did not escape observation that the Board schools were generally within beckoning distance of the old free schools, and notable additions from time to time were made to the items of instruction calculated to attract the better-to-do working and householding families of the neighbourhood. Under the increasing strain of payment by results, combined with the ill-suppressed desire of extinguishing voluntaryism, one thing after another, never before dreamt of, was added to the elementary curriculum, every supererogatory item tending further to swell the rates.

Public disappointment was heard in the repeated question, What had become of the promises so loudly vouchsafed at the beginning of the system? Why were gutter-children still left at large, while the chubby and tidy offspring of snug parents were getting brought up for clerks and governesses instead of housewives and artisans?

When the rate in London reached ninepence in the pound, espionage was found necessary to search out the little malingerers from the class-roll; and magistrates were called on to mulct indiscriminately the fathers of truants, and the widowed mothers who could scarcely scrape food and fuel together for their helpless broods. Over all was heard, ever and anon, the shrill chirrup of secularism, boasting of its progressive triumph over Christian schools, now in a fair way of extinction.

At the close of the Session of 1883, the Member for Stafford, Mr. Salt, moved: 'That the unforeseen and growing amount of the school rate, its unequal pressure upon various districts and various classes of the community, its failure in some cases to meet the requirements of the most necessitous classes, and the circumstance that it involves expenditure not originally anticipated, call for the serious consideration of her Majesty's Government, with a view to the relief of the burdens of the ratepayers, while maintaining, in accordance with the original intention of the Education Act of 1870, the efficiency of elementary education.' Many Conservatives and not a few Liberals supported the resolution.

The desire I had long felt to see some effectual curb put upon the imposition of school rates and the excess of School Board expenditure would not have induced me to second this motion if it were of a party or sectarian character. Great and grievous discontent prevailed among the rate-paying community, especially in London, at the breach of the conditions on which the Act of 1870 was passed; and, as far as I knew, there was hardly a subject on which there was more unanimity of feeling. But as one of those who steadily supported that measure, and who did not shrink, when difficulty arose regarding its application in the Metropolis, from lending aid which was frankly accepted by Government, and from taking his full share of work in bringing the Act into operation, I felt bound to raise my earnest remonstrance against the gradual perversion of the system to purposes that were never avowed, and I hoped were never intended.

We were asked to impose on the occupiers of rateable property, the bulk of whom might be fairly designated as the struggling classes, a charge, previously unknown, in aid of primary education. Voluntary schools, with the help of grants from the Privy Council, had done a great deal; but confessedly they were unable to reach a poor and helpless outlying mass; and Parliament was asked by the right hon. member for Bradford and the Prime Minister to set up Board schools—not to supplant those existing, but to supplement them, and to gather up the waifs and strays of childhood, so that nothing should be lost to the usable strength of the State.

As far as that purpose was really meant and to whatever extent it had been attained, I was ready to sustain it as cordially as ever. But I regretted to be compelled to say that, like the spirit of other young institutions, that of the Board schools had wandered frequently and far from the straight path of its duty. The questionable and quixotic ambition to obtain control of higher education, for which it was unadapted, and which it had no just means of supporting, diverted continually its thoughts and its resources from the proper objects of its care, and caused a yearly augmentation of burdens, which ratepayers, already overtaxed, felt to be unreasonable.

Rates, we are sometimes told, come out of rent; if a man pays so much more rate he gets an abatement of rent, and so there is no hardship. But in a rising market for houses this is not true; and when it was proposed to put on a rate for the first time for primary schools, it was probable enough that the charge would come out of the householder's pocket.

I well remember that, in a conference at the house of Mr. Goschen, the fitness of rates to bear the newly-proposed burden was fully discussed, upon the ground that, if primary instruction is a public duty, it is a national obligation, and ought to be discharged out of the ways and means of the nation at large. The objection was overborne. But, speaking as I was, for one of the largest portions of the ratepaying community represented in Parliament as part of the Metropolitan area, I said deliberately and distinctly that if the positive inducement had not been held out that the rates should never exceed threepence in the pound, I for one would not have agreed to the Act of 1870; and I do not believe that my

Metropolitan colleagues would have been authorized by their constituents to give that measure their support.

I was not making any charge of wilful breach of faith—I deprecate language to that effect whenever it is used. Our duty was to deal with tendencies and results, not with intentions or miscalculations. It was right, however, that the fact should be recalled when we were taking stock of our progress, and seeking to bring back daily practice to the original design.

The threepenny maximum rate did not rest upon vague recollection of words spoken in debate, but was capable of absolute proof, as I undertook to show. I held in my hand the original Elementary Schools Bill, introduced on February 17, 1870, and not finally passed until the end of the Session. The 84th clause of that Bill promised and guaranteed that when, in any parish, the threepenny rate did not produce more than £20 a year, the deficiency should be made up, not by an extra rate, but by an extra grant from the Privy Council. In a word, the great, broad, and wholesome principle was professed, and, as we hoped and believed, faithfully laid down, that primary instruction of the needy classes was the duty of the whole community, and was to be undertaken substantially for the national good.

Localities were to pay a limited rate in order to create a check on expenditure; but it never was whispered that localities were to be left to the caprice of transitory, and therefore irresponsible, School Boards; or that these were to be used by the Government as a machinery for trying fantastical experiments and empirical theories in the system of over-cram. It never was contemplated seriously by Parliament that, under the plausible pretence of screwing up the general standard of book knowledge, tested by competitive examination, a subtle and insidious means might be found for sapping and mining religious schools.

At first, when the legal limit of local rates was exceeded, excuses were made that the excess was only a little; and when all sorts of subjects of higher education were one by one added under the expanding code, we were told that it did not signify, for it was only this, and only that, and only t'other. A college friend of mine accused his servant once of making free with what did not belong to him. The man protested his innocence often; but being at last found out, declared he meant no harm, for he never meddled with any but three things, which he really thought were allowable—tea and sugar were one, wine and spirits were two, and coals and candles were three. But public patience was wearing out at last, and endurance approached its limit. The Committee of Council stimulated rather than checked the overstrain, which I believed to be a most pernicious infatuation; and in this and other ways egged on the School Boards to ever-augmenting expense.

In London the rate was already more than double what we stipulated for; and new schools on the most expensive pattern were continually erecting where they were not really wanted, apparently to break the heart of the existing voluntary schools. In the parish of St. Giles's, Bloomsbury, what had occurred? Many years before a central building was raised at a great expense, capable of accommodating from 900 to 1,000 children, and when the Act of 1870 was passed, I could bear witness that it was constantly full. A portion of the parish, however, was greatly over-crowded with poor, and the London School Board, of which during the first year I was a member, along with Mr. S. Morley, Lord Sandon, and Mr. W. H. Smith, were told that an additional schoolhouse was wanted. To provide for the wastrels and the necessitous, arrangement was accordingly made, part out of rates, part out of fees, and part out of grants—no one, as far as I knew, complaining.

Other Board schools were built in adjoining parishes, and the general effect on the old establishment in Endell Street was to drain it of half its scholars. Still we forbore to complain; but what was the result? Within the parish, whose population had greatly diminished in the previous decade, the Board supplied accommodation for 2,892 children, though the average attendance was but 2,100. They were going to add 441 additional places, at a cost of £24,470 for site and building, with a probable outlay besides of £4,500 for a new playground—and this while 400 places were actually vacant in the old voluntary school.

It was impossible to persuade an intelligent people that this was all needful and right, or that we ought thus egregiously to trifle with the means of livelihood of the peaceful and hard-toiling community, while one-half the kingdom was wholly exempt from liability to the burden thus mounting up year after year.

From the supplementary function assigned in 1870 of gleaning the Metropolitan field, and garnering the waifs and strays of childhood for the common good, the London School Board has manifested an inappeasable ambition to become the sole educational authority not only for the labouring, but for the middle classes. It already boasts that it 'has to deal with a population in excess of that of Scotland, and directly to manage schools containing children in the proportion of three to four in Scottish Public Schools, which are managed by 979 separate School Boards.' A new competitor for the control of Secondary and Technical Education being feared in the County Council for London, such divided or dual authority is vehemently deprecated as fraught with 'results disastrous to educational progress. The confusion already existing is not, it is said, the result of a policy, the ultimate effects of which have been carefully thought out, but the outcome of allowing things to drift through simple want of thought.'* Departmental zeal for sole authority and absolute uniformity of teaching, outweighs all other considerations, and managers of voluntary schools must be dull indeed if they mistake respite for permanent immunity.

Nineteen out of twenty common-sense people you talked to, whether Anglican, Catholic, or Wesleyan, declared that you were rather unfitting than fitting thousands of poor children for honestly earning their bread; and I grieved to add that the suspicion deepened daily among men of various creeds that the rates were misapplied with the unconfessed purpose of steadily reducing all primary instruction to the French dead level of secularism.

I did not say that all who were engaged in the operation realized the ultimate purpose; but I said that the experiment thus making was unwarrantable and unwise, and that, silence on the subject being at last broken, I was convinced that Parliament would have no peace until means were taken to bring back the expenditure of School Boards within proper bounds.

* Statement of Chairman, adopted by the Board, September 29, 1892.

Voluntary schools, by the help of earnest and munificent friends, were indeed trying to keep their ground; and it was to their infinite credit that in some cases they still succeeded in doing so. But everyone who watches steadily what is going on around him, and who candidly tells what he sees, must own that the high pressure of Board school competition daily threatens to squeeze the voluntary schools out of existence. Members of School Boards, and all who hold office under the Committee of Education, recognise the course of events, but say it is inevitable. Inevitable is the most good-for-nothing word in the language. Nothing in legislation, unjust, inexpedient, or wrong, is inevitable, if we only make up our minds to arrest or amend it. If you will not make rates universal instead of partial and local, and if you will not allow each parent to pay his rates, like the fees of his children, into whatever school he pleases, then there is the other alternative of charging the whole expense between fees, benefactions and public grants, which I, for one, believed would be a fairer and wiser plan.

Difficulties of detail would no doubt arise in the working of any system in a community intersected by differences of race and creed; but there were worse dangers than those entailed by the duty of adapting institutions to the conscientious convictions of the governed. The first, if not the best, of Greek historians says he weighed with care the conflicting views of those who praised Cambyses as a ruler and those who thought him insane; and he sums up the controversy in the warning words: 'I think that he was mad; and for this reason, that he tried to impose laws contrary to the religious feelings of the people.'

Mr. Forster, no longer in office, exulted in the general success of his Act, under which the average attendance in primary schools throughout the kingdom had risen from 1,150,000 to 3,000,000. The unprecedented efforts made by religious denominations to vie with those established under elective boards justified his promise in 1870, that the system of rating and compulsion would be found to supplement, not to supplant, that which previously prevailed. For himself he hoped the day was far distant when there would not be alongside secular teaching that of Scriptural education. But in compulsion we were much behind France, where the percentage was ninety-five, while in England it was but eighty. He did not deny the assurance held out in carrying the Bill, that the cost should not exceed threepence in the pound; he had, however, since then had so much experience in political life, that he should not be inclined on any subject to venture upon prophecy again. The Vice-President of the Council, Mr. Mundella, rejected as groundless the apprehension that secular was superseding religious teaching, and relied upon statistics that showed how large a proportion of the children attending Board schools were in certain places pupils likewise of Sunday-schools. It was true that special subjects — Latin, French, botany, chemistry, and elementary science — had been added to the code, and that prizes and rewards for proficiency were paid for out of the rates; but he did not think it mattered very materially. The discussion was prolonged by members on opposite sides, and by 102 to 74 Government prevailed.

Thus secured immunity, as they doubtless believed, from Parliamentary censure, the School Boards, and specially that of London, pursued their lavish and latitudinarian way. New buildings, more costly than ever, were declared to be indispensable; sites in prominent situations were said to be preferable, though at a higher price; and architectural economy was discarded, as betraying want of zeal for educational progress. The old-fashioned practice of open competition in estimates was superseded by that of sealed tenders for building contracts; and how insufficiently works were executed in many instances the public now are beginning to be aware. The Budget of the London Board in 1884 amounted nearly to a million sterling, entailing another advance in the rates.

Notwithstanding vast sums expended on the extension and improvement of voluntary schools, the outlay of the Board has since continued at an average rate of a shilling in the pound, while grievous discoveries have been made of defective buildings, demanding replacement and repair, and losses incurred by lax supervision in the supply of necessaries of various kinds in the department. But neither remonstrance in the press, protests of public meetings, nor petitions to Parliament could abate prodigality or check subversive zeal. In one Board after another throughout the country the semblance of neutrality towards religious schools was thrown aside; and even where hostile expressions were eschewed, the ultimate purpose was boldly proclaimed, and the prospect held out of all schools whatsoever being placed by law under the direct control of locally-elected Boards. These we were significantly told must be multiplied, as the encompassing drill-sheds and redoubts of disestablishment; and to further the eventual aim, all recognition of religious teaching, whether Anglican, Catholic, Presbyterian, or Methodist, must, as was said, be repudiated by the State. When called upon by the extremists to abet this total change of front on the education question, I replied that, beside the breach of faith with Parliament which was involved, I was wholly averse from the policy proposed. The oldest influence in the life of England—older than the common law, older than Parliament, older than the literature we prize or the language we speak—is the national recognition of Christianity. By its teachings as the supreme test of right and wrong, princes and nobles, lawgivers and judges, merchants and soldiers, founders of hospitals and subjects of the State, have time out of mind professed to be bound. Uproot it if you will, uproot it if you can, but do not be deluded with the vain conceit that, without anything wiser or better to put in its place, suffering and struggling society can be healthfully held together, or will long be content to grope its way without the light it has lost. Just a century ago France, at Rousseau's bidding, tried the experiment, but in a brief space she was glad to be reclothed with the old traditions of reverence, which through all the frenzy of revolutionary change she has never since abjured. Voltaire himself, who had spent a life in reviling religion, confessed when near his end that, if the popular sense of it died out, we must create it anew. And yet we hear it said that realism in art, hand to mouth inconstancy in statesmanship, competition without compunction in work, ambition, trust and love is the highest duty of enlightened and utilitarian man. Let us eat, drink, and grow rich, for to-morrow we die.

If the majority of ratepayers in any locality choose to tax themselves for a neutral Board school, and on examination the pupils earn the subsidy offered by the Privy Council, they can have what they desire; and if instead of a separate Board they prefer to vest its management and control in the Corporation or the County Council, I should regret it, but I should not object. I am doing to others as I would they should do unto me. But what is the fairness or liberality or need of trying to yoke the voluntary schools in the same team? Municipal bodies in county or town cannot be expected to govern two sets of schools on different principles; or if, by good-natured whim or the predominance of tolerant men in a committee here and there, Christian books and Christian teaching be not inhibited, what security in general can there be that the prevalent rule will not ere long be made strictly secular? And what is this but intolerance in latter-day form? Intolerance of our neighbours' opinions and belief has a wonderful knack of shedding its skin, but its poison is the same at all times. Henry VIII. cut off the head of Thomas More, the best of his Ministers, because he would not accept a new dogma; Elizabeth made Parliament pass an Act fining everybody a shilling for absence from the parish church; women were burnt for witches in later times under the sentence of learned and upright judges, and the penal laws against Catholics for saying Mass or marrying their people would fill volumes. All creeds and churches, parties and sects, have been bigoted in their turn, but none have been more intolerant and domineering than the nothing-at-all-ians: and it is because I would not accord them in future the power of injuring or affronting their neighbours in matters of education that I should refuse to hand over voluntary schools to the County Council or the School Board.

It is plausibly said that the public Treasury cannot be expected to vote vast sums in aid to bodies not subject to local control. I do not, however, admit that municipalities or councils elected from time to time for the management of roads and bridges, hospitals and water supply, and a score of other like matters, are the best qualified guardians or guides in primary education. On the contrary, I believe that the more legitimate and natural resource would be found in committees of half a dozen or half a score of parents of the children receiving instruction, who, with the ministers of religion taking part in that instruction, should be held responsible for the conduct and efficiency of each seminary, and who would, of course, be ready to confer or correspond with the Government inspector on every question that might arise. Such a system would resuscitate the sense of parental right and duty, which has too much been suffered to fall into abeyance.

But this and other questions that in more tranquil times had been kept out of the sphere of party politics were made the storehouse of electioneering missiles against which it was vain to guard. The novel and showy inducements held out to unreasoning heads of families to send their children to the over-bidding seminaries, where they were to learn so many things that had not been offered them before, even though not accompanied with the threat of magisterial fines for absence, had the anticipated effect to a very great extent. Metropolitan members, not hitherto deemed unworthy, were everywhere beset with querulous interrogatories as to what they thought and what they would vote in future discussions at Westminster respecting education; and if their answers were not framed with sufficient versatility to meet inconsistent demands, it was evident they must calculate upon a diminution of support at the poll not otherwise to be accounted for.

As I could neither be bamboozled by anonymous letters nor bullied by railing associations of a dozen or a score of violent partisans to support measures occasionally which the sober and intelligent bulk of my people disapproved, the underminers persisted in assuring persons connected with Government that I could be easily deprived of my seat. I took little notice of these intrigues, believing that Ministers would not seriously listen to what seemed an artifice so transparent. But I was mistaken.

Early in May, 1884, I received a letter from a leading member of the Administration stating that he had been pressed by Liberals in Finsbury to obtain a declaration from me that I would not stand again, as preparations would soon be made for a contest. On asking the meaning and motive of his inquiry, he told me that he had been assured that the great preponderance of the electors desired a candidate of much more advanced views, and that in all parts of the borough the prevailing opinions were expressed by the new organization.

I replied that his official friends might repeat the experiment they had made before with signal ill-success, to give over the representation of half a million of people to an intolerant and ultra clique, but that it would assuredly fail, whether I were a candidate or no. Before the impending dissolution the Act of Redistribution took effect. I withdrew from the thankless contention, and of the seven divisions of Finsbury five returned Conservatives!

INDEX.

THE END.

BILLING AND SONS, PRINTERS, GUILDFORD.
J. D. & Co.

www.ingramcontent.com/pod-product-compliance
Lightning Source LLC
Chambersburg PA
CBHW030902270326
41929CB00008B/537

* 9 7 8 3 3 3 7 1 5 3 2 7 4 *